How Carrots Won the Trojan War

HOW CARROTS WON THE TROJAN WAR

Curious (but True) Stories of Common Vegetables

Rebecca Rupp

Storey Publishing

*The mission of Storey Publishing is to serve our customers by
publishing practical information that encourages
personal independence in harmony with the environment.*

Edited by Deborah Burns
Art direction and book design by Mary Winkelman Velgos
Text production by Jennifer Jepson Smith
Illustrations by © Gilbert Ford
Indexed by Samantha Miller

© 2011 by Rebecca Rupp

Storey Publishing
210 MASS MoCA Way
North Adams, MA 01247
www.storey.com

Printed in the United States by Versa Press
10 9 8 7 6 5 4 3 2 1

Library of Congress Cataloging-in-Publication Data

Rupp, Rebecca.
  How carrots won the Trojan War / by Rebecca Rupp.
    p. cm.
  Includes index.
  ISBN 978-1-60342-968-9 (pbk. : alk. paper)
  1. Vegetables—History. 2. Vegetable gardening—History.
  I. Title.
SB320.5.R87 2011
641.3'5—dc23
                              2011020049

For Randy,
who runs the rototiller

The greatest service which can be rendered to any
country is to add a useful plant to its culture.
THOMAS JEFFERSON

CONTENTS

radish

onion

Cabbage

Celery

potato

eggplant

corn

turnip

spinach

peas

melon

carrot

asparagus

Vegetables In and Out of the Garden

Did you ever know anyone who was not delighted by a garden?
JOHN SANDERSON

Nineteenth-century gardener Samuel Reynolds Hole, Dean of Rochester, dwelling cheerfully on the subject of his craft in 1899, wrote:

"I asked a schoolboy, in the sweet summertide, 'What he thought a garden was for?' and he said, *Strawberries*. His younger sister suggested *Croquet*, and the elder *Garden-parties*. The brother from Oxford made a prompt declaration in favor of *Lawn Tennis* and *Cigarettes*, but he was rebuked by a solemn senior, who wore spectacles, and more back hair than is usual with males, and was told that 'a garden was designed for botanical research, and for the classification of plants.' He was about to demonstrate the differences between *Acoty-* and *Monocotyledonous* divisions, when the collegian remembered an engagement elsewhere."

Nowadays there's no better agreement on the purpose of gardens. According to the latest poll sponsored by the National Gardening Association in Burlington, Vermont, a gourmet 58 percent of respondents garden for better-tasting food; a thrifty 54 percent garden to save money; a worried 48 percent cite food safety concerns; and a generous 23 percent garden so that they'll have food to share. Exercise, after healthful food, was among top reasons for gardening, according to a University of Illinois survey — the figure-conscious pointed out that an hour of moderate digging burns off a waist-whittling 300 calories.

Nobody mentioned fun, though it would be nice to think that the unclassifiable 9 percent in the NGA poll who listed their gardening reasons as "Other" are lighthearted fans of strawberries and croquet.

All told, such gardeners make up nearly half of all American households, a grand total of forty-three million home vegetable gardens. Top vegetable in these gardens, by a considerable margin, is the tomato, followed in dwindling order by cucumbers, peppers, beans, carrots, squash, and onions. All grow pretty well for us, too: nationally, home vegetable gardens generate an annual 21 billion dollars' worth of food, which is no mean feat in these tricky times when every stray billion counts.

❀

Vegetables, just as our mothers told us, are good for us. In fact, they're essential. Fruits and vegetables, according to various estimates, supply 90 percent of our daily allotment of vitamin C, 50 percent of vitamin A, 35 percent of vitamin B_6, 25 percent of magnesium, and 20 percent each of niacin (B_3), thiamine (B_1), and iron. A diet heavy in vegetables reduces risks of cancer and cardiovascular disease, prolongs life expectancy, and makes us skinnier. And as author Michael Pollan points out, vegetables — unlike a lot of the questionable processed, manufactured, and additive-laden stuff found today in supermarkets — are real honest-to-God food.

For a substantial chunk of human history, however, a lot of people have turned their noses up at vegetables. In Europe, vegetables — unflatteringly dubbed "rude herbs and roots" — have a long history of disdainful neglect, with the exception perhaps of the ubiquitous onion. Medieval peasants made do for the most part with grain porridges and cheese, while their social superiors feasted carnivorously on swan, crane, and peacock, piglet draped in daffodils, chicken doused in almond milk, quail, partridge, pigeon, rabbit, venison, and veal.

Nutritionally, there's a lot to be said for crane, peacock, and roasted rabbit. Protein analyses show that meat, in terms of supplying our necessary amino acids, is a nearly perfect food, almost the equivalent of that nutritional gold standard, the egg. The Neanderthals subsisted nicely on red meat, and Methuselah's steady diet of it supported his legendary lifespan of 969 years.

A dinner party thrown by Samuel Pepys in 1663 — an annual celebration on the anniversary of his successful operation for kidney stones — featured "rabbets and chicken," a boiled leg of mutton, roasted pigeons, "Lampry pie," and a dish of anchovies, without a vegetable in sight. Roast beef was the proper food for Englishmen, thundered Robert Campbell in 1747, protesting the "Depraved Taste" of the French, who liked to gussy things up with sauces and salads. Even nutritionists admit that if we could take only one food to a desert island, we'd be better off packing hotdogs than Brussels sprouts.

Roast beef was the proper food for Englishmen, thundered Robert Campbell in 1747, protesting the "Depraved Taste" of the French, who liked to gussy things up with salads.

On the other hand, although meat eating has its nutritional advantages, vegetable eating traditionally has been considered far better for the good of the soul. Among the earliest proponents of vegetarianism was the eighth-century BCE Greek poet Hesiod, who preached, but probably did not practice, a rural diet of mallow and asphodel. He was followed, after a two-hundred-year lag, by Pythagoras, sometimes called the "Father of Vegetarianism," who urged a meatless diet upon his disciples in the sixth century BCE. The "Pythagorean diet"— the going term for meatless meals until the word "vegetarianism" was invented in the mid-1800s — was intended to promote peace of mind and suppress distracting animal passions among budding philosophers.

In colonial America, one of the earliest vegetable advocates was Benjamin Franklin, who bravely experimented with a vegetarian diet in his youthful days as a Philadelphia printer, in company with Samuel Keimer, his employer. They tried it for three months, and Franklin later recalled: "I went on pleasantly, but poor Keimer suffered grievously, tired of the project, long'd for the flesh-pots of Egypt, and order'd roast pig. He invited me and two women friends to dine with him; but, it being brought too soon upon the table, he could not resist the temptation and ate the whole before we came. . . ."

Franklin himself held on longer but finally fell off the wagon on a sea voyage from Boston. The boat became stranded off Block Island, vegetarian victuals were in short supply, and the hungry Franklin gave in to a meal of fried codfish.

Thomas Jefferson was a vegetable fan, explaining in a letter of 1819 that he ate "little animal food, and that not as an aliment, so much as a condiment for the vegetables, which constitute my 'principle' diet." More common, however, was the experience of English visitor Frances Trollope, touring the United States in the 1830s, who commented in appalled tones on the unrelenting American diet of pork, salt fish, and cornbread.

In nineteenth-century America, foremost among vegetable proponents was the vociferous Sylvester Graham, whose name survives today in the graham cracker. Graham was born in 1794 in West Suffield, Connecticut, youngest child in a family of seventeen. He was ordained a Presbyterian minister in 1826, but soon abandoned the cloth for the job of general agent with the Pennsylvania Society for the Suppression of Ardent Spirits, based in Philadelphia. During his tenure as temperance agent, Graham studied anatomy, physiology, and nutrition, and evolved the dietary theories that became the basis of the "Graham system."

According to Graham, the "enormous wickedness and atrocious violence" preceding the Flood were the result of excessive meat eating. Similarly, indulgence in meats, fats, salt, spices, ketchup, mustard, and Demon Rum was drastically weakening the present American populace, leaving citizens open to crime, sexual sin, and mental and physical disease. The cholera epidemic of 1832 seemed to prove his point and the chastened public seized upon dietary reform.

Reform was no matter for wimps. The Graham system encompassed an unappetizing regimen of oatmeal porridge, beans, boiled rice, unbuttered whole-grain bread, and graham — originally Graham — crackers, plus cold baths, hard beds, open windows, and vigorous exercise. Despite opposition from physicians, raw vegetables and fruits were on Graham's approved list, to be washed down with the recommended Graham drink: water.

Grahamite boardinghouses dedicated to this masochistic program — residents rose by a 5:00 AM bell — opened in New York City and Boston, and university students formed campus Graham clubs (by most accounts, small and short-lived). The trustees of the Albany Orphan Asylum adopted the Graham system for their charges, a move which, according to one source, "aroused great controversy in the periodical press."

❀

For all its ascetic peculiarities, Grahamism did effectively further the cause of garden-fresh vegetables in a notably vitamin-deficient society. Salad greens, tomatoes, radishes, cauliflowers, asparagus, green beans, and spinach began to appear on everyday tables, though often cooked to mush: Eliza Leslie, author of *Directions for Miss Leslie's Complete Cookery, in Its Various Branches* (1840), the best-selling cookbook of the nineteenth century, recommends that peas and asparagus be boiled for at least an hour; green beans for an hour and a half; and carrots and beets for three.

Full-blown vegetarianism was embraced by some, including such celebrities as Richard Wagner, Leo Tolstoy, and George Bernard Shaw, who abandoned meat at the age of twenty-five, announcing, "A man of my spiritual intensity does not eat corpses." (Opponents of the idea included British journalist J. B.

"Vegetarians have wicked, shifty eyes and laugh in a cold, calculating manner. They pinch little children, steal stamps, drink water, and favor beards."

Morton, who wrote: "Vegetarians have wicked, shifty eyes and laugh in a cold, calculating manner. They pinch little children, steal stamps, drink water, and favor beards.")

Also noticeably resistant to vegetables were athletes. Ancient Olympic runners ate onions and Roman gladiators dined on barley bread, but nineteenth-century sports competitors favored red meat and dark beer. From a pro-vegetable point of view, the meat/beer regimen was annoyingly successful. In 1809, British athletic champion Robert Barclay walked one thousand miles in one thousand successive hours, nourished on nothing but heaping plates of beef and mutton.

In a similarly telling episode of the 1860s, the Oxford rowing crew trained exclusively on beef, beer, bread, and tea, with an occasional suppertime helping of watercress, while the opposing Cambridge team ate unrestricted amounts of salad greens, potatoes, and fresh fruits. The years from 1861 to 1869 produced an unbroken succession of meat-fed Oxford victories. Fueled by such incidents, the red-meat mystique persisted well into the twentieth century, when nutritional research found high-carbohydrate meals like pasta and potatoes to be more efficient sources of rapid energy.

Americans today still aren't eating enough of their vegetables. A 2009 U.S. Department of Agriculture (USDA) report showed that the average American eats 92 pounds of fresh vegetables a year — depressingly down from the 101 pounds we each ate in 1999 — and that only about a quarter of us eat more than three servings of fruits and veggies a day. (The recommended goal is five to eight.) Two-thirds of Americans are now either overweight or obese, and 54 million of us suffer from prediabetes.

The favorite vegetable of American toddlers, according to one recent study, is the French fry. In the words of the Joni Mitchell song, we've got to get ourselves back to the garden.

In Woody Allen's 1973 sci-fi comedy *Sleeper*, protagonist Miles Monroe, erstwhile owner of the Happy Carrot health-food store, is cryogenically frozen and wakes up two hundred years in the future, where he baffles a team of physicians by demanding wheat germ and organic honey for breakfast. In the twenty-second century, the definition of health food has been turned on its ear.

"Oh, yes," says one doctor, chuckling knowledgeably, "those are the charmed substances that some years ago were thought to contain life-preserving properties."

"You mean there was no deep fat?" replies his appalled colleague. "No steak or cream pies or . . . hot fudge?"

❋

An undisputed advantage of the garden is that it produces no cream pies. Instead it generates what activist Michael Pollan calls real food — stuff any alert hunter-gatherer would recognize as dinner — as opposed to processed food, which nowadays includes such commercial weirdities as DayGlo-orange cheese, cereal with lavender marshmallows, and fried chickenoid chunks in buckets.

Real food, Pollan points out, is not fast. Like all good things, it takes time: one way or another, it grows, and the closer we are to that process, the healthier and happier we're likely to be.

"For all things produced in a garden, whether of salads or fruits, a poor man will eat better that has one of his own, than a rich man that has none," wrote Scottish botanist John Loudon

Real food, Pollan points out, is not fast.

in *The Encyclopedia of Gardening* in 1822. Separated from her vegetable garden during her husband's first presidential term, Martha Washington wrote home to Mount Vernon: "Impress it on the gardener to have everything in the garden that will be necessary in a house keeping way — as vegetables is the best part of our living in the country."

Of course there's more to gardening than vegetables, and gardens have always fed far more than hungry stomachs. They also feed the soul. I'd be willing to bet that even those first staggered rows of Neolithic barley delighted their planters. It's "a love that nobody could share or conceive of" who has "never taken part in the process of creation," wrote Nathaniel Hawthorne of his Concord garden. "It was one of the most bewitching sights in the world to observe a hill of beans thrusting aside the soil, or a row of early peas just peeping forth sufficiently to trace a line of delicate green." I know just what he means.

"It is not graceful, and it makes one hot," wrote Elizabeth, Countess von Arnim, busily planting her German garden in the 1890s, "but it is a blessed sort of work, and if Eve had had a spade and known what to do with it, we should not have had all that sad business of the apple." In Barbara Cooney's enchanting picture book *Miss Rumphius*, the redoubtable title character sets out to make the world more beautiful, and so she plants flowers.

To make the world a better and more beautiful place: that's why we garden.

That's what I think gardens are for.

ASPARAGUS SEDUCES THE KING OF FRANCE

plus

*Sanskrit Sex, Persian Poets,
Mr. Ramsbottom's Fatal Mistake,
An Abbé's Apoplexy, and Madame
Pompadour's Underwear*

Asparagus inspires gentle thoughts.
CHARLES LAMB

Pray how does your asparagus perform?
JOHN ADAMS TO HIS WIFE ABIGAIL

asparagus

To my mind, the problem with asparagus is the planting instructions, which begin: "Dig a trench." Experts disagree as to the precise size of trench — some recommend a relatively feasible six-inch-deep furrow; others demand an excavation a foot deep and a foot and a half wide; and Martha Washington's *Book of Cookery* directs hopeful asparagus growers to "digg ye earth out a yerd deepe, & fill up ye place againe with old cows dung."

Still, a trench is a trench, and *trench* — face it — smacks of heavy labor, misery, mud, and World War I. "Dig a trench" is the dark side of gardening, the stuff of blood, sweat, back sprains, and blisters.

That said, once you've dug your asparagus trench, you won't have to do it again for a good long time. Unlike most denizens of the vegetable garden, asparagus is a perennial, and the average asparagus bed, once established, will continue to produce asparagus spears for twenty to thirty years.

Even better, asparagus isn't particularly picky. It adapts cheerfully to a wide range of circumstances and soils and could even thrive, NASA scientists tell us, in the chilly red dirt of Mars. A sample of Martian soil, pinched up in 2010 by the robotic arm of the Phoenix Mars Lander, was found to be mildly alkaline, with traces of magnesium, sodium, and potassium — potentially fertile ground for diehards like asparagus and turnips, though future Martians may not be able to grow strawberries.

The bottom line is that asparagus is one tough cookie. Beds can be started from seed — a long-term proposition — but a better bet is from crowns, which are the base and roots of one- to two-year-old plants. Even so, you won't have harvestable asparagus spears for at least three years, so be prepared.

I'm sensitive to this, having moved multiple times and left behind a cross-country trail of immature asparagus beds. In fact, I've become suspicious of asparagus. "Plant it and you'll move" has been our rule to date, and we're awfully fond of where we're living now. Still, it's such a scrumptious vegetable that I hate to pass it up. And easy too, once you get past the trench.

�֍

Historically, asparagus is pure sex food. Its aphrodisiacal renown dates to antiquity and is derived from the undeniably penile shape of the emerging stalks, which pop suggestively out of the ground in early spring, just as a young man's fancy lightly turns to thoughts of love. Pliny the Elder, in his formidable thirty-seven-volume *Natural History*, written in the first century CE, cites asparagus as a sex booster, as does the near-legendary second-century Sanskrit sex manual, the *Kama Sutra* of Mallanega Vatsyayana. In the latter, a chapter titled "On Personal Adornment; On Subjugating the Hearts of Others; and On Tonic Medicines" provides a lengthy list of recipes to bolster lackluster lovers, among them a paste of asparagus boiled in milk, with pepper, licorice, honey, and butter.

In western Europe, asparagus was among the touted remedies for the low-libido Renaissance man, along with prunes, garlic, nettle seed in wine, and dried fox testicles. In nineteenth-century France, bridegrooms were fed three courses of asparagus in anticipation of their wedding nights, and the salacious stalks were banned from the menu in girls' schools, for fear of inflaming the imaginations of susceptible teens.

Despite — or perhaps because of — its propensity for provoking unbridled lust, people have been cooking asparagus at least since the time of the ancient Greeks and Romans. Ripe and ready for the pot, asparagus is pictured in murals on the walls of Pompeii, and Plutarch describes Julius Caesar feasting on asparagus in northern Italy, though somewhat unhappily, since his host had drenched the spears in myrrh instead of olive oil.

The Asparagus Family Tree

Traditionally, asparagus has been considered a member of the Lily family (Liliaceae), an immense taxonomic conglomerate comprising some 280 genera and 4,000 species. Among these are such botanical kissing cousins as the tulip, the Easter lily, the onion, the fall crocus, and the dragon tree, whose bright-red resin — known as dragon's blood — is used as a varnish, possibly in the finish applied to Antonio Stradivari's famous violins.

Some taxonomists, however, now suggest that asparagus deserves a family all to itself — Asparagaceae, a smaller, cozier grouping of a mere handful of genera and a couple of hundred species. Among these last are the edible garden asparagus, *Asparagus officinalis*, and the asparagus fern, *Asparagus densiflorus*, the feathery green stuff often found fluffing out florists' bouquets.

The Romans seem to have liked their asparagus *al dente*, since "quicker than it takes to cook asparagus" is a catch-phrase from the time of the Emperor Augustus meaning "lickety-split." The first-century *Apicius*, the oldest known Roman cookbook, sometimes titled *De Re Coquinaria* (*The Art of Cooking*), recommends that "to be most agreeable to the palate," asparagus spears should be peeled, washed, and immersed in boiling water backwards, by which the author means cooked in a tall narrow pot such that the spears stand upright with their tips poking out of the water. He doesn't specify how long one boils — presumably not very, unless using the asparagus in his subsequent recipe, which involves mushing it up and baking it in a pie along with pepper, wine, oil, fish sauce, and figpeckers, which are European warblers.

❋

As well as a vegetable Viagra, asparagus was touted as a specific for everything from congestive heart failure to kidney stones. According to Pliny, asparagus sharpened the eyesight and alleviated elephantiasis. It was also a preventive for pains in the chest and spine, a remedy for diseases of the intestines, a cure for jaundice and "the stings of serpents," and, Pliny reports solemnly, "It is said that if a person is rubbed with asparagus beaten up in oil, he will never be stung by bees."

The sad truth is that asparagus, medically, isn't good for anything much, though recent research from Korea's Cheju National University School of Medicine indicates that it may ease the miseries of hangovers. Asparagus extracts were found to increase the activity of crucial enzymes in the liver and expedite the metabolism of alcohol, suggesting that a hefty meal of asparagus should precede a binge at the neighborhood bar.

Cultivated asparagus largely vanished from Europe with the fall of Rome, though it remained a favorite in the Middle East. A tenth-century Persian history, *Muraj al-Dhahab* ("Meadows of Gold"), includes a lush description of a literary symposium on cooking held at the court of the Abbasid caliph Al-Mustakfi in which poets struggled to outdo each other with mouthwatering descriptions of dishes. The offering of Baghdadi poet Kushajim (nicknamed "the Scribe") was a twenty-two-line paean to asparagus in sauce, which, after luscious comparisons of asparagus to gold, silver, pearl rings, and cream embroidery, ends with, "Should pious anchorite see such repast / In sheer devotion he would break his fast." The drooling caliph promptly sent to Damascus for asparagus spears.

❈

Invading Arabs, who occupied Spain from the eighth to the fifteenth centuries CE, brought asparagus with them. Reportedly its popularity at the Iberian dinner table can be traced to one man: Ziryab ("the Blackbird"), a musician at the ninth-century court of Córdoba, whose charisma and creativity allowed him to establish himself as an arbiter of culture and home decor. His closest modern equivalent is Martha Stewart, and, like Martha, Ziryab's knack with table settings and window treatments made him enormously rich. Along with the joys of asparagus, he is said to have introduced the Spaniards to tablecloths, toothpaste, the lute, crystal (instead of metal) wine glasses, the style of wearing one's hair "with a fringe on the forehead" (bangs), and the custom of starting a multicourse meal with soup and ending it with dessert.

Asperges à la Pompadour

The legendarily lovely Jeanne Antoinette Poisson, Madame de Pompadour, became King Louis XV's mistress at the age of twenty-four and remained the royal favorite until her death in 1764. A shade of pink and an upswept hairstyle are both named after her, and the French champagne glass was supposedly based on the shape of her breasts. An eighteenth-century British army regiment was named after her, nicknamed "The Pompadours" for the purple facings of their uniforms — reputedly the color of her underwear. It was also the color of her asparagus, a particularly salacious plump Dutch white variety with purple tips.

This version of her famous recipe comes from the great gourmet Alexandre Grimod de la Reynière (1758–1837):

"Dress and cook the asparagus in the normal way, plunging them into boiling salted water.

"Slice them diagonally into pieces no longer than the little finger. Take only the choicest sections, and, keeping them hot, allow them to drain in a warm napkin while the sauce is being prepared.

"In a *bain-marie* (water bath), work ten grams of flour and a lump of butter together, a good pinch of nutmeg, and the yolks of two eggs diluted with four spoonfuls of lemon juice. After cooking the sauce, drop in the asparagus tips and serve in a covered casserole."

From Spain, Ziryab's asparagus spread to France, where its prime proponent was Louis XIV, during whose seventy-two-year reign — which extended from 1643 to 1715 — the Palace of Versailles was built and the accompanying Potager du Roi (King's Kitchen Garden) was planted. The 25-acre Potager surrounded a courtyard with a fountain, and was overlooked by a terrace from which the king, who was fond of plants, could watch his gardeners in action. It was presided over by Jean-Baptiste de la Quintinie, a lawyer turned master gardener, whose duty it was to oversee the 29 individually enclosed gardens, the 12,000 fruit trees, including 700 of the king's favorite figs, and the 6,000 asparagus plants in the royal hotbeds, from which the court was able to enjoy asparagus as early as December.

Equally appreciative of asparagus was Madame de Pompadour, by far the cleverest of Louis XV's many mistresses, who served it in a sauce of butter, egg yolk, nutmeg, and lemon, a dish still known today as "Asperges à la Pompadour." (See page 17.) She may even have occasionally cooked it herself: in the heyday of the royal affair, Madame de Pompadour maintained a summer house at Versailles to which the king would periodically repair — disingenuously announcing to the court that he was going hunting — for private suppers.

Asparagus reached England by the sixteenth century and was in commercial cultivation by the seventeenth, when it was grown primarily around the village of Battersea and sold in London markets as "Battersea bundles." Samuel Pepys's diary for April 20, 1667, finds the author buying asparagus — "brought home with me from Fenchurch Street a hundred of sparrowgrass, cost 18d" — which he and his wife ate for supper with salmon. Asparagus was on the menu for the coronation feast of James II in 1685, along with a hundred and forty-five other (largely nonvegetable) dishes, among them pickled oysters, pigeon pie, rabbit ragout, and roast fawn.

In the early nineteenth century asparagus was immortalized by Jane Austen in *Emma* (1815), when the chattery Miss Bates has a disappointing encounter with a fricassee of sweetbreads and asparagus. The dish, untasted, was snatched from under her nose at the table and returned to the kitchen at the behest of Emma's hypochondriacal father.

❄

Nobody knows exactly where the ancestral asparagus came from. It appears to be a native of the eastern Mediterranean and Asia Minor — wild asparagus (*Asparagus protratus*) is found scattered along the sandy cliffs of the European coastline. Scattered is the operative word: due to cliff erosion, trampling tourists, and competing scrub plants, wild asparagus is now an endangered species.

The "wild" asparagus stalked by American forager Euell Gibbons, however, is still up for grabs. Unlike many modern garden plants — the needy and dependent corn, for example — asparagus thrives perfectly well without us. It is not native to North America; our widespread wild plants are domestic runaways, offspring of cultivated *A. officinalis* that hopped the garden fence and headed for the wide-open spaces.

Asparagus arrived in North America early and did well. John Josselyn, author of *New-Englands Rarities Discovered* (1672), describes it as thriving "exceedingly," and in John Lawson's *A New Voyage to Carolina* (1709), an account of his 600-mile trek through the wilderness on foot and by canoe, he comments that "Asparagus thrives to a Miracle." By the time Swedish botanist Peter Kalm began his North American travels in the late 1740s, he saw asparagus growing wild through New Jersey, Pennsylvania, and New York. A testy letter of 1737 from Thomas Hancock — uncle of John, of the memorable signature — to his English seed dealer is a backhanded tribute to the resilience of asparagus: ". . . the Garden Seeds and Flower Seeds which you sold Mr. Wilks for me and Charged me £6.4s2d Sterling were not worth one farthing. Not one of all the Seeds Came up Except the Asparrow Grass."

The part of the irrepressible asparagus plant that we eat is the early shoot or sprout; if left alone, such sprouts develop into tall ferny branches bearing small bell-shaped greenish yellow flowers. The ferny foliage looks leafy but, strictly speaking, isn't: the narrow fronds are actually modified photosynthetic stems called cladodes or cladophylls.

The flowers are gender-specific. *A. officinalis* is dioecious, bearing male and female flowers on separate plants. Following pollination by visiting bees, female plants produce bright red berries, each containing up to eight seeds. The berries are adored by birds, who have been the prime movers in liberating garden asparagus into the wild.

Traditional asparagus cultivars, such as the heirloom Mary and Martha Washington varieties, produce half male and half female plants. Newer cultivars, however, such as Jersey Giant, Jersey Knight, and Jersey Prince, are all male. Male asparagus is generally bigger, yummier, and three to four times more productive than female, which shows the advantages of putting one's energy into brawn rather than seeds.

❄

"Not one of all the Seeds Came up Except the Asparrow Grass."

Colonial America appears to have eaten a lot of asparagus. In 1709, Virginia planter William Byrd II noted in his diary, "At noon I ate nothing but squirrel and asparagus," and planter Landon Carter complains in 1777 of feeling "very heavy and Sleepy" after his dinners, which condition he blames — repeatedly — on asparagus. George Washington grew asparagus in the "boxed Squares" of his garden at Mount Vernon; and Thomas Jefferson planted it, along with two hundred and fifty other varieties of vegetables, in his 1,000-foot kitchen garden at Monticello, where it was painstakingly mulched with tobacco leaves and fertilized with manure. Since asparagus, like crocuses and robins, is a harbinger of spring, Jefferson annually recorded the dates when it first appeared on the Monticello table — usually, in balmy Virginia, by the first week in April.

He also seems to have been fussy about its preparation. Mary Randolph's cookbook *The Virginia Housewife, or Methodical Cook*, first published in 1824, and known to contain many Jefferson family recipes (Mary was a cousin), advises scraping the asparagus stalks, tying them into bundles of twenty-five, and tossing them into boiling water containing a handful of salt. "Great care must be taken to watch the exact time of their becoming tender," Mary cautions, "take them just at that instant, and they will have their true flavour and colour; a minute or two more boiling destroys both." She suggests serving asparagus on buttered toast.

Commercial asparagus is pricey because, since the stalks appear over a period of weeks, the harvest is prolonged and has to be done by hand. Historically it has been considered a food for the tables of aristocrats, sometimes nicknamed the "royal vegetable" or the "food of kings." Jean Anthelme Brillat-Savarin, French epicure and author of *The Physiology of Taste* (1825), was appalled to find asparagus selling for 40 francs a bundle, at a time when the average workman earned 2½ francs a day. "They are certainly very fine," he snapped, "but at such a price no one but the King or some prince will be able to eat them." John Loudon writes in *The Encyclopedia of Gardening* (1822): "The asparaginous class of esculents may be considered comparatively one of luxury. It occupies a large proportion of the gentleman's garden, often an eighth part; but does not enter into that of the cottager."

As late as the 1930s, asparaginous esculents were apparently still the preserve of the sophisticated rich. In "Asparagus," a poem of that period by comedian Marriott Edgar, his hero Mr. Ramsbottom wins five pounds at the races and decides to bring a present home to his wife.

> He saw some strange stuff in a fruit shop
> Like leeks with their nobby ends gone.
> It were done up in bundles like firewood —
> Said Pa to the Shopman, "What's yon?"
>
> "That's Ass-paragus — what the Toffs eat"
> Were the answer, says Pa "That'll suit,
> I'd best take a couple of bundles
> For Mother's a bobby for fruit."

Being ignorant of asparagus, however, Mr. Ramsbottom ends up giving away all the green tips to friends who (suddenly, suspiciously) claim to raise rabbits. He comes home with a handful of woody ends, which his wife mistakes for kindling, and then pronounces too damp to light the kitchen fire.

Most who got their hands on asparagus were both savvier and less willing to share. Among the best of asparagus stories is the one told of Bernard le Bovier de Fontanelle, irrepressible French writer and gourmand, who died in 1757, just one month short of his hundredth birthday. (He attributed his longevity to strawberries.) Planning a private asparagus feast, Fontanelle was dismayed to receive an unexpected guest, the Abbé Terrasson, whom he felt compelled to ask to stay to dinner. Resignedly, he ordered his kitchen staff to prepare half of his treasured asparagus with the abbé's favorite white sauce, and the other half, as he himself preferred, in an oil dressing.

Just before the meal was served, the abbé suddenly crumpled to the floor in a fit of apoplexy. Fontanelle dashed to the kitchen, shouting frantically, "The whole with oil! The whole with oil!"

An almost inevitable adjunct to a feast of asparagus is funny-smelling pee. Asparagus transforms "my chamber-pot into a vase of aromatic perfume," enthused Marcel Proust, but most of those who experience it are a lot less complimentary. Dr. Louis Lemery wrote in his *Treatise of All Sorts of Foods* (1702) that "Sparagrass" causes "a filthy and disagreeable Smell in the Urine." "A few Stems of Asparagus eaten, shall give our Urine a disagreeable Odour; and a Pill of turpentine no bigger than a Pea, shall bestow on it the pleasing Smell of Violets," wrote Benjamin Franklin in a little-known piece of Frankliniana titled "Fart Proudly," originally sent as a snarky letter to the British Royal Society in 1781.

A common comparison of the disagreeable odor is to the smell of rotten cabbage, which as everybody knows is perfectly awful. Studies of the phenomenon are complicated, however, by the fact that not everybody produces an asparagus odor, and of those who do, not everybody can smell it. Experiments to determine which is which involve either analyzing urine samples by gas chromatography or, more subjectively, persuading volunteers to sniff pots of pee. The culprit in asparagus appears to be asparagusic acid, which in the human digestive tract is converted to a handful of noxious sulfur-heavy compounds, among them the particularly pungent methanethiol, the nose-assaulting essence in skunk spray.

Along with asparagusic acid, asparagus contains a raft of more congenial components, notably folate, fiber, potassium, and vitamins K, A, and C. It also contains a good deal of asparagine, one of the twenty amino acids that serve as the building blocks for proteins. Ten of these, including asparagine, are nonessential amino acids, meaning that our bodies can synthesize them from other compounds; another ten are essential, meaning we can't produce them on our own, but must acquire them through eating. Asparagine was the first of the amino acids to be isolated, discovered in 1806 by French chemists Louis Nicolas Vauquelin and Pierre Jean Robiquet, who extracted it from and named it after asparagus juice.

How to Eat Asparagus

"Although asparagus may be taken in the fingers, don't take a long drooping stalk, hold it up in the air and catch the end of it in your mouth like a fish. When the stalks are thin, it is best to cut them in half with the fork, eating the tips like all fork food; the ends may then be taken in the fingers and eaten without a dropping fountain effect! Don't squeeze the stalks, or hold your hand below the end and let the juice run down your arm."
Emily Post's *Etiquette*, 1922

American asparagus is almost invariably green, though it is also available in an anthocyanin-laden purple and a bleached and ghostly white. White asparagus is simply green asparagus, buried. Popular in Europe for its smooth buttery taste, white asparagus is created by mounding sandy soil over the beds to shield the growing plants from direct exposure to the sun, which ordinarily induces the manufacture of chlorophyll and turns the stalks green.

Germans are so passionate about their pallid crop that during the spring asparagus season — *Spargelzeit* — visitors annually converge on the Asparagus Triangle in Baden-Württemberg, where the town of Schwetzingen styles itself the "Asparagus Capital of the World." The point of Spargelzeit is, of course, to eat as much asparagus as possible, preferably at every meal, though the area also features asparagus celebrations with chosen Asparagus Queens, asparagus-peeling contests, an Asparagus Cycling Trail, and a three-story Asparagus Museum in a fifteenth-century tower in Freistaat Bayern.

The actual asparagus capital of the world these days is in Peru. The recent Peruvian asparagus boom is an example of the Law of Unintended Consequences, a beefed-up and academic big brother of Murphy's Law, which states that intervention in a complex system often leads to unanticipated and sometimes disastrous results. In this case, the complex system was the global economy, the intervention was the U.S. government's War on Drugs, and the unanticipated consequence was the fall of American asparagus.

In the early 1990s, the American government, in an attempt to persuade Peruvian farmers to grow something other than coca — the immensely profitable raw material of cocaine — began to subsidize Peruvian asparagus. Under the tenets of the Andean Trade Preference Act (ATPA), passed in 1991 and renewed in 2002, Peru is allowed to export its asparagus to the United States tax-free — a financial advantage of such magnitude that American asparagus farmers, faced with it, have toppled like dominoes. Pre-ATPA imports of Peruvian asparagus totaled 4 million annual pounds; today we bring in 110 million pounds each year. It's not clear that this vegetarian windfall has made much of a dent in the Peruvian coca industry, but American asparagus growers in the top asparagus-producing states of California, Washington, and Michigan have taken a dive.

There's even a movie about it. In the spirit of Michael Moore's 1989 documentary *Roger and Me*, which chronicled the economic collapse of Flint, Michigan, after the closing of the General Motors auto factories, Anne de Mare and Kirsten Kelly's *Asparagus!* traces the awful impact of governmental drug-war policies on Michigan's rural Oceana County. Once the "Asparagus Capital of the Nation," Oceana has traditionally made its living from asparagus, while developing an accompanying local asparagus culture, featuring an annual Asparagus Festival, an asparagus-costumed dance troupe, an asparagus comic-book hero (Super Stalk), and the world's tallest asparagus cake.

Today not only the farmers of Oceana but hundreds of asparagus farmers nationwide have gone out of business, taking with them a distinctive way of life. Community pride and sense of identity, writes De Mare, often center around local crops. When we lose them, we lose sight of who we are.

❀

The grassroots solution to the erosion of local food and farms is to eat locally. Local eaters now even have a name all their own — *locavore* — selected as the Word of the Year in 2007 by the *Oxford American Dictionary*. The term was coined by California local eater Jessica Prentice, cofounder of the online community Locavores, but the concept has been promulgated since the 1970s by Alice Waters, founder of Berkeley's famous Chez Panisse restaurant. Waters's passionate support of organic, locally grown, and seasonally appropriate food has changed the nature of American eating — although, admittedly, local eating calls for more ingenuity and self-sacrifice in some places than in others. Where we live in northern Vermont, for example, local eating in February means last summer's canned tomatoes and the hope that maybe the cat will catch a squirrel.

Still, today more and more people are tackling "100-mile diets," from the book of the same name (*The 100-Mile Diet: A Year of Local Eating*) by Alisa Smith and J.B. MacKinnon of Vancouver, British Columbia. The couple, who began their local-eating project on the first day of spring in 2005, resolved to eat nothing that could not be obtained within a 100-mile radius of home.

Still, the most environmentally friendly local eating undeniably comes from one's own backyard. Which is why, this season, I'm going to dig an asparagus trench.

CHAPTER TWO
In Which

BEANS BEAT BACK THE DARK AGES

plus

*An Old Testament Swindle,
A Pythagorean Dilemma, Siege Stew,
Boston's Sunday Dinner,
A Soupçon of Cyanide,
and A Pressing Social Problem*

I was determined to know beans.

HENRY DAVID THOREAU

In the late nineteenth century, an enterprising American distributor marketed his green beans as "the Ninth Wonder of the World." It's not certain how this appealing slogan affected the case-hardened American consumer, but it did catch the jealous eye of P. T. Barnum, who claimed that he had coined the term himself to describe such phenomena as General Tom Thumb, the Feejee Mermaid, Jumbo the Elephant, and Chang and Eng, the Siamese Twins. Barnum sued and beat the bean, which subsequently qualified its Wonder status by adding a cautious "of Food" in smaller print.

The wondrous bean that figured in this legal brouhaha was *Phaseolus vulgaris*, the so-called American, French, kidney, or common green bean. *P. vulgaris* has been cultivated for thousands of years, perhaps originally domesticated from a wild ancestor resembling the uncivilized-sounding *P. aborigineus*, native to Argentina and Brazil. Bean seeds from archaeological sites in Peru and Mexico have been radiocarbon-dated respectively to 8000 and 5000 BCE, and by the time of the Spanish conquest, Montezuma was taking in 5,000 tons of beans a year in tribute from his devoted subjects.

Columbus noticed the American beans ("very different from those of Spain") in Cuba on his first voyage to the New World. Giovanni da Verrazano, flushed with success after his North

American voyage of 1524, described the Indian beans as "of good and pleasant taste;" Samuel de Champlain, in his 1605 account of the Indians of the Kennebec region in Maine, mentioned their cultivation of "Brazilian beans" in different colors, three or four of which were planted in each hill of corn to grow up the supporting cornstalk. Thomas Hariot mentioned beans (in two sizes) grown by the Indians on Roanoke Island, and John Smith and Powhatan went on record as sharing a macho meal of beans and brandy in the early days of the settlement at Jamestown.

✿

Beans, for the Indians of eastern North America, were relatively new. According to Bruce D. Smith, archaeobiologist at the Smithsonian National Museum of Natural History, the Eastern woodlands tribes had established themselves as farmers by 2000 BCE, and had domesticated a handful of promising local plants, among them squash (crooknecks and pattypans), sunflowers, lamb's-quarters (*Chenopodium berlandieri*), and marsh elder (*Iva annua*).

Of the traditional "three sisters" — squash, corn, and beans, which, as every schoolchild knows, were the principal crops of the American Indians — squash, in the northeast and mid-Atlantic regions, was for some two millennia an only child. Beans and corn were laggardly imports from Mexico, slowly moving their way from vegetable patch to vegetable patch across the country and up the Eastern seaboard. Corn is believed to have made it to the eastern United States by 200 CE; beans arrived somewhat later. In both cases, it was another 600 years or more before cultivation really took off. If Leif Erikson, scudding along the North American coast in year 1000, had looked farther south or farther inland, he might have found farmers growing squash. He might not yet have found beans.

It seems to have been the Spanish who brought the American bean to Europe, sometime in the sixteenth century, where it was grown as an ornamental — which isn't surprising. Bean flowers are gorgeous, described in the botanical literature as "papilionaceous," because their petals look like butterfly wings. One story claims that the introduction of the American bean to European cuisine was sheer serendipity: at some point, a bunch of neglected pods accidentally toppled from an ornamental vine into a peculiarly placed soup pot, where they remained long enough to be cooked and eaten. This seems unlikely, since the American beans — though admittedly a little funny-looking to the novice — were readily recognizable as beans, and the Old World was used to beans. It had been living with beans for ten thousand years.

❀

Beans are legumes, members of the family Fabaceae — the third largest of the families of flowering plants (after the Orchid and Daisy families), and the second most important to the human diet after Poaceae, the grasses. Fabaceae contains more than 600 genera and nearly 19,000 species, an unwieldy batch of friends and relations that includes beans, peas, lentils, and soybeans, carob and tamarind trees, and alfalfa, kudzu, licorice, jicama, and peanuts.

Gardenwise, the oldest of the bunch may be the lentil (*Lens culinaris*), whose name comes from the contact-lens-like shape of the dried bean. Lentils, along with barley and einkorn wheat, were among the first plants domesticated some 10,000 years ago in western Asia's lush Fertile Crescent, a vaguely boomerang-shaped swath of territory between the Tigris and Euphrates rivers, stretching from the Mediterranean Sea to the Persian Gulf.

Lentils, along with barley and einkorn wheat, were among the first plants domesticated some 10,000 years ago in western Asia's lush Fertile Crescent.

The Sumerians grew them, and the oldest known legume recipe — found in a trio of Babylonian culinary cuneiform tablets dated to 1700–1600 BCE — is for a porridge of lentils, simmered in beer. Remains of lentil dinners have been found in Bronze Age Swiss lake dwellings, and lentils are featured in the most egregious example of shysterism in the Old Testament, when the cagey Jacob talks his older twin brother Esau into trading his birthright for a bowl of lentil soup.

Almost as old is the Old World's only cultivated bean, the fava or broad bean (*Vicia faba*), to which Pliny the Elder awarded "the highest place of honor" among leguminous plants. Domesticated in the late Neolithic period, the fava probably originated somewhere in the Mediterranean region or Near East, though its wild progenitor is apparently now extinct. Favas have been found in Egyptian tombs and in the ruins of Troy, and in the Old Testament, Ezekiel ate them between prophecies. The Greeks used fava beans as voting tokens in magisterial elections, a custom later remarked upon by Plutarch, who claimed that the proverbial dictum "Abstain from beans" had nothing to do with diet, but meant keep out of politics.

Among the rules adhered to by the vegetarian followers of Pythagoras, whose quasireligious sect settled in Croton on the coast of southern Italy by 530 BCE, were strictures that forbade stirring fires with iron pokers or eating meat, fish, or beans. The bean ban is usually attributed to the Pythagoreans' belief in the transmigration of souls, in which human beings could not only be reborn as animals, but — just possibly — as beans. Certainly it wasn't worth taking the chance: eating a bean, according to Pythagoras, was like biting off the head of one's mother.

Alternatively the Pythagorean avoidance of beans may have had its roots in the genetic disease known as favism. Particularly common in individuals of Mediterranean ancestry, favism results from a deficiency in the enzyme glucose-6-phosphate dehydrogenase (G6PD). The deficiency, carried on the X chromosome, renders the red blood cells of unlucky males and homozygous females sensitive to hemolysis (breakdown) by the oxidants found in fava beans. Fava bean consumption, or even a stroll through the field when the bean plants are in flower, brings on a severe allergic-type reaction, and in extreme cases rapid hemolytic anemia, shock, and death. Beans, in other words, may have made Pythagoras so sick that he simply didn't want them anywhere near him.

Political meddling — Plutarch's forbidden indulgence in beans — eventually led to Pythagoras's downfall. The unpopular Pythagoreans were shunned, persecuted, and eventually driven from Croton. One story holds that beans ultimately brought about Pythagoras's death. Trapped while on the run, he refused the only available means of escape, which involved trampling through a bean field, and so was captured and killed by his enemies.

Despite this awful warning, Pythagoras's banned bean was a prime edible of the Middle Ages. Italian scholar and author Umberto Eco, in fact, hypothesizes that Europeans emerged from the so-called Dark Ages — the bleak and impoverished period extending from the fall of Rome to the end of the first millennium — because of the fava bean. His essay, "How the Bean Saved Civilization," appeared in a special issue of the *New York Times Magazine* on the theme of the best inventions of the past one thousand years.

The evidence for the redemptive role of the bean comes from babies. Though numerical estimates vary, it's clear that a population boom began as Europe entered the tenth century. In the seventh century — possibly the nadir of the miserable Dark Ages — the population of Europe had sunk to a hungry and disease-ridden 14 million. By the year 1000, however, it had more than doubled; by the fourteenth century, it had doubled — even tripled — again. Eco argues that the upswing in population size, energy, intellect, and the economy all derived from a new crop. It was in the tenth century that Europeans began the widespread cultivation of beans.

Legume comes from the Latin verb *legere*, meaning "to gather," and when it comes to gathering, legumes — such as beans and peas — are well worth the effort. Nicknamed "the poor man's meat," beans and peas contain 17 to 25 percent protein, two to three times that found in cereal crops. The influx of protein into the previously parsimonious Dark Age diet made for stronger, healthier people, who lived longer and had more children. The quality of daily life improved, countries grew richer, and the expanding and better-fed population was able to support the specialization of labor, the growth of cities, the burgeoning of the arts, the emergence of science, and the launching of ships to the New World.

Furthermore, the benefits of beans lie not just in beans as food, but in the baggage the growing bean brings with it.

Leguminous plants are distinguished by their ability to fix nitrogen — that is, to convert atmospheric nitrogen to a form in which it can be used by plants and animals to synthesize such life-essential molecules as DNA, RNA, and proteins. (See box.)

Medieval beans were such an essential article of diet that the penalty for robbing a beanfield was death. In England, ghosts were said to fear broad beans — to banish specters, one spat beans at them — and those same beans, roasted, were believed efficacious in the treatment of toothache and smallpox.

"Three blue beans in a blue bladder" was a tongue twister long before she sold seashells by the seashore, and the tale of Jack and the Beanstalk — though nobody knows exactly where it came from — is of ancient origin.

❈

Anthropologist Solomon H. Katz points out that, despite their obvious benefits, people historically have been ambivalent about beans, viewing them with "mingled respect and dread." Beans could give you nightmares. Lunacy was said to be on the rise when the beans were in blossom, and anyone silly enough to fall asleep in a beanfield could wake up irrevocably insane. Seventeenth-century cleric John White, of whom not much seems to be known except that he was once tossed out of his post as vicar of Cherton, wrote in *Art's Treasury: Or, a Profitable and Pleasing Invitation to the Lovers of Ingenuity* (1688) that if a pregnant woman indulged in "Onions, or Beans, or such vaporous Food," her offspring would be "Lunatic, or Foolish."

Sixteenth-century physician Baldassare Pisanelli claimed that beans "make the senses stupid, and cause dreams full of travails and perturbations." It's possible that Saint Jerome thought the same: he declared beans aphrodisiacs ("they tickle the genitals") and forbade nuns to eat them.

Modern pharmacologists believe they may have found the biochemical explanation for beans' restless and mentally unbalanced reputation. Fava beans contain up to 0.5 percent by weight L-dopa (1-3.4-dihydroxyphenylalanine), a novel amino

Beans, Peas, and Nitrogen

Chemically, nitrogen fixation is a heroic feat. Nitrogen, which makes up about 70 percent of the air we breathe, ordinarily exists in the form of molecular N_2 — two atoms of nitrogen held together by a powerful triple bond, the chemical equivalent of Gorilla Glue. Practically nothing unhinges N_2. In its triple-bonded form, it is stubbornly unreactive, which means that it simply sits there sullenly and can't be used to make anything else. If nitrogen were a food, it would be a coconut — delicious, nutritious, and maddeningly uncrackable. Eighteenth-century French scientist Antoine Lavoisier, who first named nitrogen, originally called it "azote," which means lifeless. In the atmosphere, the only thing that rips apart that triple bond is a bolt of lightning.

In the garden, however, this feat is performed by beans, peas, and their leguminous relatives. Strictly speaking, legumes don't fix nitrogen themselves; rather, they serve as cooperative incubators for organisms that do. Legumes nurture symbiotic *Rhizobia* bacteria in nodules on their roots, which — by virtue of an enzyme called nitrogenase — are able to convert unusable atmospheric nitrogen (N_2) into usable ammonia (NH_3). Plants without such bacterial buddies require another nitrogen source, which in the case of modern commercial crops is often provided by expensive and environmentally damaging chemical fertilizers.

A time-honored alternative to these unnatural additives is crop rotation. Since Roman times, farmers have periodically planted their fields with *Rhizobia*-toting legumes to add fixed nitrogen to the soil.

acid first isolated from bean seedlings by Marcus Guggenheim in 1913. L-dopa was initially thought to be a mere chemical curiosity, until research in the 1950s showed it to be a precursor of dopamine, an essential neurotransmitter.

Dopamine, if present in abnormal quantities in the human brain, can have disastrous effects. Too much appears to be a corollary of schizophrenia; too little is the hallmark of Parkinson's disease, the debilitating ailment first described by physician James Parkinson in 1817 as "the shaking palsy." Dopamine cannot cross the blood-brain barrier — that is, injected into the human body, it can't get into the brain — but L-dopa, a more agile molecule, can. Today L-dopa is the drug of choice for alleviating the symptoms of Parkinson's disease, for which discovery Swedish scientist Arvid Carlsson won a Nobel Prize.

It seems likely that L-dopa may account for the classical reports of sleep disturbances, vivid dreaming, and enhanced sexuality associated with fava bean eating. Today most L-dopa is obtained not from favas, but from the even more L-dopa-heavy velvet bean (*Mucuna pruriens*), so named for its fuzzy golden pods. A native of India, the velvet bean, a pharmacological powerhouse, contains up to 7 percent L-dopa.

❈

Pliny the Elder, annoyingly, does not prescribe beans for palsy, which makes some medical sense, but instead recommends white bread and baths. He does, however, list sixteen other bean-based remedies: beans parched in vinegar are good for "gripings of the bowels;" beans boiled with garlic are good for coughs; and even the ashes of beanstalks are useful for soothing sciatica.

Most Romans ate beans, in one form or another. The first-century cookbook *Apicius* (*De Re Coquinaria*) — possibly written by the flamboyant gourmet Marcus Gavius Apicius, known for throwing lush parties during the reign of Tiberius — devoted an entire section to legumes, with recipes for mushes, porridges, soups, gruels, and bean-stuffed suckling pigs. Among these, and less awful than most Roman concoctions, is *Lenticulum de castaneis*, a dish of mashed lentils and chestnuts with spices and olive oil, which sounds vaguely like hummus. My favorite, however, is *Apicius's* beans "Boiled, Sumptuously," in which the boiled beans are served as a salad with hard-boiled eggs, fennel, pepper, and a little wine and salt. Or, the author adds generously, serve them up "in simpler ways as you may see fit."

Beans, to the ancients, were primarily cheap peasant food, the classical equivalent of Wonder bread and Hamburger Helper. Martial, the first-century Roman poet best known for his twelve catchy (and occasionally obscene) books of epigrams, describes inviting a friend to dinner, with the caveat that, as a poet, he's too broke to provide luxuries and flute girls. All he can spring for is leeks, boiled eggs, cabbage, and beans — to accompany "a kid snatched from the jaws of a savage wolf," which sounds suspiciously like the first-century equivalent of roadkill.

The fourteenth-century *Forme of Cury* (*Manner of Cookery*), compiled by the cooks of England's Richard II — the book to consult if you need to gild a peacock — includes recipes "For to

Beans, to the ancients, were primarily cheap peasant food, the classical equivalent of Wonder bread and Hamburger Helper.

make grounden benes," "For to make drawen benes," and "Benes yfryed," which, in Gothic script, looks pretty much like refried beans. Similarly, *Le Menagier de Paris*, written in 1393 by a helpful husband for his inexperienced teenage bride, includes — along with instructions for eradicating flies (whack them with paddles), choosing a fresh rabbit (snap its back legbone), and cleaning birdlime off a sparrowhawk (dunk its feathers in milk) — detailed instructions for cooking beans and preventing them from sticking to the bottom of the pot.

Johannes Bockenheim — cook to Pope Martin V and author, sometime in the 1430s, of *Registrum coquine* (*The Cookery Register*) — explains not only how to prepare a dish, but also what sorts of persons each of his seventy-four recipes is intended to serve: peasants or princes, Italians or Englishmen, priests or prostitutes. His bean soup, a mix of stewed favas, onions, olive oil, and saffron, is recommended for Lollards and pilgrims — that is, for both heretics and the ultradevout — which seems emblematic of the comfortable ubiquity of the bean.

❀

Almost every culture has its signature bean cuisine. In France, the most famous of bean dishes is *cassoulet*, a stew of fava beans, meat, and spices, named for the flat earthenware dish or *cassole* in which it is traditionally baked. The story goes that the original cassoulet was invented during the siege of the town of Castelnaudary during the Hundred Years' War. In 1355, with England's Edward, the Black Prince, at their gates, the inhabitants of Castelnaudary decided to fortify themselves for battle with stew. Everything they had, including beans, duck, goose, and pork sausage, went into the communal pot. The nicer version of the story holds that the well-fed French then rose up and beat off their English enemies, though history reports that the Black Prince sacked the town, burned most of it, and massacred the populace. The cassoulet tradition, however, survived, and today, according to food writer Alexander Lobrano, Castelnaudary is the heart of southwestern France's "cassoulet belt," an 80-mile stretch of bean cookery where every restaurant serves some version of cassoulet.

By the seventeenth century, cassoulet was no longer made solely with fava beans, but with *Phaseolus vulgaris*, the exciting new bean from the recently discovered Americas. American beans reputedly came to France with the fourteen-year-old Catherine de Medici, when she arrived from Italy in 1533 to marry the future Henri II. Maguelonne Toussaint-Samat's *History of Food* (2009) describes how Catherine brought a humble little bag of beans in her trousseau, tucked in among her laces, ropes of pearls, gold-embroidered gowns, and black-and-crimson silk sheets. (Catherine also gets credit for introducing the French to forks, sorbet, olive oil, Chianti, macaroons, artichokes, and the ballet.)

The American bean was known in France as the *haricot*, even though, according to Toussaint-Samat, the original *haricot* or *hericoq* had nothing to do with beans. Instead the word referred to an entirely beanless turnip-and-mutton stew, popular in France since at least the fourteenth century. Following the introduction of *Phaseolus vulgaris*, however, the American beans ousted turnips from the traditional dish, and in fact became so overwhelmingly popular as an *haricot* ingredient that the bean

Kidneys and Canoes

While the scientific name *Phaseolus* derives from the Greek for "little boat" (supposedly from the canoelike shape of the seedpods), the common name *kidney bean* comes from the anatomically suggestive shape of the seeds. Medically, this was thought significant: the medieval Doctrine of Signatures held that the shapes of plants constituted a broad hint from the Almighty as to their uses in healing.

The Doctrine maintained, for example, that walnut kernels, being crinkly and convoluted, had "the very figure of the Brain," and thus were good for headaches; lungwort, whose attractively speckled leaves reminded some depressed observer of diseased lungs, was a specific for pulmonary infections; and the kidney bean was a cure for urinary disorders. Physician Nicholas Culpeper, in his *Complete Herbal* (1653), recommended beans, dried, ground to a powder, and dissolved in white wine, as a treatment for kidney stones.

subsequently grabbed the name for itself. (An alternative source suggests that haricot comes from the Aztec word for bean, *ayacotl*.) To distinguish the haricot dried (the edible bean seed) from the haricot fresh (the young bean, pod and all), precise cooks further adopted the term *haricot vert* ("green bean").

A charming story holds that the *haricot vert* and its associated recipes reached England in company with fleeing French Huguenots during the reign of Elizabeth I. In gratitude for religious freedom, they made a gift of green beans to the Queen, who found them "much engaging to the royal taste" and ordered some planted in her garden at Hampton Court. A brief movement then flared up among patriotic British farmers to rename the new and presumably French vegetable the "Elizabeth bean."

Unfortunately, like the tale of the bag of beans tucked in Catherine de Medici's lush luggage, there's little (if any) supporting historical evidence for this – and frankly, the bean plug doesn't sound like Elizabeth I, whose food passions were candy and cake. Still, American beans were both grown and eaten in Elizabeth's England, if not enthusiastically by the Queen.

John Gerard includes the *Phaseolus* or "Kidney Beane" in his encyclopedic 1597 *Great Herball, or Generall Historie of Plantes*, in which he finds it vastly superior to the familiar fava or "great garden Beane." Boiled, buttered, and eaten in the pod, he writes, the American beans are "exceeding delicate meate and do not ingender winde as other Pulses do." Ripe, however, "they are neither toothsome nor wholsome," and thus should all be picked "whilest they are yet greene and tender."

❄

American bean cookery owes a lot to the Indians who, by the time the European colonists arrived, had been cooking and eating beans for at least 600 years. The original of Boston baked beans was a New England Indian dish in which dried beans were soaked in water until softened, mixed with bear fat and maple sugar, and baked overnight in a "beanhole" — a hole dug in the earth and lined with hot stones.

Slow overnight baking particularly appealed to the Puritans of Massachusetts Bay, for whom cooking was prohibited on the Sabbath. Beans, tossed into the pot on Saturday night, seemed a neat solution to the problem of Sunday dinner, and soon became a Boston tradition. Boston, accordingly, acquired the nickname Beantown — though somewhat unfairly, since the top baked-bean eaters in the world are the British, who consume 800 million tons of them a year, a lot of them for breakfast.

By the eighteenth century, the "Indian Beans" had acquired varietal names. Thomas Jefferson grew twenty-seven varieties of kidney beans at Monticello, including Arikara or "Ricara" beans, collected by Lewis and Clark from the Dakota Arikara tribe during their 1804–1806 cross-country Voyage of Discovery.

In the first published American cookbook, Amelia Simmons's 1796 *American Cookery* — in which the longest recipe is a three-page account of how to dress a turtle — the author lists nine varieties of beans, among them the Clabboard, the Crambury, the Lazy, and the English or horse bean, this last so easily cultivated that it "may be raised by boys." Not much is known about Amelia Simmons, not even where she came from, but best guess places her in either Connecticut or New York. She describes herself as "a poor solitary orphan," and admits modestly to being "circum-scribed in knowledge," for which in her preface she solicits the "Candor of the American Ladies." (She received it, apparently, since subsequent printings of *American Cookery* include corrections to her original recipes.) The recipes indicate that vegetables are not Amelia's strong suit: in fact, she lists only two for beans, one for French (American or green) beans and one for broad (fava) beans. Instructions are the same for both: boil them.

❀

Amelia does differentiate among string, shell, and dried beans, the three uses to which the edible bean is still put today. The string bean — stringless since 1894, when Calvin Keeney of New York bred a bean free of the fibrous "string" that ordinarily runs the length of the pod — is eaten whole, green and immature, while the outer pod is still tender. At this stage the beans are also called snaps because they crack crisply when broken in two. Not all are actually green: the wax or golden-podded bean was introduced in the 1830s, developed by sequentially selecting for lightened pod color.

Most colonial string beans were pole types or "runner" beans, often planted in the cornfield Indian-style, so as to clamber up the cornstalks. Bush string beans were also apparently cultivated by the North American Indians: the Omahas, for example, raised "walking beans" (pole types, which climbed or crawled) and "beans-not-walking" (bush varieties, which stayed put). Still, bush beans were rare in gardens before the nineteenth century, when New York seedsman Grant Thorburn offered one of the first named bush varieties in his catalog in 1822. It was called Refugee, since it was (supposedly) among the beans brought to England by the refuge-seeking Huguenots in the 1500s.

Somewhat older adolescent beans are eaten as "shell" beans. By the shell stage, nine to eleven weeks after planting, the bean pods have become inedibly rubbery, but the enclosed seeds are still tender and immature, prime candidates for the cooking pot. The bean generally reaches adulthood (the dry-bean stage) after twelve to fourteen frost-free weeks on the vine. Designated "best for winter use" by Miss Simmons, these include such traditional baking beans as the small white oval-shaped bean so commonly found in ships' stores that it is best known today as the navy bean.

❈

While *Phaseolus vulgaris* is by far the dominant species of the cultivated American beans — worldwide, we produce some 25 million tons of it each year — it's not the only bean on the

Phaseolus family bush. Also grown today are *P. lunatus*, the lima bean; *P. coccineus*, the scarlet runner bean; and *P. acutifolius*, the tepary bean.

I'll admit, right up front, that I'm not a fan of lima beans. Everyone else in my family loves them, so clearly it's my fault and has nothing to do with the beans. Lima beans have "a wonderful plush texture," writes Martha Rose Shulman in the *New York Times*; and Laurie Colwin in *More Home Cooking* (1995) admits to being addicted to them. "They are pillowy, velvety, and delicious," Colwin writes, "and people should stop saying mean things about them." But I just can't see it, and in my lima-bean blindness, I'm not alone. Bart Simpson hates lima beans; and in Judith Viorst's picture book *Alexander and the Terrible, Horrible, No Good, Very Bad Day* (2009) — in which life is so awful that Alexander is prepared to throw in the towel and move to Australia — one of the bad-day disasters is lima beans for dinner.

The species *Phaseolus lunatus* includes both large-seeded limas and small-seeded sieva or butter beans. The species name (*lunatus*) comes from the moon-like shape of the moon-colored seeds; the common name (lima) is from their city of approximate origin in Peru, where archaeologists estimate they were under cultivation 6,000 years ago. The domesticated lima bean thus considerably pre-dates Lima, founded in 1535 by Francisco Pizarro in the valley of the river known to generations of Peruvian natives as the Rimac. (The lima thus might better be

"They [lima beans] are pillowy, velvety, and delicious, and people should stop saying mean things about them."

known as the Rimac bean.) The Spaniards, who liked them, sent samples of the local beans back to Europe, and then distributed them, as a sideline of their numerous voyages of exploration, to the Philippines, Asia, Brazil, and Africa.

Lima beans reached the United States in the early nineteenth century, by one account picked up in Peru by naval officer John Harris, who first grew them in his garden in Chester, New York. If so, they caught on like wildfire. Lima beans are mentioned in the 1812 diary of Benjamin Goddard, a gardening resident of Brookline, Massachusetts; and a recipe for "Lima, or sugar beans" appears in Mary Randolph's *Virginia Housewife* of 1824. Chances are there were multiple introductions: the varieties grown today can be traced back to a range of original South American imports.

Most eaters, unlike Bart, Alexander, and me, find them scrumptious. Eliza Leslie, in her *Directions for Cookery, In Its Various Branches* (1840), declares limas "the finest of all the beans." Frances Trollope, a visiting English author who loathed everything on the continent, including the American view of Niagara Falls, declared lima beans "a most delicious vegetable: could it be naturalized with us it would be a valuable acquisition."

Hands-down most spectacular of the cultivated American beans is the scarlet runner, *P. coccineus*, which was first domesticated in Central America and Mexico. Nicknamed "painted lady" for its gorgeous and gaudy flowers, the scarlet runner was first adopted by Europeans as an ornamental. It was grown in sixteenth-century England as "garden smilax," so called because, as it climbs, it twines counterclockwise like smilax or honeysuckle. John Gerard grew it in his garden, on decoratively positioned poles, although it was equally popular over the "arbors of banqueting places" to lend

a note of glorious color to the upper-class picnic. In Germany it
was known as *Feuerbohne* or "fire bean." Thomas Jefferson reports
planting some in 1812 on the "long walk" of the garden as "Arbor
beans, white, crimson, scarlet, purple."

P. acutifolius, the tepary bean, is the ancient *Phaseolus* of the
American Southwest. The tepary is a rapid grower, notably resistant to drought, ideally suited to the hot, dry climates of western
Texas, Arizona, and New Mexico. It was domesticated in Mexico
at least by 5000 BCE and was intensively cultivated by the Hopis,
who deliberately selected for the widest possible range of colors: yellow, tawny, brown, garnet, blue-black, white, and speckled.
Tepary beans, before the advent of the playing card and the poker
chip, figured as counters in an ancient Indian gambling game.

❀

Gambling aside, we all know the real problem with beans.
Both Old and New World beans — and, to be fair, bran, onions,
cucumbers, raisins, cauliflower, lettuce, coffee, and dark beer —
have a reputation for eliciting a condition known delicately
in the sixteenth century as "windinesse." Flatulence, for much
of human history, has been a pressing social concern: Robert
Burton, in his 1621 *Anatomy of Melancholy,* lists sixty-four
proposed remedies for sufferers. The embarrassing aftereffects
of bean eating are due to an assortment of oligosaccharides —
short chains of two to ten linked sugars — which the body is
unable to break down into metabolizable form. The bacteria of

the lower intestinal tract, however, can digest these tidbits just fine, producing in the process an accumulation of bloating gas.

One possible solution to the bean problem is to nuke the beans. Jammala Machaiah and Mrinal Pednekar, researchers in the food science laboratory at the Bhaba Atomic Research Centre (BARC) in Trombay, India, have found that zapping beans with low-intensity gamma rays eliminates up to 80 percent of the pesky oligosaccharides. Another method — the recipient of U.S. Patent No. 6,238,725 in 2001 — involves soaking and boiling, though not in the helter-skelter manner as performed in the average kitchen, but under carefully calibrated conditions involving mathematical formulae.

While hardly the pinnacle of social acceptability, flatulence is not ordinarily dangerous — except perhaps in the case of a Roman aristocrat under the emperor Claudius who reportedly endangered his health by embarrassed retention. Other bean components can be much nastier.

Foremost among the evils are the cyanogens, harmless sugar complexes that in the presence of a specific enzyme are cloven to release cyanide, an effective and deadly inhibitor of the respiratory system. Cyanogens are found in the seeds of apples, pears, peaches, and apricots, as well as in lima and kidney beans — the last two owing their appealing flavor to a soupçon of cyanide. Wild beans are generally higher in cyanogens than are their cultivated relatives, and some cultivated varieties have more poisonous potential than others. The colored lima beans, for example, of the sort popular in early Peru, contain up to thirty times the cyanogen concentration of the all-white lima beans grown today.

Red Wine, Chocolate — and Beans

Air isn't good for us. Breathe it long enough, points out Nick Lane, author of *Oxygen: The Molecule That Made the World* (2002), and it inevitably does us in. Oxygen is a killer.

The culprits here are a class of sinister oxygen offshoots called free radicals — highly reactive molecules with itchy unpaired electrons. Free radicals are products of normal body metabolism — each one of our body's cells generates 20 billion of them a day — and they're also found floating around in the environment, constituents of air pollutants and cigarette smoke. Left to themselves, free radicals — like tiny gobbling Pac-men — destroy cellular integrity and wreak havoc with DNA.

Our bodies ordinarily fight free radicals off with a pair of antioxidant enzymes, catalase and superoxide dismutase (rudely abbreviated as SOD). Over time, however, our lifelong accumulation of free radicals overwhelms our normal defenses. Free-radical-induced damage has been implicated in cardiac disease, long-term memory loss, macular degeneration, and cancer. One theory of aging holds that it's all the fault of free-radical-generated oxidative stress.

We can beat free radicals off, however — with food. Red wine, dark chocolate, green tea, fruits, and vegetables are all — in varying degrees — rich sources of protective antioxidants such as vitamins E and C, carotenoids, and flavonoids. The total antioxidant content of a food is determined by ORAC (Oxygen Radical Absorbance Capacity) analysis — a test-tube test that determines how effectively various foods can block the oxidative destruction of a fluorescent test molecule. In theory, the higher the ORAC score, the better, though in actual practice there are variations depending on whether a food is raw, boiled, baked, steamed, or juiced.

Top of the list, according to a 2004 U.S. Department of Agriculture (USDA) study: blueberries, artichokes, apples, potatoes, and red beans.

Along with cyanogens, bean seeds contain protease inhibitors — complex protein molecules that interfere with the enzymatic processes of digestion — and lectins, which bind to sugar receptors on the surfaces of intestinal cells, with ensuing ill effects. Black turtle beans, for example, contain a hefty dose of the toxic lectin phytohemagglutinin, which induces a lethal clotting of the blood. Luckily, both cyanogens and phytohemagglutinin are defused by cooking, which means there's no need to fear black bean soup. Perhaps, as one anthropologist suggests, cooking developed in the first place to detoxify the otherwise irresistibly nutritious seeds of wild legumes.

Such piddling negatives as poisons, however, are hardly enough to put a dent in the popularity of beans. In comparison to the egg — the acknowledged *ne plus ultra* of human foods — beans pack 34 percent as much protein, and they're a whole lot easier to carry. Daniel Defoe's stranded Robinson Crusoe, discovering a "parcel of money" in gold and silver on his desert island, is thoroughly dismayed: "I would have given it all for a sixpenny-worth of turnip and carrot seed out of England, or for a handful of peas and beans, and a bottle of ink."

"Not worth beans" has meant "utterly valueless" since the thirteenth century, which shows that, historically, we haven't had a clue as to the value of beans. A lot of us are here only because of them.

Chances are, even you and me.

CHAPTER THREE
In Which

BEETS MAKE VICTORIAN BELLES BLUSH

plus

The Smell of Rain, Charlemagne's Christmas List, A Clever Use of Wine Lees, A Recipe for Longevity, and An Infamous Doctor

The beet is the most intense of vegetables.
TOM ROBBINS

beet

Alot of us don't like beets.

According to an AOL food preference poll of 2008, beets are among Americans' top ten most-hated foods. They were seventh in awfulness, to be exact, which means they were less loathed than liver (the worst of the worst), lima beans, mayonnaise, mushrooms, eggs, and okra, but were definitely more despised than Brussels sprouts, tuna fish, and gelatin.

Just 11 percent of home gardeners grow beets. Among the beetless majority is the White House: no beets were planted in 2009 in the White House organic vegetable garden because President Barack Obama and First Lady Michelle can't stand them. Irwin Goldman, master beet researcher and professor of horticulture at the University of Wisconsin in Madison, estimates that just 8,000 acres of land in the United States are devoted to growing beets — we use more for turnips (11,500 acres), radishes (14,600), and macadamia nuts (17,800) — and the National Agricultural Statistics Service (NASS) barely bothers to track them.

The problem with beets, beet-haters say, scrunching up their noses and making "blech" expressions, is their taste. Beets, they claim, taste like dirt. And they do, actually, although most beet aficionados prefer the term "earthy." The crucial chemical that gives beets their distinctive flavor is the same substance that makes the garden smell so good after a rain. Called geosmin, it's officially a terpene — one of a vast class of hydrocarbon molecules that also puts the tang in turpentine and the zip in hops. In nature, geosmin is produced by a number of microorganisms, including blue-green algae and soil bacteria.

People are surprisingly sensitive to it. We can detect geosmin in nanogram quantities — that is, in amounts as low as ten parts per trillion. In very tiny doses, geosmin can be a flavor plus. (One optimistic wine seller compared the touch of it in his vintage to dried apricots.) Too much of it, however, makes water, wine, catfish, and beets taste like mud, and, though it won't actually hurt us, we don't like it.

❄

The garden beet, *Beta vulgaris*, is said to get its formal name from the Greek letter *beta*, because the swollen root more or less resembles a Greek B. Less is more like it: as any casual student of the Greek alphabet can plainly see, the average beet looks a lot more like an omicron (O), theta (Θ), or even a lower-case sigma (ς) than a beta. However, Carl Linnaeus — the father of modern taxonomy — swallowed it, and then assigned the beta-shaped beet to the Goosefoot family (Chenopodiaceae), so called because the leaves of some of the more prominent members resemble the flat flappy feet of geese.

In 2003, however, following extensive morphological and phylogenetic analyses, modern taxonomists demoted the chenopods from family status, and incorporated them into the previously somewhat puny family Amaranthaceae, thus nearly tripling its size. Beet relatives now include some 2,400 species, among them the potherbs Good-King-Henry and lamb's-quarters; leafy garden spinach; quinoa, a chenopod used by natives of the high Andes to make porridge and beer; and tumbleweed or Russian thistle, a pest in the American West, immortalized in song ("Driftin' along with the tumbling tumbleweed") in the 1940s by the Sons of the Pioneers.

Botanists recognize three subspecies of beets: *B. vulgaris* ssp. *vulgaris*, which includes the familiar fat red beetroot, the sugar beet, and the outsized mangel-wurzel; *B. vulgaris* ssp. *cicla*, the leaf beets or chards; and *B. vulgaris* ssp. *maritima*, the uncivilized sea beet, a native of the coasts of Europe and the Middle East, believed to be the ancestor of all modern domesticated varieties.

The oldest of cultivated beets were probably the chards, which have nothing remarkable in the way of roots, but are eaten much like spinach, for the leaves. The ancient Greeks, said to have offered chard on silver platters to the god Apollo, referred to the leafy beet as *teutlion* because, according to science writer Stephen Nottingham, its foliage resembled squid tentacles. Whatever it looked like, it was healthy stuff: a cupful of cooked greens provides an entire adult daily requirement of vitamin A.

Pliny the Elder, who ate his beets as leaves, spoke slightingly of the "crimson nether parts" as the preserve of doctors and druggists.

The Romans were the first to develop beets with bulbous roots, though initially these were used only as medicine. Pliny the Elder, who ate his beets as leaves, spoke slightingly of the "crimson nether parts" as the preserve of doctors and druggists. His *Natural History* lists twenty-four remedies based on beetroot: soaked in water, beets were good for "the stings of serpents"; boiled and eaten with raw garlic, they were used to treat tapeworm. Beet juice cured headaches and vertigo, or, injected into the ears, tinnitus; and various decoctions were used for ulcers, pimples, erysipelas, chilblains, toothache, and — peculiarly — both constipation and diarrhea. The food-loving author of *Apicius* (*De Re Coquinaria*), however, lists at least two recipes for beetroot: in one, beets are boiled with leeks, cumin, coriander, and raisin wine; in another, they are pickled with vinegar, oil, and mustard seed.

❀

By the late eighth or early ninth centuries, beets were certainly being grown in northern Europe. Around that time they appear in Charlemagne's *Capitulare de villis* — a lengthy imperial administrative directive, divided into helpful *capitula*, or chapters — that describes the makeup and management of the royal estates.

No detail, apparently, was too small for the king. The *Capitulare* calls for annual accounting statements (at Christmas) from each of his many stewards, who were required to calculate total estate income, assess amounts of land under cultivation (both by "our own plowmen" and tenants), sum up stocks of pigs, turnips, mulberry wine, beer, and beeswax, and even note the number and nature of recorded poaching incidents.

It sounds much like our annual required report to the Internal Revenue Service, and doubtless drove a lot of French stewards equally mad.

Also included in the *Capitulare* is an extensive list of the flowers, herbs, fruit and nut trees, crop plants, and vegetables grown in the royal fields and gardens. Among these last are "Salads" (cucumbers, melons, lettuce, parsley, radishes, and celery), "Roots" (carrots, parsnips, onions, leeks, and garlic), and "Pot-herbs" (mint, chicory, endive, savory, cabbages, and beets). The inclusion of beets with the potherbs (not roots) suggests that Charlemagne's was a leaf beet or chard; the bulbous bright red beetroot, known as the "Roman beet" or "Blood Turnip," seems to have become common in European gardens only in the sixteenth century.

The Elizabethans ate their beets boiled in stews, pureed and baked in tarts, and occasionally roasted whole in the embers. White beets seem to have been more common, and consequently less desirable, than red. In 1577, Thomas Hill, author of *The Gardener's Labyrinth*, in which he supplies would-be horticulturalists with a lot of bizarre advice, addressed himself to unhappy white-beet growers: "To have the Beete growe redde, water the plant with redde Wine Lees." Hill also included his personal technique for producing bigger beets, by placing a "broad Tile, potshearde, or some other thing of weight" on top of the developing stalk, which naturally makes one wonder about the state of the Hill family beet patch.

"To have the Beete growe redde, water the plant with redde Wine Lees."

Red, in most plants, comes from anthocyanins, a class of red and purple pigments that puts the color in apples, grapes, and eggplants, and make roses red and violets blue. The beet, on the other hand — though relatively impervious to red wine lees — is made red by betalains, a class of brilliantly colored molecules peculiar to beets, bougainvillea, and the prickly pear cactus.

Betalains, of which there are many, come in two major kinds: betacyanins, which are red and purple, and betaxanthins, which are yellow, orange, and gold. Betacyanins are what led nineteenth-century belles to use beet juice as rouge; and today betanin — the reddest of the betacyanin reds — is used commercially to color a wide range of products from sausages to Kool-Aid. Not everyone, incidentally, is able to metabolize betacyanin properly, which means that after an orgy of red beet eating, they pee pink.

✸

Beets are not only beautiful, but also beneficial. They're rich in folic acid, a B-complex vitamin, and in free-radical-scavenging antioxidants, which prevent cell damage and combat aging. The Hebrew Talmud — a collection of rabbinical writings generally dated to 300–500 CE — presciently recommends eating beetroot for long life (along with drinking mead and bathing in the Euphrates River). Modern juice diet advocates claim that a daily dose of beet juice cleanses the body of environmental toxins, lowers blood pressure and cholesterol levels, and reduces the risk of cardiovascular disease and colon cancer.

Pro-beet claims, however — maybe the color inspires irrational passions — can be dangerously overblown. In the 1950s, for example, Hungarian physician Alexander Ferenczi reported miraculous success in treating assorted advanced malignant cancers with a quart of raw beet juice a day, a result that still — despite lack of medical backup — pops up all over the Internet. Most notorious of medicinal beet advocates, however, is certainly South Africa's late health minister, Manto Tshabalala-Msimang, nicknamed "Dr. Beetroot" for her promotion of traditional but wholly ineffective beetroot, lemon, and garlic remedies in lieu of antiretroviral drugs as a treatment for AIDS.

The European colonists toted beets across the Atlantic to North America, where both chard and beetroot, in red, white, and yellow, were well established by the eighteenth century. Thomas Jefferson planted beets at Monticello; and Mary Randolph mourns that they "are not so much used as they deserve to be," and recommends that they be boiled and served with salt fish.

Amelia Simmons mentions them in *American Cookery*, casting in her lot with the red: "The *red* is the richest and best approved; the white has a sickish sweetness, which is disliked by many."

Red as a Beet

To turn *as red as a beet* has been a synonym for an embarrassed blush since colonial times — appropriate not only for the hot-faced hue, but because beet red, exactly like a blush, is impermanent. Betacyanins are water-soluble: used as fabric dye, beets produce an initial deep rosy red that, disappointingly, promptly comes out in the wash. Better are red beans, which dyers use to produce a rich red-brown, and better yet is madder, *Rubia tinctoria*, a sprawling perennial of the same plant family as coffee and quinine. The British red coats were dyed red with madder root, as were the beet-red stripes in Betsy Ross's famous flag.

Achard promised outflows of tobacco, molasses, rum, coffee, vinegar, and beer, all from the miraculous beet.

❈

The sickish white, on the other hand, was viewed more positively by European chemists who, in the eighteenth century, were in the process of developing the sugar beet. In 1747 German chemist Andreas Marggraf found that white beetroots contained sucrose, the same profitably sweet ingredient produced by sugarcane. Subsequently Marggraf's student Franz Achard instituted a program to improve the sugar potential of the existing beet crop and devised an industrial process for efficiently extracting sugar from beets — a scientific accomplishment that overexcited him to the point of promising future outflows of tobacco, molasses, rum, coffee, vinegar, and beer, all from the miraculous beet.

The King of Prussia, who took much of this hype with a grain of salt, still offered Achard a subsidy to establish a sugar beet industry, and the first processing plant was constructed at Kunern, Silesia, in 1801. The beets processed were Silesian fodder beets, which contained up to 6.2 percent sugar, as opposed to the relatively measly 2 percent sugar content of the run-of-the-mill garden beet.

Over the next decade, the sugar beet industry soared in importance, notably in France, where Napoleonic warmongering and the resultant British blockade of French seaports had cut off the French supply of West Indian cane sugar. In the ensuing scramble for sweeteners, factories manufactured syrups from everything from raisins to honey — distressingly unsatis-factory substitutes for table sugar — until pharmacist Nicolas Deyeux, who seems to have kept current with the scientific lit-erature, proposed using Achard's sugar beet. The first imperial French sugar beet factory was established in 1812, three years before the imperial French government went under at the Battle of Waterloo.

Today sugarcane and sugar beets together account for most of the world's sugar, with a little help from corn and sorghum, sugar maples, and honeybees. The modern improved sugar beet, *B. vulgaris* var. *saccharifera*, contains an impressive 20 percent sucrose by weight and is now in sixth place on the UN Food and Agriculture Organization's list of the world's major crops. (Number one is sugarcane.)

❄

The eighteenth century also saw the introduction of the mangel-wurzel, like the sugar beet an offshoot of the earlier white fodder beet. It was developed in Germany and Holland as a livestock feed and introduced to England in the 1770s, where an unfortunate mistranslation of the German *Mangold-Wurzel* ("beet root") as *mangel-wurzel* ("scarcity root") fostered the belief that these beets would make a dandy food for the poor in periods of famine.

They were better suited to cows. Martha Washington experi-mented with them at Mount Vernon, and by 1888 W. Atlee Burpee's *Farm Annual* offered customers seven different types of mangels, including the Golden Tankard, which in the illustration looks like a gallon jug with a ridiculously undersized topknot of leaves. Cows fed on it, says Mr. Burpee, give higher-priced milk.

The *Farm Annual* also offers twelve varieties of garden beets and a lone cultivar of chard, the stems and midribs of which, the accompanying description explains, can be either cooked "like Asparagus" or pickled.

All are, of course, delicious.

And they taste, just a little bit, like good garden dirt.

CABBAGE CONFOUNDS DIOGENES

plus

*Robert Burton's Black Vapours,
Samuel Pepys's Dismal Dinner,
Captain Cook's Sauerkraut,
A Roman Broccoli Binge, and
The Vegetable Variation of
Johann Sebastian Bach*

Oh thrice and four times happy those who plant cabbages!
FRANÇOIS RABELAIS

Cabbage

The original ancestor of the edible cabbage was a seaside dweller, a native of the Mediterranean and the northern European coast. Some cabbage students believe it was sea kale, a tough, bitter, loose-leafed plant still found growing wild along the temperate seaboard; others believe that the modern cultivated cabbage is a multifaceted mongrel, with combined genetic input from a number of assorted — and now impossible to sort out — wild relatives. Whatever the case, as of the present day some prolific great-granddaddy *Brassica oleracea* has spawned kale, kohlrabi, head cabbage, broccoli, cauliflower, and Brussels sprouts, plus the phenomenal ten- to fifteen-foot-tall tree cabbage, stalks of which once served as rafters to support the thatched roofs of cottages in the Channel Islands.

The cultivated cabbage has been around for thousands of years. The Greeks ate it and the Romans positively doted on it. The Romans claimed that their prized cabbages originated from the sweat of Jupiter, shed while attempting to explain away the rival pronouncements of a pair of opposing oracles, a plight with which any parent of two or more children can sympathize. An alternative and less pleasant tale involves Lycurgus, king of the Edonians, who banned the cult of the wine god Dionysus and, wielding an ox goad, imprisoned the Bacchae, the god's drunken followers. In revenge, Dionysus drove Lycurgus mad, which caused the king to chop his son to pieces, thinking the boy was a grapevine. The outraged Edonians then had their king torn apart by wild horses. Bereaved and awaiting his unspeakable punishment, he wept, and his tears became cabbages.

Roman soldier and statesman Cato the Elder, whose *De Agri Cultura* (*On Agriculture*) dates to the second century BCE and is the oldest surviving book of ancient Latin prose, waxed ecstatic over the cabbage, to which he attributed his formidable health and longevity. (He lived well into his eighties, reportedly fathering twenty-eight sons.) Others were less enthusiastic. One story holds that the fourth-century BCE Greek philosopher Diogenes — famed for wandering about with a lantern, vainly searching for an honest man — once remarked to a pleasure-loving young friend, known for sucking up to the rich, "If you lived on cabbage, you would not be obliged to flatter the powerful." The young man promptly replied, "If you flattered the powerful, you would not be obliged to live on cabbage."

The author of *Apicius* (*De Re Coquinaria*), whose tastes were usually fancier, listed at least five different ways of preparing cabbage, variously accompanied by cumin seed, mint, coriander, raisins, wine, leeks, almond flour, and green olives; and the Emperor Claudius, the story goes, once convoked the Senate to vote on whether corned beef and cabbage was the best of all possible dinner dishes. The senators, no fools, voted a unanimous yes.

Medicinally, cabbage eating was said to prevent drunkenness or at least to alleviate hangovers, both recurrent Roman problems; it was also the vegetable of choice for curing colic, paralysis, and the plague. Pliny the Elder, who lists eighty-seven remedies involving cultivated cabbages, recommends it as a palliative for everything from gout to hiccups to shrew-mouse bites, and claims that a child, washed in the urine of a cabbage eater, will "never be weak or puny." He also points out dampeningly that cabbage, eaten, makes the breath smell.

❀

The earliest of cultivated cabbages was almost certainly kale, *B. oleracea* var. *acephala*, a curly-leaved nonheading cabbage akin to the American Southern favorite, collard greens. The thick leaves branch from fibrous stalks, which, according to Irish legend, the fairies ride for horses on moonlit nights. Kale arrived early in colonial America and was firmly established by the late eighteenth century, when an advertisement for "Dutch kale of various Colours; Scotch ditto" appeared in the *Maryland Journal and Baltimore Daily Advertiser.*

"Scotch ditto" seems an offhand tribute to the top kale consumers of Europe. "To be off one's kale" is the Scottish equivalent of "to be off one's food," and in Scotland, a "kaleyard" is what anyone else would call a kitchen garden. Scotland's kale broth is one of the few survivors of traditional kale cuisine, a school of cookery that admittedly was never extensive, even at its peak.

Historically, kale has been a more popular food for livestock than for people, though for both it is notably nutritious, rich in calcium and vitamins K, A, and C. It's also a rich source of antioxidants, containing a hefty 1,770 ORAC units per 100 grams, twice as much as Brussels sprouts, broccoli, or beets.

The Romans may have had kohlrabi. Pliny describes "a Brassica in which the stem is thin just above the roots, but swells out in the region that bears the leaves, which are few and slender"

Cabbage and Co.

The cabbage, *Brassica oleracea*, is a member of Brassicaceae, the Cabbage or Mustard family, along with such other edible goodies as rutabagas, radishes, horseradish, watercress, true mustard, and wasabi. The family itself contains some 330 genera and nearly 4000 species. Distant cabbage cousins include such unlikely cabbagoids as candytuft and indigo.

— which certainly sounds like kohlrabi, though at least one latter-day interpreter thinks he was talking about cauliflower. Kohlrabi is sometimes called cabbage turnip or turnip-rooted cabbage because of its turniplike shape, but the more anatomically correct nickname is stem cabbage, since the edible portion is actually an aboveground swelling of the stem, modified for starch storage. The official scientific name is the tongue-twisting *B. oleracea* var. *gongylodes* sub-var. *caulorapa*.

Charlemagne ordered kohlrabi to be planted in his domains but fed it only to cattle, under the urgings of the royal physician, who warned that it would turn his soldiers unaggressively bovine. Kohlrabi is fairly bland in flavor — Alice B. Toklas of the notorious marijuana-laden brownies (actually "Hashish Fudge") ascribed to it "the pungency of the high-born radish bred in a low-brow cucumber"— and it has traditionally been best liked on the dinner tables of Germany and Eastern Europe. It never made much culinary headway in America, where nineteenth-century seed catalogs usually carried it with the proviso that if the family spurned it, it would do just fine as livestock feed. W. Atlee Burpee, in 1888, offered three cultivars, green, white, and purple, and had little to say about any of them.

Heading cabbages, *B. oleracea* var. *capitata*, the solid balls that, chopped, dominate New England boiled dinner, were known to Pliny, who mentions heads measuring a foot across. When Julius Caesar's troops invaded Britain they brought it along, in two colors, red and green.

In heading cabbage, the leaves are larger and thicker than those of nonheading varieties and are tightly wrapped around an enlarged terminal bud on a truncated stem. The result is about the size and shape of a human head: the scientific name *capitata* thus comes from the Latin *caput*, "head," as in *capitalist* and *decapitate.* The common name cabbage similarly comes from the Old French word for head, *caboche*. Attractive as cabbage heads are, being called one is not a compliment: according to lexicographer Stuart Berg Flexner, "cabbagehead" has meant a perfect idiot since 1682.

By the late sixteenth century, John Gerard in his *Great Herball* (under "Of Coleworts") lists sixteen different kinds of cabbages in cultivation, among them the "open coles" (kales and collards), "curled savoys" (broccoli), and "collie flours," and credits them with a host of medicinal virtues, including the ability to clear the complexion and cure deafness. He warns vineyard owners off them, however, since cabbages reputedly killed grapevines.

Robert Burton, in *The Anatomy of Melancholy* (1621), cautioned depressives to keep away from cabbages: "Amongst herbs to be eaten I find gourds, cowcumbers, coleworts, melons

"Cabbage causeth trouble-some dreams and sends up black vapours to the brain."

disallowed, but especially cabbage. It causeth trouble-some dreams and sends up black vapours to the brain." And Samuel Pepys was simply disappointed in them. His diary entry for Sunday, March 10, 1660, records dismally, "Dined at home on a poor Lenten dinner of coleworts and bacon" — after which things didn't get much better, since in the afternoon he went to church and the sermon was dull.

Not everyone, however, regarded cabbages as negatively as did Burton and Pepys. In fact, the early English cabbage is boastfully commemorated in stone on the 1627 tomb of Sir Anthony Ashley in Wimborne St. Giles, Dorset. Sir Anthony lies in effigy with an impressive cabbage at his feet, though no one these days is sure just why; the legend that he was the first cabbage planter in England is certainly wrong. One food historian has suggested that perhaps he made some useful improvement in the existing cabbage breeds.

If so, Ashley's improved cabbage may have eventually reached the American colonies — though not with the first lot of transatlantic cabbages, which were planted in Canada in the 1540s by French explorer Jacques Cartier. John Winthrop, Jr., setting out to join his father in Massachusetts Bay in 1631, packed a chest of garden seeds, along with "bookes and cloth," gunpowder and butter, and leather, rope, and ironware. His seed list ("Bought of Robert Hill Grocer dwelling at the three Angells in lumber streete") is an excellent indication of what was planted in the early colonial garden. Included are seeds of "Cabedg," "Colewort" (probably kale), and "Culiflower." This last was the most expensive item on young John's list: while most of his picks cost pennies, he forked over five shillings for two ounces of cauliflower seed.

Over the course of the next century, cabbages, gamely multiplying, became a staple of the American garden and table. By the mid-eighteenth century, garden writer and designer Batty Langley announced that "to make an Attempt of informing Mankind what a Cabbage, Savoy, or Colly-flower is, would be both a ridiculous and simple Thing, seeing that every Person living are perfectly acquainted therewith . . ." Among those perfectly acquainted was the indefatigable Thomas Jefferson, who grew eighteen varieties at Monticello. Frequently mentioned in his records are drumhead cabbages, which had flattened tops reminiscent of the percussion instrument, and the darkly ruffled Savoys, which Jefferson described in glowingly classical terms as having a "wrinkled jade green head with a surface like crackled faience." It was their resemblance to the Savoy that led flower-growers to dub the old-fashioned damask roses "cabbage roses."

W. Atlee Burpee's seed company was essentially founded on a cabbage, the Surehead, introduced to American gardeners in 1877. Response was enthusiastic: R. McCrone of Sykesville, Maryland, said his Sureheads were as large as water buckets; Seth Fish of Monmouth, Maine, called them "the finest sight on my farm"; J. M. Carroll of Springville, Alabama, said modestly that his gave entire satisfaction; and S. C. Stratton of Leetonia, Ohio, who wrote that "The Surehead Cabbage cannot be beat," boasted that his weighed thirty-five pounds apiece. By 1888, Burpee was offering thirty-one cabbage cultivars in addition to the Surehead, as opposed to one each of "Brocoli" (in purple) and Brussels sprouts.

The Self-Cleaning Cabbage

Biomimetics is the science of snatching good ideas from nature, which people have been doing ever since we started draping ourselves in sabertooth-tiger fur. Velcro (from burdock burrs), sticky tape (from gecko toes), and the sharkskin-style swimsuits worn by Olympic swimmers are all human exploitations of designs that nature thought up first. Water- and dirt-repellent protective sprays like Scotchgard were inspired by the cleanliness-conscious cabbage.

When scrutinized under an electron microscope, cabbage leaves prove to be covered with minuscule lumps and bumps, which in turn are coated with tiny water-shedding wax crystals. Water, poured on a cabbage, simply rolls down the surface of these waxy bumps, collecting grime as it goes, which is why cabbage leaves are so sparklingly clean after a rain.

❄

Abraham Lincoln, a cabbage lover, demanded and got corned beef and cabbage for his inaugural dinner in 1861, but by the late nineteenth century, the culinary cabbage had been banished from polite tables. Food writer M. F. K. Fisher, in *Serve It Forth* (1937), describes an acquaintance's encounter with a dish of cabbage at a little Swiss restaurant. "'What — *what* is that beautiful food?' Mrs. Davidson demanded. . . . At the word spinach her face clouded, but when I mentioned cabbage a look of complete and horrified disgust settled like a cloud."

The turn-of-the-century cabbage had hit social rock bottom. It was peasant food, served forth on the tables of the poor and the vulgar, the sort of people who kept pigs in the parlor. Its fall from favor was largely the fault of cabbage b.o., the penetratingly unpleasant smell generated by cabbage cooking. Mrs.

Davidson, encountering it for the first time, describes how she staggered, gasping, down the street, pressing her muff to her face. Then realization dawned.

"*Oh!*' I cried. 'Oh, we're in the *slums!*'"

The odoriferous culprits in simmering cabbage are sulfur-containing compounds, volatile by-products of mustard oil and isothiocyanates. When heated, these normal constituents of cabbage break down and release repellent vapors of ammonia, methyl sulfide, mercaptans, which smell of skunk, and hydrogen sulfide, which smells of rotten eggs.

For the garden cabbage plant, the noxious mustard oils are the vegetable equivalent of heavy artillery. As defensive chemicals, they act to repel cabbage-eating pests. In undisturbed cabbage tissue, the oils are bound to sugar molecules and, as mustard oil glycosides, are peacefully benign. When the cells are broken, however, as by predatory nibbling insects, enzymes clip off the restraining sugars and release the burning oils. These oils are devastating to bugs. Relatively low-key in cabbage, broccoli, and cauliflower, higher concentrations of mustard oils put the pepper in radishes, the spice in hot-dog mustard, and the explosive burn in horseradish and wasabi.

As well as mustard oils, members of the cabbage family contain goitrins, capable of blocking iodine uptake by the thyroid gland, and antivitamins, which bind to or mimic the real McCoys, preventing their uptake by the body. Neither is present in particularly threatening concentrations in the cultivated cabbage plant, which has been defused by centuries of human selection. Wild cabbages, however, can contain up to four times the amount of the milquetoast house-and-garden cabbage varieties.

While the nineteenth-century cabbage was most commonly subjected by the poor and vulgar to prolonged boiling, the cabbage-fancying Pennsylvania Germans turned theirs into sauerkraut. Sauerkraut is an ancient food tradition: the laborers who built the 1,500-mile-long Great Wall of China were nourished on rice and cabbage pickled in wine. Centuries later, Genghis Khan's cohorts added salt and took the portable result along on their invasion of eastern Europe. The concoction, adopted by the invadees, outlasted the Mongol hordes.

Rich in vitamin C, sauerkraut was carried as an antiscorbutic on early sea voyages. The British navy gave it a try before latching onto limes, and found it a success. Captain James Cook, on his second voyage on the *Resolution* from 1772 to 1775 — during which he circumnavigated New Zealand and just missed Antarctica — fed his men on fermented cabbage, noting in his log:

"Sour Krout, of which we had also a large provision, is not only a wholesome vegetable food, but, in my judgement, highly antiscorbutic; and spoils not by keeping. A pound of it was served to each man, when at sea, twice a week, or oftener when it was thought necessary ... These, Sire, were the methods, under the care of Providence, by which the *Resolution* performed a voyage of three years and eighteen days, through all the climates from 52 degrees North to 71 degrees South, with the loss of one man only by disease, and who died of a complicated and lingering illness, without any mixture of scurvy."

Sauerkraut was claimed (by royalty-courting Pennsylvanians) to have been a favorite food of Charlemagne, and President

James Buchanan, a Lancaster boy, was famed for the sauerkraut suppers served at Wheatlands, his Pennsylvania estate. During World War I, nobody gave it up, but ate it under the patriotic sobriquet "Liberty Cabbage." To this day, in Maryland, sauerkraut is a standard accompaniment to the all-American Thanksgiving turkey.

❆

Garden broccoli, *B. oleracea* var. *italica*, was loved by the Romans. The common name is derived from the Latin *bracchium*, meaning branch, although Roman growers themselves referred to the plant poetically as "the five green fingers of Jupiter." Drusus, oldest son and heir of the Emperor Tiberius, is said to have been positively addicted to it. One story holds that the broccoli-besotted prince once refused to eat anything else for an entire month, at which point his urine turned a bright broccoli green. His annoyed father upbraided him for "living precariously" and ordered him to cease and desist.

A Bolt of Broccoli

There's a kind of lightning that looks like broccoli. Discovered in 1989 when physicist John Winckler and colleagues at the University of Minnesota inadvertently captured it on video, this breed of bolt, rather than heading earthward, shoots upward into the stratosphere, forming eerie pink-and-blue electrical apparitions towering 30 miles or more above the tops of thunderclouds. Winckler dubbed these "sprites" after the flighty fairies of Prospero's enchanted island in Shakespeare's *The Tempest*. Like fairies, they're elusive, lasting barely a millisecond — less than the time it takes a hummingbird to flap its wings. Some viewers compare them to jellyfish, but any meteorologist with a garden will see a resemblance to broccoli.

Broccoli was introduced to France in the mid-1500s — some credit the bevy of creative Italian cooks who arrived with Catherine de Medici — and soon after made its way across the Channel to England, where it appeared on Elizabethan menus as "Brawcle." Phillip Miller mentioned it as "Italian asparagus" in his *Gardener's Dictionary* (1731), and Virginian John Randolph described it in 1765 in his anonymously published *Treatise on Gardening*. "The stems will eat like Asparagus," said Randolph, "and the heads like Cauliflower."

Although it sounded yummy, broccoli didn't truly catch on in the United States until the 1930s — and even then it met pockets of suspicious resistance. President George W. Bush dug in his heels on broccoli, famously announcing, "I haven't liked it since I was a little kid and my mother made me eat it. And I'm the President of the United States and I'm not going to eat any more broccoli."

A well-known *New Yorker* cartoon of the early broccoli period, captioned by E. B. White, shows a vegetable-proffering mother and an uncooperative child:

"It's broccoli, dear."

"I say it's spinach, and I say the hell with it."

Kids these days seem more accepting of broccoli. It's not at the top of the juvenile list — favorite childhood vegetables are carrots and potatoes — but it's not at the bottom either. Nearly 60 percent of kids like it, which puts it well up on green beans, spinach, asparagus, and eggplant.

Both broccoli and cauliflower are edible modifications of the cabbage flower. Botanists hypothesize that one of these is an early developmental form of the other, though considerable chicken-or-egg-like confusion exists over which came first. The edible portions of the broccoli plant include both fleshy stalks and clustered flower buds. These buds, left to themselves, will eventually open — hence "sprouting broccoli" — while the cauliflower head, a degenerate and sterile inflorescence, lacks this ability and, like Peter Pan, florally speaking, never grows up. To some scientists this suggests that broccoli appeared on the scene first. Today most broccolis are green, but common nineteenth-century garden varieties were more colorful, in purples, browns, reds, and creams.

Cauliflower, *B. oleracea* var. *botrytis*, was somewhat better accepted by the public, though it was censured by Mark Twain as "nothing but a cabbage with a college education." This most intellectual of cabbages is a precocious annual, whose edible buds, in lieu of opening, solidify into a tightly packed head technically called a curd. An early description of the cauliflower — at least, it might be cauliflower — dates to the twelfth century, when an Arab botanist spoke of a "flowering Syrian cabbage." It was mentioned by John Gerard as "Cole flowery," and commented upon in seventeenth-century French documents as "*chou-fleur.*" In Spain, according to Bert Greene, cauliflowers were grown ornamentally and it was customary for young women to wear small samples titillatingly tucked in their cleavages.

"Of all the flowers in the garden," announced Samuel Johnson, the way to whose heart was through the stomach, "I like the cauliflower best."

More commonly, however, the cauliflower was eaten — raw, boiled, or pickled — and by the eighteenth century, in any one of these manifestations, it was a highly regarded addition to the dinner table. "Of all the flowers in the garden," announced Samuel Johnson, the way to whose heart was through the stomach, "I like the cauliflower best." In France, the cauliflower was popularly eaten in soup — at court as the delectable Crème du Barry, a cream-of-cauliflower soup named for the equally delectable mistress of Louis XV.

Nowadays most cauliflower cultivars are white or cream-colored — the curds were once routinely blanched by wrapping them in the outer leaves to prevent unwanted discoloring by chlorophyll-inducing sunshine. Eighteenth-century gardeners also grew red and purple cauliflowers, which seem to have gone out of fashion by the late 1800s. Burpee's 1888 *Farm Annual* offers eleven cauliflower cultivars, all white.

❁

The latest of the versatile cabbages is Brussels sprouts, *B. oleracea* var. *gemmifera*, which serendipitously burst upon the garden scene in mid-eighteenth-century Belgium. Earlier possible descriptions exist: some sources hold that the Romans had Brussels sprouts, known as *bullata gemmifera* or diamond-makers, from their putative ability to enhance mental prowess. (Mark Antony is said to have eaten them, without effect, before being trounced by Augustus Caesar at the Battle of Actium.) Others suggest that the Roman references actually describe a tiny form of heading cabbage. In fact, the sprouts are axillary buds, compact miniature cabbage heads sprouting from the stalk, which is topped by a rosette of large loose leaves. From these multiple buds comes the nickname "thousand-headed cabbage."

When it comes to the multitudinous cabbages, we eat leaves, stems, buds, flowers, and roots — all but the fruit. The cabbage fruit, called a silique or siliqua, is a dry and unappetizing seed capsule — seldom seen in the garden, since most cabbages are picked and cooked before they have a chance to produce any. The cabbage-related *Lunaria annua*, however — variously known as "honesty," "money plant," and "moonwort" — is grown for its lovely translucent siliques, which resemble flat silvery coins.

Also prized for siliques is *Arabidopsis thaliana* or thale cress, a nondescript-looking cabbage cousin native to Europe, Asia, and North Africa that goes from seed to sprout to flower to seed-stuffed silique in a mere six weeks. With its tiny genome — just five chromosomes — and (for a plant) its lightninglike growth rate, *Arabidopsis* has established itself as a model organism for studies of plant genetics, development, and evolution. Plant scientists describe it as the greenhouse equivalent of those other boons to biology, the mouse and the fruit fly.

The modern cabbage is also a candidate for a future life in space. NASA's Contained Environmental Life Support System (CELSS) program, established in the 1980s, analyzes food-plant production in sealed spaces, of the sort likely to be available on future space stations and colonies. So far, lettuce, spinach, strawberries, chives, and potatoes are high on the extraplanetary list. Researchers are testing a wide array of additional crop and garden species, including tomatoes, corn, sorghum, rice, wheat, peanuts, radishes, squash, cucumbers, carrots, and cabbages.

Bach's Classical Cabbage

German composer Johann Sebastian Bach drank brandy and beer (we know this from surviving bar bills), and he almost certainly ate cabbage, turnips, and potatoes. His music, however, suggests that he may have preferred sausage and sauerbraten. Variation 30 of his famous *Goldberg Variations* is based on an old German folksong, "Kraut und Rüben," which begins "Cabbage and turnips have driven me away/Had my mother cooked meat, I'd have opted to stay."

One story, on the other hand, holds that cabbages have already headed off to explore new worlds on their own. An old tale from northern Germany claims that the man in the moon is a larcenous peasant who sneaked out to cut cabbages from his neighbor's garden on Christmas Eve. Caught in the act by the passing Christ Child, he was sent to the moon as punishment for his sin. There he still sits, cabbages and all.

CHAPTER FIVE
In Which

CARROTS WIN THE TROJAN WAR

plus

*A Badly Behaved Rabbit,
Henry Ford's Food Fetish, A Dose of
Devil's Porridge, The Amazing Career
of Cat's-Eyes Cunningham, and
A Royal Embroidery Contest*

Large, naked raw carrots are acceptable as food only to those who lie in hutches eagerly awaiting Easter.

FRAN LEBOWITZ

Carrot

Beatrix Potter's Peter Rabbit, certainly the most famous rabbit in literature, didn't eat carrots. No, really. He didn't. Once he wiggled under Mr. MacGregor's garden fence, he gorged on lettuces, French beans, and radishes, and then, feeling sick, he went off in search of parsley. At that point he rounded a cucumber frame, encountered the justifiably enraged Mr. MacGregor, and spent most of the rest of the book running. That evening, still without a carrot in sight, his well-behaved siblings, Flopsy, Mopsy, and Cottontail, got blackberries and milk for supper, while the reprehensible Peter was put sternly to bed with a dose of chamomile tea.

Rabbits *will* eat carrots but, frankly, carrots don't seem to be all that high on the rabbit food list. Their preferred vegetables are peas, beans, and beets, and if you grow any or all of these, the only way to keep rabbits from munching up the lot is to put a two-foot fence around your garden. Alternatively you can sprinkle the perimeter with dried blood or fox urine — or you can get a ferret. Not that these are guarantees. Rabbits are pushy, persistent, and tough.

People, on the other hand, not only eat carrots, but apparently adore them. Each of us consumes about twelve pounds of carrots a year (up from a mere four annual pounds in 1975); and kids, who turn up their noses at squash and spinach, routinely list carrots among their vegetable favorites. Historically, foremost among American carrot fans was industrialist Henry Ford, whose passion for vegetables was perhaps second only to his fondness for the automobile.

Ford was anti-milk ("the cow is the crudest machine in the world") and anti-meat (he promoted soybeans in lieu of beef and oatmeal crackers as a substitute for chicken), but he was devoted to the carrot which, he was convinced, held the secret to longevity. At one point he was the guest of honor at a twelve-course all-carrot dinner, which began with carrot soup and continued through carrot mousse, carrot salad, pickled carrots, carrots au gratin, carrot loaf, and carrot ice cream, all accompanied by glass after glass of carrot juice.

One story holds that Ford became interested in the painter Titian when his son Edsel donated a Titian painting ("Judith and the Head of Holofernes") to the Detroit Institute of Arts. It wasn't the artist's work that interested him; it was the fact that Titian had reportedly lived to be ninety-nine. He wanted to know if Titian ate carrots.

❀

The first carrots, botanists believe, came from Afghanistan and were purple. Scrawny, highly branched, and unpromising, these wine-colored roots belonged, like their plump cultivated descendants, to the Apiaceae family, some 300 genera and 3,000 species of aromatic plants commonly known as umbellifers. As well as the crunchy carrot (*Daucus carota*), the Apiaceae include celery, parsnips, anise, caraway, chervil, cilantro, cumin, dill, fennel, lovage, parsley, and poison hemlock — this last, known in Ireland as "Devil's porridge," an infusion of which killed Socrates. Characteristically, the umbellifers have hollow stems: Yann Lovelock in *The Vegetable Book* (1972) describes how the stalks of wild parsnip were once used as straws for sipping cider and weapons for shooting peas.

The ancestral carrot probably looked very much like Queen Anne's lace, the ubiquitous wild carrot of present-day fields and roadsides. The cultivated Greek and Roman carrots were probably still branched — a witchy characteristic referred to by modern breeders as "a high degree of ramification" — but were most likely larger, fleshier, and less bitter than their wild relatives. Experiments in the late nineteenth century by French seedsman Henri Vilmorin demonstrated the relative ease with which primitive farmers could have developed the cultivated carrot. Starting with a spindly-rooted wild species, Vilmorin was able to obtain thick-rooted equivalents of the garden carrot in a mere three years.

The conical root shape characteristic of carrots today seems to have shown up in the tenth or eleventh century in Asia Minor, and may have reached Europe in the twelfth century by way of Moorish Spain. No one, however, seems to have rushed to adopt it: John Gerard, in the sixteenth century, remarks that as nourishment goes, the carrot is "not verie good," although botanist John Parkinson, author of *Paradisus in Sole Paradisus Terrestris* (1629),

The emperor Caligula, who had a fun-loving streak, once fed the entire Roman Senate a feast of carrots in hopes of watching them run sexually amok.

who seems to have liked it better, says it can be "eaten with great pleasure" if boiled in beef broth. The roots, he added, are "round and long, thicke above and small below," and come in either red or yellow, while the dark green foliage, in autumn, turns red or purple, "the beautie whereof allureth many Gentlewomen oftentimes to gather the leaves and stick them in their hats or heads, or pin them on their arms instead of feathers."

※

The primitive purple, violet, red, and black carrots owed their color to anthocyanin, a pigment that dominated the carrot world until approximately the sixteenth century, when a pale yellow anthocyanin-less mutation appeared in western Europe. It thus must have been an anthocyanin-laced purplish carrot that Agamemnon's soldiers legendarily munched (presumably quietly) inside the Trojan Horse "to bind their bowels," and that Greeks on the home front used to concoct an aphrodisiacal potion or *philtron*. Like any vegetable even vaguely resembling a penis, the carrot was thought to be a passion promoter. Devious Roman soldiers boiled carrots in broth to release the sexual inhibitions of their female captives, and the emperor Caligula, who had a fun-loving streak, once fed the entire Roman Senate a feast of carrots in hopes of watching them run sexually amok.

The purple carrot quickly fell from favor with the advent of the yellow and, later, orange varieties. The cultivated purples, though tasty, turned an unappetizing muddy brown when cooked, which put off even the most stolid of chefs. The aesthetically appealing orange carrot is said to be a late-sixteenth- or early-seventeenth-century development of the Dutch, who were the dominant European carrot breeders. Some evidence for this comes from the sudden appearance of orange carrots in period oil paintings: Dutch painter Joachim Wtewael's "Kitchen Scene" (1605), for example, a detailed portrayal of a crowded and active kitchen complete with kids, dogs, cats, and a flirtation going on in the corner, features a large bunch of orange carrots sprawled, dead center, on the floor.

From the first orange original, Dutch growers soon produced the even deeper-colored Long Orange, a hefty carrot intended for winter storage, and the smaller and sweeter Horn. The Horn was further fine-tuned to yield, by the mid-eighteenth century, three breeds of orange carrot varying in earliness and size: the Late Half Long, the Early Half Long, and the smaller Early Scarlet Horn. Collectively, these 200-year-old Dutch carrots are the direct ancestors of all orange carrots grown today.

Carrots owe their orange to carotenoids, a collection of some five-hundred-odd yellow and orange pigments that function in plants to protect the all-important green chlorophyll from sun damage. About 10 percent of carotenoids are also vitamin

No matter what your grandma told you, carrots won't give you full-fledged nocturnal vision, any more than bread crusts will make your hair curl.

Raw or Stewed?

A single orange carrot provides the average adult with more than his or her recommended daily allotment of vitamin A. In terms of beta-carotene, however, the carrot cooked is far more forthcoming than the carrot raw. Crunched down à la Bugs Bunny, raw carrots release only about 3 percent of their total beta-carotene to the human digestive system. In boiled carrots, where the cooking acts to break down the root's thick cell walls, up to 40 percent is released; and blended or juiced carrots release up to 90 percent.

A precursors, and beta-carotene — the most prominent carotenoid in carrots — is one of these. In the human digestive tract, beta-carotene is clipped in half by a helpful enzyme to form two molecules of vitamin A, also known as retinol.

❊

Vitamin A plays a number of essential roles in the human body, among them the support of cell growth and reproduction and the regulation of the immune system — but it is perhaps best known for its effect on eyesight. In the retina of the eye, vitamin A binds to a protein (opsin) in the rod cells to form the visual pigment rhodopsin, which allows us to see — more or less — in the dark. In fact, the first hint of vitamin A deficiency is impaired dark adaptation ("night blindness"), and a severe or prolonged lack of vitamin A can lead to permanent blindness.

No matter what your grandma told you, however, carrots won't give you full-fledged nocturnal vision, any more than bread crusts will make your hair curl. The carrot-based night vision hype can be traced to the Battle of Britain in World War II, when Britain's newly installed radar network, which effectively

During World War II, innovative home front housewives produced carrot toffee, carrot marmalade, carrot fudge, and a drink called Carrolade made from crushed carrots and rutabagas.

tracked incoming German bombers, began to give a distinct advantage to the fighter pilots of the Royal Air Force.

Legendary pilot John Cunningham, nicknamed "Cat's Eyes" for his reputed ability to see in the dark, was the first person to shoot down an enemy plane with the aid of radar, and he soon went on to chalk up an impressive record of kills. The RAF, in an attempt to distract German attention from the bristling radar towers along the British coast, spread the story that Cunningham and his fellow night-flying pilots owed their success to a prodigious diet of vision-enhancing carrots. It's not clear how the carrot con went down with the German high command, but the British civilian population swallowed it, in the belief that eating carrots would help them navigate in the blackout.

Although carrots can't give you bona-fide night vision, they can, if you eat enough of them, turn you yellow. This syndrome, known clinically as carotenemia or carotenosis, results from the deposition of carotene pigments in the subcutaneous fat, just beneath the skin. Though visually somewhat startling, carotenemia seems to be physically harmless and disappears within a few weeks if the victim lays off carrots.

Carotene also gives cream its rich yellowish hue. In the seventeenth century, cows fed on the champion Dutch carrots were said to yield the richest milk and the yellowest butter in Europe, which in turn was held to be responsible for the famous rosy-cheeked Dutch complexion. Butter makers in colonial America, starting with less well-fed cows, often colored their butter after the fact by adding carrot juice to the churn.

✳

As well as beta-carotene, carrots are also high in minerals, notably potassium, calcium, and phosphorus. In 2008, Kendal Hirschi and his team at Baylor College of Medicine in Texas created a genetically engineered high-calcium "super carrot," capable of delivering to the eater over 40 percent more calcium than the ordinary carrot. Super carrots may eventually help stave off such conditions as brittle bone disease and osteoporosis.

Carrots also contain a lot of sugar. A single 7½-inch carrot contains some seven grams of carbohydrate, most of it — as in honey — in the form of fructose and glucose. Carrot carbs were made much of by the British Ministry of Food during World War II, when sugar was essentially unobtainable. The Ministry's "War Cookery Leaflet 4," devoted to the preparation of carrots, included recipes for carrot pudding, carrot cake, and carrot flan. Under the urging of the government's vegetable-promoting "Dr. Carrot," a gigantic carrot tricked out in a lab coat and top hat, innovative home front housewives produced carrot toffee, carrot marmalade, carrot fudge, and a drink called Carrolade, made from crushed carrots and rutabagas.

Because of their lip-smacking sweetness, carrots historically have been used in desserts. A recipe for carrot conserve — a sweet jam — survives in the fourteenth-century *Menagier de Paris*. The conserve, whose carrots are referred to as "red roots," also contains green walnuts, mustard, horseradish, spices, and honey. John

Evelyn's 1699 *Acetaria: A Discourse of Sallets* contains a recipe for a distinctly unsaladlike carrot pudding, a luscious-sounding mix of cream, butter, eggs, sugar, nutmeg, and grated carrot. The Irish, who doubtless found carrots a welcome relief from a relentless diet of potatoes, called them "underground honey."

❄

Even sweeter than the carrot is the related parsnip, *Pastinaca sativa*, which Ogden Nash, not a parsnip lover, compared dampingly to an anemic beet. Historically, it fared better: cheap, sugary, and substantial, the parsnip was a prime entrée in the Middle Ages, especially during the lean days of Lent.

The parsnip, like the bustle, began to fall from favor in the nineteenth century when, along with the Jerusalem artichoke, it was ousted from gardens by the more versatile Irish potato. Pre-potato, however, it was a garden staple: the rich ate parsnips in cream sauce and the poor ate them in pottage. John Gerard and Sir Francis Bacon both put in a good word for them; and Sir Walter Scott wrote sardonically that fine words don't butter any parsnips, meaning that flattery is worth diddly-squat.

Most parsnips are long, pale, funnel-shaped roots, a sort of oversized khaki-colored carrot. (Round turniplike varieties, introduced to the United States in 1834, never really caught on.) The large meaty types known as hollow-crown parsnips were

Aunt Hannah, having passed through port and rum, hit the parsnip wine, which led her to sing "a song about Bleeding Hearts and Death, and then another in which she said her heart was like a Bird's Nest."

developed in the Middle Ages; still grown today, these have a saucer-shaped depression at the top of the root (the "hollow crown") from which sprout the stems and leaves. Parsnips contain, root for root, about twice as much sugar as carrots, most in the form of sucrose, the sugar of sugarcane.

Historically, the sugary parsnip has been boiled down into syrup and marmalade and, with the help of a little yeast, brewed into beer and wine. One early nineteenth-century source directs hopeful winemakers to boil twelve pounds of sliced parsnips, strain through a sieve, add loaf sugar and yeast, and then age for twelve months. Modern winemakers, however, according to biologist (and parsnip fan) Roger Swain, opt for aging up to ten years, and a lot of wine connoisseurs suggest never, under any circumstances, taking the stuff out of the cask.

Drunk, however, it seems to be effective: in *A Child's Christmas in Wales*, Dylan Thomas's susceptible Aunt Hannah, having passed through port and rum, hit the parsnip wine, which led her to sing "a song about Bleeding Hearts and Death, and then another in which she said her heart was like a Bird's Nest."

The sweeter the parsnip, the more efficient the fermentation process — which means that winemakers should harvest their parsnips in the spring. Many plants, including parsnips, cabbages, and potatoes, sweeten after exposure to temperatures below 50 degrees F (10 degrees C). As early as the first century CE, Pliny the Elder commented on the phenomenon: "Turnips are believed to grow sweeter and bigger in cold weather," and "With any kind of cabbage, hoarfrosts contribute a great deal to their sweetness."

Low-temperature sweetening occurs in leaves, shoots, and roots of responsive plants. The sugar content of cabbages doubles after thirty days in the cold; overwintered parsnips contain nearly three times more sucrose by weight than their autumn-harvested buddies.

No satisfactory explanation yet exists for this sweetening process. One hypothesis suggests that the increased sugar acts as a cryoprotectant, a species of natural antifreeze. A similar explanation has been advanced to account for the increased spring sugar content of some tree saps, like that of the syrup-generating sugar maple.

✳

Carrots and parsnips are biennials. The starches and sugars of the fat storage roots are meant to support the development of flowers and seeds in the second year of growth. Permitted to progress to year two, carrots produce lacy compound umbels on two- to six-foot stalks, similar to the flowers of Queen Anne's lace. The largest flower, which ripens first, is called the king umbel, followed by a lesser array of side umbels, from all of which develop carrot seeds.

The edible taproot, for which gardeners routinely forfeit the aesthetic delights of carrot flowers, consists of a central core of vascular tissue and an outer layer called the cortex, composed of storage tissue. In the carrot, as increasing amounts of starch are accumulated, the central core pushes outward, maintaining a two-part pattern, which is why the carrot in cross-section looks like a slice of hard-boiled egg. In the beet, in contrast, vascular and storage tissue are laid down in alternate rings, like those of

*Queen Anne, the story goes, challenged her
ladies-in-waiting to make a piece of lace
as fine as the flower of the wild carrot.*

a tree trunk, while in the radish and turnip, vascular and storage cells are indistinguishably intermixed.

The taproots of today's garden carrots average five to eight inches long. These are weenie by ancestral standards. Nineteenth-century growers boasted of two-foot roots, a foot or more in circumference at the thickest, and weighing up to four pounds. Amelia Simmons, in her 1796 *American Cookery*, after a discussion of the superiority of the yellow carrot over the orange and the red, advises the "middling sized" carrot for cooking, by which she means a hefty vegetable a foot long and two inches across at the top. She recommends it as an accompaniment for veal, though it is also "rich in soups" and "excellent with hash." Carrots in Mary Randolph's *Virginia Housewife* (1824) require three hours of boiling, which implies a vegetable of substantial size.

❄

The carrot arrived in North America with the first settlers. The Jamestownians planted them between tobacco crops; and John Winthrop, Jr., included "Carrets" on his seed list of 1631. Carrots figured in the earliest of American seed advertisements: in 1738, one John Little offered orange carrots for sale along with his other "new garden seeds"; in 1748, "Richard Francis, Gardner, living at the sign of the black and white Harre at the South end of Boston" offered the gardening public carrots in a choice of orange or yellow. Jefferson grew carrots in several colors at Monticello.

From all of these widespread colonial gardens, the carrot promptly escaped and reverted to the wild. The ubiquitous American Queen Anne's lace of fields and country roadsides descends from ex-cultivated escapees.

The Queen of these lacy flowers is said to be Anne of Denmark, wife of England's James I and an expert needle-woman. Queen Anne, the story goes, in an attempt to allevi-ate the mind-crushing boredom of court living, challenged her ladies-in-waiting to make a piece of lace as fine as the flower of the wild carrot. The Queen herself, not surprisingly, won hands down, and the flower was rechristened in her name. Less roman-tically, it is known as bird's nest or devil's plague.

On both sides of the Atlantic, the 1870s were a banner decade for carrots, ushering in both the Danvers carrot, a dark orange, medium-long variety with exceptionally high yields, developed in Danvers, Massachusetts, and the Nantes carrot, named for its town of origin in France. Burpee's 1888 *Farm Annual* neglected the Nantes in favor of the equally French Chantenay ("of more than usual merit") and Guerande ("of very fine quality") — but reserved special praise for the homegrown Danvers, vari-ously described as "handsome" and "first-class." Also offered by Burpee were the Early Scarlet Horn and the related Golden Ball, a stumpy little vegetable that looked less like a carrot than a deep-yellow radish.

French seedsmen Vilmorin-Andrieux, in *The Vegetable Garden* (1885), diplomatically mention both the Danvers and the Nantes varieties along with some twenty-three other carrots, in a range of shapes and sizes. Impressive among them is the English Altringham carrot, whose bronze or violet roots measured over twenty inches long.

Garden carrots today generally belong to one of four major types: Imperator, Danvers, Nantes, or Chantenay. In general, Imperator and Danvers carrots are long and pointed; Nantes and Chantenay carrots, shorter and blunt; but the vast number of carrot cultivars available today tend to blur distinctions. Most carrot eaters agree that Nantes and Chantenay types are best for eating raw, while Danvers types — known for "broad shoulders" — are best for slicing and popping in stew.

It's safe to say, however, that there's a carrot out there for everybody. In fact, the online World Carrot Museum, an extraordinary collection of all things carrot, includes a list of common carrot varieties that includes at least one for (almost) every letter of the alphabet, from the New Zealand Akaroa to the (good for juicing) Zino.

CELERY CONTRIBUTES TO CASANOVA'S CONQUESTS

plus

*Mrs. Astor's Dinner Table, Besotted Bees,
A Trimming for Tombs, Boar Sauce,
John Evelyn's Unfinished Masterpiece,
and Airborne Magicians*

Genuineness only thrives in the dark.
Like celery.
ALDOUS HUXLEY

Celery

Celery tonic is still around. Nowadays it's called Cel-Ray and is made by Canada Dry, but it's still basically the same brew — soda water flavored with crushed celery seeds — that went on the market in Brooklyn in 1868 as Dr. Brown's Celery Tonic. It's not clear that there ever actually was a Dr. Brown — the name may simply have been invented for customer appeal, like General Mills's housewifely but nonexistent Betty Crocker. Real or no, however, he was at the forefront of the nineteenth-century celery craze, an enthusiasm that eventually produced not only celery soda, but also celery gum, celery soup, and Elixir of Celery, touted as a treatment for nervous ailments and popular enough to be offered in the 1897 Sears, Roebuck catalog.

In the Gilded Age, celery was also in vogue on the posh tables of the rich, whose meals, served by footmen, lasted more than two hours and involved twenty-four pieces of silverware and six wineglasses per place setting. Celery, in the heyday of the Astors and Vanderbilts, was served — not in little flat dishes with the olives, as on everybody's grandmother's dinner table — but in towering glass or silver celery vases, such that the leafy tops loomed impressively over the gravy boats, soup tureens, epergnes, and fancy floral centerpieces. Celery, once upon a time, was a fashion statement. It was pricey, and if you had it, you wanted to show it off.

The high cost of celery, which put it well out of the range of the average pocketbook, was due to its labor-intensive mode of cultivation. Nineteenth-century celery was routinely blanched, a whitening and sweetening process that involved piling dirt around the developing stalks to block exposure to sunlight. With the introduction of self-blanching varieties — Burpee's Golden Self Blanching Celery came on the market in 1884 — celery rapidly became more affordable. It was soon immensely popular across the social board; a late-nineteenth-century French tourist peevishly wrote that the celery-obsessed Americans "almost incessantly nibble" from the beginning to the end of their repasts. Inevitably, as celery entered the common clutches, it lost its prestige, and by the end of the century had been demoted from the boastful vase to the aforementioned unobtrusive flat dish.

The subject of all this social heartburn is a member of the family Apiaceae (along with the related carrots, parsnips, parsley, caraway, coriander, dill, and fennel). Its scientific name, *Apius graveolens*, derives from the Latin *apis*, or "bee," because bees go dotty over its tiny fragrant white flowers. Modern edible celery is believed to have originated in the Mediterranean area and Eurasia, where, in wild form, it established itself in the marshlands adjacent to the seacoast. Wild celery is colloquially known as smallage, derived from an older term for celery — *ache* (pronounced "ash") — which evolved into the Old English *small-ache*. More strongly flavored than cultivated celery, smallage today is the source of culinary celery seed.

In ancient times celery was prized as a pharmaceutical, and one linguistic theory holds that its common name derives from its remedial reputation — from the Latin *celer*, meaning quick-acting or swift, as in *celerity* and *acceleration*. Medically, celery has a long and versatile history. The Egyptians used celery stalks to treat impotence; the Romans used them to treat constipation and wore the leafy tops to alleviate hangovers. Apicius, who doubtless suffered many in the course of his expensively decadent career, recommended that morning-after victims "wear a wreath of celery round the brow to ease the pain." Pliny recommends celery (or parsley) as a treatment for lumbago; and reports that celery (or parsley), tossed in a fish pond, revives sickly fish.

In the Middle Ages, celery was used as a laxative or diuretic, as a treatment for gallstones, and as a palliative for wild animal bites. In the eighteenth and nineteenth centuries it was recommended (in tea) for digestive upsets and insomnia, and (in conserve) for chest pains. The nineteenth edition of the *Dispensatory of the United States of America* (1907) listed a "Compound Elixir of Celery," recommended for its sleep-inducing and calmative properties, though this may have had less to do with celery than with the elixir's other ingredients, which included alcohol and cocaine. Madame de Pompadour, with celery's rumored aphrodisiac effect in mind, fed Louis XV on celery soup, and legendary eighteenth-century lover Giacomo Casanova is said to have eaten celery to improve his sexual stamina.

Some modern research indicates that Casanova, at least, may have had it right. Doctors Mark Anderson, Walter Gaman, and Judith Gaman, coauthors of *Stay Young: Ten Proven Steps to Ultimate Health* (2010), have dubbed celery "Vegetable Viagra." The secret, they explain, is androsterone, a naturally occurring steroid found in human sweat and urine, boar saliva, and celery.

In people and boars, androsterone acts as a pheromone, which makes the males exuding it more attractive to females. A few stalks of celery before a date, the authors of *Stay Young* suggest, may be the difference between a cold shoulder and a hot night.

❇️

For all its aphrodisiacal potential, celery has some dismal associations. The ancient Greeks associated it with death, trimmed tombs with it, and coined the ominous saying "He now has need of nothing but celery" to mean imminent demise. Seventeenth-century poet Robert Herrick, better known for such sensual and upbeat works as "To the Virgins, to Make Much of Time" ("Gather ye rosebuds while ye may"), wrote a gloomy celery-featuring ditty titled "To Perenna, A Mistress" that begins, "Dear Perenna, prithee come / And with smallage dress my tomb." Wild celery was found among the funeral garlands in King Tutankhamen's sarcophagus.

The innocent-seeming celery does indeed have distinctly ominous features. Prominent among these is its content of chemical compounds known as psoralens or furocoumarins. Psoralens, present in appreciable amounts in celery, parsnips, and parsley, are potent photosensitizers — that is, they increase the sensitivity of the skin to sunlight. In combination with ultraviolet irradiation, psoralens have been used therapeutically to treat vitiligo — a skin depigmentation condition — and psoriasis, a chronic and miserable inflammatory skin disease. (*Psoralen* shares a root with the Greek *psoraleos*, "mangy," and *psora*, "itch.") The drawback is that such treatments must be strictly limited, since psoralens are also photocarcinogens, with the potential for causing skin cancers.

In healthy celery, psoralens are present at relatively low levels and pose no threat to the human hide. Sick celery, however, is a different matter. The plant produces psoralens in response to microbial invasion; thus diseased plants possess ten to one hundred times more of these molecules than their germ-free relatives, potentially dangerous concentrations. And then there are parsnips (*Pastinaca sativa*), which, even in the pink of health, are comparatively swimming in psoralens. Consumption of 0.1 kg of parsnip (a mere 3½ ounces) necessarily involves ingesting 4 to 5 mg of assorted psoralens, a potentially risky quantity unless one lives in a lightless cellar. The chief psoralens in celery, bergapten and xanthotoxin, are capable, even at normal, low levels, of inducing severe allergic reactions, frequently afflicting celery harvesters and growers and ranging in severity from hives to outright anaphylactic shock.

Similarly implicated in celery allergies is apiol, the essential aromatic oil of the celery plant, most highly concentrated in the spicy seeds. Apiol's major constituent is a terpene compound called limonene, also present in citrus fruits and various mints. (Limonene, the *bête noire* of the fruit juice industry, turns bitter in processing, and has therefore inspired a scientific and industrial scramble to develop low-limonene oranges and grapefruits.) The allergic reaction is said to be exacerbated by exercise, a good argument for lying quietly on the couch while chewing celery stalks. Apiol, since the days of Hippocrates, has also been known to induce abortion, and was used as an effective, but frighteningly toxic, abortifacient into the mid-twentieth century.

In the culinary sense, apiol is a much more desirable proposition, giving celery and parsley their distinctive flavor. In the celery plant, it is concentrated in the seeds and in cavities between the cells of the leaves, which is why leafy celery tops are often used to flavor soups. The Romans loved it, and used celery seeds (preferably the wild, stronger-flavored variety) as a condiment. The author of *Apicius* sprinkled them liberally in a sauce to be served with wild boar.

❋

With the decline and fall of Rome, celery fell from public view. It was resurrected as an edible, according to food historians, only in the sixteenth century, and then by way of Italy, where the hefty wide-stalked varieties similar to those around today were originally developed. The Reverend William Turner chattily mentions Italian celery in his *Herbal* of 1538: "The first I ever saw was in the Venetian Ambassador's garden in the spittle yard, near Bishop's Gate Streete." (Spittle, less repulsive than it sounds, was an early English term for garden spade.) John Parkinson was not enthusiastic about it — "its evil taste and savour doth cause it not to be accepted in meates as Parsley."

By Parkinson's time, however, the culinarily adept French were in the midst of developing an elaborate celery cuisine. A recipe of 1659 describes a dish of celery cooked with lemon, pomegranates, and beets. Celery hearts — the fused base where the stalks meet — were esteemed; and the leafy stalks themselves were eaten as delicacies with dressings of oil and pepper.

❄

By 1699, British diarist and prolific writer John Evelyn had adopted the cause of "Sellery." In his *Acetaria: A Discourse of Sallets,* he praises the "high and grateful Taste" of celery, peeled, sliced, and eaten with "Oyl, Vinegar, Salt and Peper" (though he warns diners that small red worms often lurk in the stalks). Evelyn was an early proponent of the "Herby-Diet" — that is, vegetarianism.

Acetaria, a spin-off from a far more ambitious work, was originally intended as a mere chapter in Evelyn's three-volume, one-thousand-plus-page *Elysium Britannicum, or The Royal Garden,* a comprehensive account of the practices and principles of seventeenth-century gardening. The book as planned was to include detailed chapters on soils and composts, waterworks, nurseries, and bowling greens, orangeries and aviaries, garden statuary, a plan for revamping cemeteries, and a horticultural book list.

Though Evelyn worked on the project for 50 years, it was never published, and after his death Christ Church Library, Oxford,

By 1699, British diarist John Evelyn had adopted the cause of "Sellery," which he praised for its "high and grateful Taste."

acquired the manuscript — an intimidating mishmash of text; loose notes; pasted-in addenda; DIY instructions for constructing a "Transparent Bee-Hive," a garden "Thermoscope or wheather-Glass," and an artificial echo; and original sketches, among them a nice diagram of a tarantula. In the year 2000, Evelyn's *magnum opus* — or at least the surviving third of it — finally appeared in print, painstakingly deciphered and transcribed by John Ingram of the Colonial Williamsburg Foundation, some 300 years after the publication of *Acetaria* — originally slated to appear in Book II, Chapter XX, as "Of Sallets."

❊

Cultivated celery, *Apius graveolens* var. *dulce*, eaten today for its crunchy stalks, is certainly the vegetable recommended by Evelyn for his Sellery salad. Botanically speaking, the scrumptious stalks are leaf petioles rather than true stems — structural equivalents of the "stems" that attach conventional leaves to the branch of a tree. The other cultivated celery, *A. graveolens* var. *rapaceum*, also known as knob- or turnip-rooted celery or celeriac, features a starch-swollen lower stem (not root). The scientific name *rapaceum* reflects the necessary harvesting technique — unlike the more docile garden celery, celeriac clings to Mother Earth and has to be ripped from the ground by force.

Historically, it caught on best in Germany and France, where it was usually served up boiled. Stephen Switzer, an eighteenth-century English gardener and garden writer, obtained celeriac from an importer of "curious seeds," who in turn had procured it from Alexandria. Switzer grew some, and included it in his 1729 treatise titled "A compendious method for the raising of Italian broccoli,

Spanish cardoon, celeriac, finochi and other foreign vegetables," which suggests that it was at that time a vegetable oddity.

The European colonists brought celery with them to America, repeatedly and unsuccessfully, since the climate, north or south, never seemed to suit it. The gardeners of Massachusetts Bay reported that their "Celary" roots rotted over the winter, and Thomas Jefferson recorded similarly unhappy results at Monticello. Somebody eventually managed to grow it, however: talented Philadelphia horticulturalist and seedsman Bernard M'Mahon (or McMahon) — to whom Jefferson initially entrusted the plant collections of the Lewis and Clark expedition — lists four varieties common to American gardens in 1806, though it certainly never reached such heights of commonness as the bean, the pea, and the onion.

Commercial celery didn't appear until the mid-nineteenth century, the successful stock imported from Scotland to Kalamazoo, Michigan (now "Celery City") by an enterprising Scotsman named George Taylor in 1856. (Anti-Taylor sources claim the crucial seed arrived with a green-thumbed Dutch immigrant in the 1870s.)

Burpee's 1888 catalog offered ten varieties of celery, including the Incomparable Crimson and the White Walnut, so named for its rich, nutty flavor, plus celeriac or turnip-rooted celery which, Mr. Burpee adds truthfully, in parentheses, is really shaped like

As a food source, celery is so pathetic that diet dogma holds that it has "negative calories" — that is, it takes more energy to chew and digest it than it provides in the first place.

an apple. Until the 1930s most celery in this country was sold blanched and white, but the most likely denizen of the supermarket vegetable bins today is a variety called Pascal, which is green.

❋

Celery is still characteristically eaten crisply raw, much as advised by the omniscient *Ladies' Home Journal* in 1891, which directed:

"Celery should be scraped and washed and then put in iced water, to be made crisp, at least an hour before it goes on the table. It is now served in long, flat glass dishes. It should be put on the table with the meat and other vegetables, and is to be removed before the dessert is served."

In crisply raw form, there's not much to it. Celery is 95 percent water, and the average stalk delivers just 10 dietary calories. As a food source, celery is so pathetic that diet dogma holds that it has "negative calories"— that is, it takes more energy to chew and digest it than it provides in the first place. Sadly, this isn't actually true. Neither is the equally hopeful theory of Leonard J. Kelly of New York City, who hypothesized that very cold beer has negative calories, due to the energy expenditure exerted by the beer-drinking body in warming it up.

Celery also tends to be finicky to grow, though if you've got the right combination of temperature and soil, you can get a lot of bang for your buck: a single ounce of celery seed is enough to plant a full acre of celery. Failing that, the possibilities are even more exciting. Medieval magicians, the story goes, tucked celery seeds in their shoes in order to fly.

CHAPTER SEVEN
In Which

CORN CREATES VAMPIRES

plus

*Pilfering Pilgrims,
A Peculiar Baby's Rattle,
George Washington's Whiskey,
Major Lynde's Ignominious
Defeat, Pudding with
Grasshoppers, and A Test
in Table Manners*

Gardens, scholars say, are the first signs of commitment to a community. When people plant corn they are saying, let's stay here.
ANNE RAVER

The number one crop in traditionally corny Kansas, home of Dorothy, Toto, and Dwight David Eisenhower, is wheat. Number two is sorghum, and corn limps in at third place, just ahead of soybeans. Still, Kansas is part of the Corn Belt, the band of corn-rich cropland that has been steadily oozing westward since colonial days. The original American Corn Belt extended down the Atlantic Coastal Plain from Massachusetts to Georgia. It then shifted into the Piedmont, then later hopped the Appalachians and spread across Kentucky and Tennessee. Tennessee raised most of the nation's corn well into the nineteenth century, when the Belt moved again, to the territory it occupies today: fifty million acres stretching from Ohio to South Dakota and Kansas. Today the top state for American corn is Iowa.

From the Corn Belt comes most of this country's annual ten-billion-plus bushels of corn, which is enough, says one mathematically minded urbanite, to bury all of Manhattan Island sixteen feet deep in kernels. (This is a creepy image, especially if you've seen that bit in the 1985 movie *Witness*, where an evil policeman is asphyxiated in a silo under tons of corn.) About 50 percent of American corn is used as livestock feed.

Another 15 percent or so is exported, and about 25 percent is used to make ethanol.

Of the remaining 10 percent, less than 1 percent is eaten as just plain corn, by people — the rest, in more or less adulterated forms, passes into an enormous number of peripheral corn products. Among these are corn syrup, cornstarch, corn oil, and cornmeal, the last once recommended (rapidly eaten in quantity) to prevent internal damage due to inadvertently swallowed fishbones. More versatile medicinally was corn whiskey, once used to treat colds, coughs, consumption, toothache, rheumatism, and arthritis — all ailments that must have been rampant, since American whiskey consumption in the period from 1790 to 1840 has been estimated at an annual five gallons a head.

Today processed corn in various forms figures in cardboard, charcoal briquettes, crayons, fireworks, wallpaper, aspirin, chewing gum, pancake mix, shoe polish, ketchup, marshmallows, instant tea, mayonnaise, surgical dressings, cat litter, golf tees, and soap. The cobs make a dandy fuel for smoking hams and, carved, form the bowls of corncob pipes — a craft that went commercial in 1869 in Missouri. Cobs have also functioned as bottle stoppers, tool handles, hair curlers, fishing floats, and — sliced crosswise — as checkers; and creative housewives in nineteenth-century Missouri turned them into corncob jelly.

The husks stuffed early American mattresses — Abraham Lincoln was born on a bed of cornhusks and bearskins in a cabin somewhere south of Hodgenville, Kentucky — or were woven into horse collars. A process for turning cornhusks into paper was patented in 1802, although it doesn't seem to have gone much of anywhere.

Cornstalks were fed to pigs and brewed into beer; and in the seventeenth-century Massachusetts Bay colony, corn was accepted as legal tender, at least in transactions that didn't specify cold cash or beaver pelts.

※

Columbus saw vast cornfields in the West Indies, and likely brought the first samples home on his second transatlantic voyage in 1493, along with an assortment of parrots. Within two generations of discovery, the appealing new crop had spread to Africa, India, Tibet, and China, where the emperor, with a sharp eye for the main chance, was already taxing it.

Along with the seed itself, Columbus brought back the native word for the grain — *mahiz* — which survives as the correct common name for American corn, *maize*. Much early confusion relative to the historical cultivation of maize stems from the European use of the word *corn* in a generic sense to mean kernel, as in *peppercorn* and *corned beef*, which was prepared with kernels (corns) of salt. *Corn* was also the term used willy-nilly to refer to whatever the dominant grain of the country happened to be. Hence corn in England meant wheat; in Scotland, oats; and the "alien corn" in the Bible, in which Ruth stood about miserably, was most likely Mesopotamian barley. The all-purpose term promptly expanded to include the new American grain.

By 1542, when German herbalist Leonhart Fuchs published the first known maize illustration, he called it Turkish corn and claimed it came from Asia. The Turks, who denied all connection with it, called it Egyptian corn; the Egyptians called it Syrian corn; the Germans threw up their hands and called it *Welschkorn*, which means strange grain. Linnaeus, who assigned corn its scientific name in 1737, dubbed it *Zea mays* — *mays* a spelling variant of the original maize, and *Zea*, meaning "I live," from the Greeks, who lightheartedly used the term for a number of different plants, among them true wheat.

❀

Corn, along with wheat and rice, is one of the world's staple crops, providing one-fifth of the planet's total food energy. We're dependent upon it — but not nearly as dependent as it is upon us. If people suddenly vanished from the Earth, corn would vanish with us. In those fat cobs of modern corn, the kernels — seeds — are trapped within the tightly wrapped husk, which functions as a sort of malignant chastity belt. Left to themselves, corn seeds cannot be dispersed: a fallen cob eventually sprouts a collection of infant seedlings so closely packed that their intense competition for water, food, and sunlight kills them off. Without the help of humans, a cob is a reproductive dud. Botanists call corn a "biological monstrosity."

Almost the first act perpetrated by the arriving *Mayflower* colonists on the resident Indians was to pinch a stash of seed corn. To be fair, it was less an act of malice than of desperation. When the ship dropped anchor off Cape Cod on November 11, 1620, its passengers were hardly prepared for the awfulness of the New England winter, which would leave half of them dead before the spring of 1621. Already in early November it was so cold that the blowing sea spray froze on their jackets and encased them in ice — and to make it all worse, their food stores were running low.

Then — "by gods good providence" — a mission of exploration, led by the blustery Captain Miles Standish, discovered a buried store of seed corn, which they promptly appropriated, salving their consciences by vowing to make restitution to the rightful owners later. Apparently they never did, which did them no good in their future relations with the Wampanoags. And in truth, it's hard to imagine what restitution Standish and company might have made. There's no substitute for seed corn. Seed corn, saved each year for the next planting season, was the difference between tribal survival and starvation. To this day, "to eat one's seed corn" is an act of utter hopelessness.

❀

The importance of corn to people is attested to in part by our relationship's longevity. Based on recent genetic analyses, scientists now guess that corn has been under cultivation for nearly 9,000 years, first domesticated in southern Mexico from teosinte, an annual wild grass native to Mexico, Guatemala, and Honduras.

The earliest domesticated corn, though a giant agricultural step for mankind, was a pathetic production compared to the juicy cobs of today. In 1948 Herbert W. Dick, a Harvard anthropologist, unearthed primitive one- to two-inch cobs from beneath six feet of accumulated prehistoric garbage in the Bat Cave of New Mexico. Dated to 3,500 years ago by radiocarbon analysis, the Bat Cave corn held the corn age record until the 1960s, when samples of a punier and even more primitive 5,000-year-old corn — with cobs the size of pencil erasers — were discovered in the Tehuacan Valley of Mexico by Richard MacNeish of Boston University.

Since then the world's oldest corn has taken a 4,000-year leap back in time. Today the record holder consists of a collection of

8,700-year-old maize starch granules, scraped from prehistoric grinding tools and winkled out of crevices in the caves and rock shelters of Mexico's Central Balsas River Valley.

Such authentic early specimens replaced a previous corn find, a puzzlingly modern-looking ear of petrified maize that turned up in the early twentieth century in a curio shop in Cuzco, Peru. The ear, believed to be thousands of years old, was reverently dubbed *Zea antiqua* and donated to the Smithsonian Institution. There, in the 1930s, it was gingerly cut open and found to be made of pottery clay. Archaeologists guess that it was a baby's rattle.

Modern corn (maize) is a grass, a member of the Poaceae family, a collection of some 600 genera and 10,000 species, among them wheat, barley, oats, rice, sugarcane, and bamboo. As grasses go, however, corn is indisputably odd. Flemish herbalist Rembert Dodoens, hitting the nail neatly on the head in 1578, described corn as "a marvelous strange plant, nothing resembling any other kind of grayne." The "marvelous strange" was one of the rare points upon which contesting corn scientists have universally agreed. Nothing that looks much like corn is found in the wild, and nobody, for most of its history, knew where it came from.

Corn has always been a mystery, which perhaps is why so many myths surround it. The Navajos claimed that corn came from a magical turkey hen, which dropped an ear of blue corn while en route to the morning star. The Rhode Island Indians say the original corn was dropped by a supernatural crow. The Seminoles say that corn was brought by Fas-ta-chee, the dwarfish corn god, who carried it in a sack on his back, and to the

Toltecs, corn was the gift of Quetzalcoatl, the Plumed Serpent. Some tribes of the American Southwest say that corn was distributed to people by the flute-playing fertility god Kokopelli, as he traveled from village to village.

✳

Prehistoric farmers, determinedly selecting for larger, meatier ears, had developed an impressive two to three hundred different corn breeds by the time Columbus reached San Salvador, including all of the major classes of corn grown today: pop, flint, flour, dent, and sweet. The five classes differ primarily in the makeup of the corn endosperm, the food storage organ of the kernel, whose food content ranges from the iron-hard starch of pop and flint corns to the soft chewy sugar of sweet corn. Most corn kernels contain around 70 percent starch, stored in tiny granules that accumulate gradually, layer by layer, around a central nucleus.

In popcorn, these granules are embedded in a tough matrix of protein. Popcorn pops because when heated the internal water reaches the boiling point, vaporizes, and rapidly expands in volume, upping the pressure on both this protein matrix and the kernel's outer hull. When the pressure becomes insupportable, the matrix abruptly gives way and the kernel explodes — literally everting, or turning itself inside out. From this startling property comes popcorn's scientific name, *Zea mays* ssp. *everta*. Proper popping depends on water content: optimal is 13–14.5 percent. Popped, most popcorn swells to more than thirty times its starting size.

The white crispy popcorn innards, of which Americans collectively crunch 17 billion quarts per year, consist mostly of cooked starch. Popcorn was breakfast food in colonial New England, eaten with milk and maple sugar; and the Pennsylvania Dutch, who also gave us Christmas cookies and apple strudel, cooked up chicken-corn soups with popcorn floating on the top to give them extra oomph.

By the mid-nineteenth century, popcorn was no longer a mealtime staple, but it was still such a popular munchie that vendors were hawking it on the city streets. Popcorn balls, coated with molasses, caramel, or honey, moved in as candy treats in the 1870s, and soon ranked right up there with such old-time favorites as vinegar candy and saltwater taffy. Two entire buildings at the Philadelphia Exposition of 1876 were devoted to selling popcorn, which was washed down with Arctic Soda Water, elegantly dispensed from colored marble soda-water fountains with silver fittings.

Popcorn is an extra-hard form of flint corn, the somewhat larger high-protein, high-starch corn that predominated in the northeastern United States and Canada centuries before the Europeans arrived. Today it's usually colored flint corn that people use to decorate their front doors in autumn, calling it "Indian corn." Early native growers purposefully selected and bred their crops for color, producing, by the time the Europeans arrived, red, blue, black, yellow, white, and multicolored corns. Intrigued colonists continued these breeding practices and eventually grew ears of every conceivable hue, including purple, maroon, amber, chocolate brown, lemon yellow, copper, and orange.

❈

Color in corn is like fingerpaint: it's a matter of mixing. Each kernel, along with a nascent embryo, contains a stuffing of endosperm, starchy food for the infant corn plant. Surrounding the endosperm is a one- to two-cell-thick starch-packed layer called the aleurone, and topping that is the protective pericarp, which consists mostly of cellulose and is the part of the kernel that tends to get stuck annoyingly between the teeth after a corn-on-the-cob orgy. All of the above come in different colors, and the perceived color of a corn kernel is the sum of all three.

Popular fashion today narrow-mindedly limits most eating corns to yellow or white — which shades, plus orange, result from the deposition of xanthophyll and carotene pigments in the endosperm. Gaudier colors generally reside in the pericarp or aleurone. Kculli, an ancient near-black corn used by the Peruvian Indians to make dye and colored beer, has a dark red pericarp, a purple or brown aleurone, and a white endosperm.

An aleurone-based blue accounts for blue corn, prized by the natives of the American Southwest. Francisco Coronado found the Pueblo peoples growing it in the course of his ill-fated trek in search of the Seven Cities of Gold in 1540. Today it still puts the blue in blue corn chips and blue tortillas. Blue corn is a flour corn, which differs from its flinty relatives by a mutation at a single locus on corn chromosome 2. This resulted in a corn with soft endosperm, easily ground into meal.

Most common now in the fields of the modern Corn Belt is dent corn, a horticultural compromise between flint and flour, which contains a mix of hard and soft starch. The distinction between hard and soft starches lies in the makeup of the starch molecules. The hard stuff consists of straight chains of linearly linked sugar molecules and is scientifically known as amylose;

soft starch, composed of branched chains, is known as amylopectin. In dent corn, the amylopectin is concentrated at the crown of the mature kernel. As the kernel dries, this soft starch shrinks, forming a characteristic dimple — or dent.

❀

Unusual among vegetables, corn doesn't sweeten with age. "Green" or unripe corn is sweet because it hasn't yet had a chance to convert its natural sugars into starch. Ripening corn, unlike practically everything else in the garden, becomes progressively less tasty as it approaches maturity. The corn we know as "sweet" corn is a mutant, forcibly interrupted in the sugar-to-starch conversion process such that it stays permanently, youthfully, sweet. People, unsurprisingly, love it.

Sweet corn was grown in prehistoric Mexico and Peru, and by many of the North American Indian tribes. Most sources state that the pioneers didn't manage to get their hands on it until 1779, when Richard Bagnal, an officer in General John Sullivan's destructive expedition against the Iroquois, nabbed a sample from a cornfield on the Susquehanna River in western New York. If so, it spread fast: by 1810, Thomas Jefferson records growing "shriveled" corn — a sweet variety — at Monticello.

Since it's higher in sugar than starch, sweet corn produces translucent wrinkled kernels analogous to the equally wrinkled seeds of the high-sugar pea. At least three mutations govern sweetness in corn, and the earlier a mutation acts in the sugar-to-starch conversion pathway, the sweeter the resulting corn. Sweeter than sweet is supersweet corn — its real name — governed by a mutation called *shrunken 2*, identified in 1950 by researcher J. R. Laughman at the University of Illinois.

Sweetness increased yet again in the 1960s when another Illinois scientist, A. M. Rhodes, discovered a positively sinful three-way cross that he dubbed *sugary enhanced* (*se*), which is the closest corn gets to chocolate. Marketed *se* corns include cultivars in the Everlasting Heritage series — Kandy Korn, for example — and the sweet bicolor Burgundy Delight; and it may be these that Garrison Keillor had in mind when he remarked that sex is good, but not as good as fresh sweet corn.

The *se* mutation not only makes corn supersweet, but also enables it to hang onto its sugar content much longer after harvest than is usual. Classically, sugar starts going downhill the minute the corn is picked — hence the traditional adage that you can stroll out to the corn patch as slowly as you please, but you'd better run like the devil back to the house. Mark Twain took that one step further, recommending that the boiling cooking pot be taken right out to the garden. Actually, that's unnecessarily drastic; corn experts today grant pickers a twenty-minute grace period before the deterioration begins.

❋

The sugar in corn provides a fine food source for yeasts, and since prehistoric times corn has been used to make alcohol, first as beer and wine, and later as whiskey. In the starchier types of corn, the starch molecules must be broken down into their component sugars before the yeasts can go to work, which problem the ancient Peruvians solved by chewing, thus reducing corn-starch to sugar with the human salivary enzyme amylase. The resultant masticated mash was fermented to yield an alcoholic beverage called *chicha*, which was not only enthusiastically drunk but also sprinkled in the fields at corn-planting time to ensure a good harvest. Post-sprinkling, the imperial Inca himself started the sowing by breaking the soil with a golden pickaxe.

High-powered corn liquors appeared in America with the establishment of the Scotch-Irish whiskey distilleries in eighteenth-century Pennsylvania — though the first known American whiskey maker seems to have been George Thorpe, a preacher and physician, who was turning corn into alcohol in Virginia by 1620. ("Wee have found a waie to make soe good drink of Indian corne I have divers times refused to drinke good stronge English beare and chose to drinke that," he confided in a letter to a cousin back home.) Unfortunately, Thorpe's endeavors came to an end abruptly in 1622 when he was killed by the Powhatan Indians. An inventory of his belongings included "a copper still, old," valued at three pounds of tobacco.

By the next century, corn distilleries were common enough on family farms that Alexander Hamilton, strapped for funds in the aftermath of the Revolutionary War, decided to levy a tax on homemade spirits. The tax impinged on whiskey profits to such an extent that the incensed distillers of Pennsylvania banded together in the Whiskey Rebellion of 1794. They created local havoc, burning tax collectors' homes, tarring and feathering unlucky collectors, and eventually occupying Pittsburgh. George Washington countered by calling out fifteen thousand federal troops, which effectively ended the hostilities — though many unrepentant rebels subsequently packed up their stills and moved to Kentucky, where they began making bourbon.

Shortly afterward, Washington himself became a whiskey man. In 1797, with the help of his whiskey-savvy Scotch-Irish overseer John Anderson, he established a distillery at Mount

Vernon. By 1798, he had five stills and a boiler and was crank-ing out an annual 11,000 gallons of whiskey, based on a mix of corn and rye. Even Thomas Jefferson, who much preferred wine, started making corn whiskey at Monticello in 1813.

John C. Fremont carried whiskey, ostensibly as antifreeze for his surveying instruments, during his western explorations of the 1840s, and whiskey seems to have been among the "neces-saries of life" for the midcentury California mountain man. A list of provender required by a party for an eight-day trip through the mountains, reported *Hutchings' California Magazine* in 1860, included eight pounds of potatoes, nine pounds of onions, eleven pounds of crackers, seven pounds of cheese, two bottles of pepper sauce, and fourteen bottles (plus a small keg) of whiskey.

The South mourned the absence of whiskey during the Civil War, when the North captured the Tennessee copper mines and cut off the supply of metal for kettles and condens-ing tubes, although the deprivation occasionally worked in the Confederates' favor. Among the best of contemporaneous corn-whiskey stories appears in the after-action report of a Yankee major, Isaac Lynde, who in July 1862 was commanding a detach-ment of soldiers en route to Fort Stanton in New Mexico. His men turned out to have canteens full of whiskey snitched from the medical stores in the dispensary and, being in no state either to stand and fight or to run away, were promptly captured by patrolling Texans. The humiliated Major Lynde would doubt-less have thrown in his lot with Edward Enfield, whose 1866 *Treatise on Indian Corn* condemned whiskey, stating that corn "like some other best gifts of the Deity, [has] been perverted to base and injurious uses."

When not drunk in "spirituous liquors," corn was consumed in succotash, fritters, hoecakes, pone, hominy, and hasty pudding — the last so ubiquitous that colonial poet Joel Barlow wrote a poem in three excruciating cantos in honor of it. ("My morning incense and my evening meal / The sweets of Hasty Pudding. Come, dear bowl / Glide o'er my palate and inspire my soul.") The Indians made their own brand of hasty pudding, flavored with dried blueberries and grasshoppers. Benjamin Franklin, who liked it for breakfast, flavored his with honey and nutmeg, and the French, who adopted it as a political gesture during the American Revolution, flavored theirs with cognac.

Not everyone was a corn fan. Josiah Atkins, trudging through Virginia with the Continental Army in 1781, wrote home that want of provisions had reduced him to eating what "people in these parts call Hoe cakes . . . which makes my trials insupportable," and British visitor Frances Trollope, in her best-selling *Domestic Manners of the Americans* (1832), dismisses corn: "They eat Indian corn in a great variety of forms, but in my opinion all bad."

Even so, corn was historically and enthusiastically eaten as corn on the cob — a practice that arose, according to corn scientist Walton Galinat, from "man's instinctive desire to eat directly with his bare hands." Man may have wanted to, but the socially censorious did their best to see that he didn't. "The greatest drawback is the way in which it is necessary to eat it," commented Harriet Martineau in 1835.

The persnickety Charles Day, author of *Hints on Etiquette and the Usages of Society with a Glance at Bad Habits* (1844), writes, "It is not elegant to gnaw Indian corn. The kernels should be scored with a knife, scraped off into the plate, and then eaten with a fork. Ladies should be particularly careful how they manage so ticklish a dainty, lest the exhibition rub off a little desirable romance." Emily Post lists corn on the cob under "Graduating Tests in Table Manners," as one of the hurdles for the inept diner, along with asparagus, artichokes, bread and butter, and terrapin bones. In fact, Emily throws up her gloved hands regarding corn:

> "Corn on the cob could be eliminated so far as ever having to eat it in formal company is concerned. … if you insist on eating it at home or in a restaurant, to attack it with as little ferocity as possible, is perhaps the only direction to be given, since at best it is an ungraceful performance and to eat it greedily a horrible sight!"

For all the appeal of corn cuisine, corn has its nutritional drawbacks. None of the cereal grains is a complete protein source, and corn is no exception. It is deficient in both the essential amino acids lysine and tryptophan, and not too forthcoming with the vitamin niacin (B_3), which in corn kernels is tightly bound to another molecule and thus is unavailable to hopeful eaters. A lack of niacin — the name was coined to avoid the nasty cigarette-smoking connotations of the scientifically correct nicotinic acid — leads to a deficiency disease called pellagra.

Pellagra arrived in Europe neck and neck with American corn. It was first described in Spain in 1735 by physician Gaspar

Casal, who called it "Asturian leprosy;" and sufferers were some-times known as the "butterfly people" from the butterfly-shaped rash that first appeared across the nose and face before spreading to the rest of the body in hideous and painful scabs. (The name pellagra is Italian, meaning "rough skin.") Jeffrey and William Hampl, in a 1997 paper in the *Journal of the Royal Society of Medicine*, argue that the symptoms of pellagra — sun sensitivity, tongue edema, dementia, and a prolonged wasting death — were the source of the original European vampire legends. Dracula, in other words, simply needed niacin.

Most victims, however, seem to have associated the disease with corn, variously blaming it on corn's "impure Indian" nature, moldy kernels, or corn-associated insects. In the poverty-stricken American South, pellagra reached epidemic proportions by the early twentieth century: an estimated 100,000 Southerners died of the disease between 1900 and 1940. In 1909, the afflicted state of South Carolina put corn on trial, on a charge of mur-der. ("Corn stands indicted!" thundered Ebbie Watson, the state agricultural commissioner.) An alternative take, which let corn off the hook, held that pellagra sufferers were simply weak by nature and had acquired the disease in an unmentionable man-ner from sheep.

In 1915, Joseph Goldberger, a Public Health Service physi-cian, performed a series of comparative nutritional studies in prisons and orphan asylums that definitively pinpointed pellagra as a dietary deficiency disease. It was noninfectious, linked to "low-grade starchy diets," and curable by supplementing the diet with proteinaceous meat, milk, and eggs. The amino acid trypto-phan is a precursor of niacin, which means that in the absence of ready-made niacin, the body can manufacture its own, provided it is supplied with proteins rich in tryptophan. Corn in this case administers a nutritional double whammy: its niacin exists in unusable form, and it lacks tryptophan.

Once the corn/pellagra link was understood, scientists began to wonder why prehistoric societies based on corn, such as the Mayas and Aztecs, were not riddled with the disease. The answer lay in traditional corn-processing techniques. Before grinding their corn into meal, primitive societies subjected the kernels to an alkali treatment — soaking in wood ashes or lime. Called nixtamalization, this process both helped in the removal of the hulls and improved the overall nutritional quality of the corn-meal. The nutritional benefits are upped, perversely, by reducing the availability of zein, the principal storage protein in corn, and the worst of the corn proteins in terms of its rock-bottom low content of lysine and tryptophan. This in turn increases the relative availability of these scarce amino acids.

Alkali-treated corn both provides the eater with nearly three times the lysine of untreated corn and converts the bound niacin to a useful absorbable form. Corn tortillas and grits (or hominy, from the original Algonquian *rockahominie* or *tackhummin*) are thus better protein sources than corn on the cob.

Today the latest approach to the nutritional limitations of corn involves boosting lysine and tryptophan levels through genetic engineering. Before biologists started fiddling around with its DNA helix, however, corn did a reasonable job of juggling genes on its own. Among the first to notice this phenomenon was Cotton Mather, who, peering into his neighbor's garden in 1716, noticed that yellow corn plants, located down-wind from red and blue, ended up with multicolored ears. The multicolored corn was the result of cross-fertilization, to which wind-pollinated corn is promiscuously prone.

Each (male) corn tassel annually produces up to 60 million pollen grains, powdery specks that with the help of just a bit of breeze can travel half a mile in under a minute. Corn doesn't stay put, and corn pollen's gypsy-like behavior makes it more than likely that whatever is growing in your corn patch got some input from the corn patch next door. Most early corn breeding proceeded in this happy-go-lucky fashion: different varieties of corn planted next to each other cross-pollinated to yield new and occasionally better offspring.

It was in this offhand manner that Robert Reid produced his famous Yellow Dent, by interspersing a dent corn called Gordon Hopkins Red with Little Yellow, an early flint corn, on his farm south of Peoria, Illinois. Reid's Yellow Dent, cited as "the most significant stride in corn production since prehistoric times," won a prize at the Chicago World's Fair of 1893 — belatedly, since by then it had been America's favorite corn for decades.

More extensive studies of plant hybridization — in everything from cabbages to petunias — were performed by no less an authority than Charles Darwin, who published the results in 1876 under the title *The Effects of Cross and Self-Fertilisation in the Vegetable Kingdom*. This made much less of a splash than the inflammatory *On the Origin of Species by Means of Natural Selection* (1859), but it was to have a substantial impact on the world of corn. Darwin's key observation was that the offspring of crosses between related strains were weaker and less productive than those of crosses between unrelated parents — or, conversely, that the progeny of unrelated parents are healthier and more vigorous. This phenomenon is known as heterosis or hybrid vigor, and, on the human scale, is why kings occasionally marry commoners, with an eye to beefing up the royal bloodline.

In 1879, an American disciple of Darwin, William James Beal, at the Michigan Agricultural College (now Michigan State University), performed the first systematic studies of controlled crosses in corn. Beal planted his cornfield with two different varieties of corn, then put one over on Mother Nature by detasseling — emasculating — corn number one, thus making certain that any ears would result only from cross-fertilization with pollen from the tassels of corn number two. The hybrid offspring of this carefully directed interaction, right on cue, were healthier, happier, and higher-yielding than the wimpish progeny of closely related parents.

George Harrison Shull, a farm boy from Ohio, is usually credited with introducing hybrid corn to the commercial cornfield. One of eight children from a poor family, Shull managed to work his way through college as a janitor, graduated at the top of his class, and went on to earn a PhD in plant genetics from the University of Chicago.

His corn hybrid experiments began in the early 1900s at the Station for Experimental Evolution in Cold Spring Harbor, New York, where he planted his first corn patch as a vegetable-garden demonstration for tourists of the principles of Mendelian genetics. From this showplace garden came the corn that was to become his major contribution to the world of agriculture: pure inbred parental strains, painstakingly developed by repeated generations of self-fertilization.

Once his collection of pure lines was established, Shull tried a cross and in one fell swoop obtained vigorous, high-yielding, first-generation hybrids. Hybrid corn seed — the plant version of Superman — went on the market in the 1930s, and by the end of the decade high-yielding hybrids occupied the vast majority of American cornfields.

Unfortunately, farmers have paid for their increased production figures with decreased genetic diversity — which means that in the 1970s, more than 70 percent of American corn acreage was planted with just six varieties of corn. Such a degree of specialization was asking for trouble, and in 1970, when a new strain of southern leaf blight fungus appeared on the scene, identically susceptible corn plants dropped like flies across the nation. Sensitivity to the attacking fungus was correlated to possession of the otherwise useful Texas (T) cytoplasmic male sterility factor, a genetic element that functions like a vegetable vasectomy, eliminating the need for painstakingly detasseling the plants by hand to prevent self-fertilization. The result was an overall 15 percent loss of the corn crop, and up to 50 percent in some unlucky states.

Even more than a vacuum, it seems, Nature abhors uniformity. In light of this painful lesson, research efforts now are directed toward incorporating a greater range of characteristics into existing corn varieties, and toward preserving corn's genetic heritage, notably Mexico's landrace corn, a reservoir of biodiversity developed by indigenous farmers over the past 9,000 years.

❄

Corn in America is often still eaten three meals a day, although the morning dollop of cornmeal mush has now been replaced by the bowl of cornflakes. The name most commonly associated with this breakfast treat is Kellogg, of whom originally there were two, the brothers John H. and Will K.

John H. Kellogg was a doctor who, fresh out of medical school in 1876, took over the directorship of the Western Health Reform Institute at Battle Creek, Michigan. Under his rule, the Institute became famous for its specially designed vegetarian diets: the skinny were fed twenty-six meals a day and made to stay in bed with sandbags on their stomachs; the hypertensive were served nothing but grapes; and everybody was encouraged to gnaw on zwieback, for health of gums and teeth.

Within the first year, Kellogg was also plying patients with his first toasted cereal creation — a mix of mashed-up biscuits of oats, wheat, and cornmeal known as Granose. It took him until 1895 to come up with the first flake cereal, a wheat preparation made by rolling partially cooked whole grains out flat, then toasting until crisp and dry. (The idea, said Dr. Kellogg, had come to him in a dream.) The public turned up its collective nose at wheatflakes, but cornflakes, brought out several years later, were a success. In fact, cornflakes were so popular that by the early 1900s some forty-four cereal companies — some of them in tents — were in business in and around Battle Creek.

Prominent among cereal promoters was C. W. Post, a suspender salesman turned health-foods manufacturer, whose personal brand of cornflakes went on the market in 1906 under the name Elijah's Manna. Both name and carton — which showed an assortment of heavenly ravens dropping cornflakes into the hands of a hungry prophet — were considered blasphemous by clergymen, and turned out to be downright illegal in Britain, where it was forbidden to register Biblical names for commercial purposes. Post reissued his flakes in 1908 as Post Toasties.

Kellogg's cornflakes (flavored with barley malt) were the foundation of the enormous Battle Creek Toasted Corn Flake Company, established in 1906 by Dr. Kellogg's entrepreneurial brother Will. John and Will seldom saw eye to eye over the proposed direction of the breakfast food industry, and their differences of opinion landed them in court for twelve years of legal tussling over who was legally entitled to the use of the Kellogg name. Will K. won (with a few limited privileges to John), which is why it's Will's signature that gives the seal of approval to the modern cornflakes box. Both John and Will, nourished on cornflakes, lived well into their nineties. Will died in 1951; his tombstone, suitable for the prototypic morning man, is a sundial bearing a bronze robin pulling up a bronze worm.

"Plough deep, while Sluggards sleep / And you shall have Corn, to sell and to keep," wrote Ben Franklin in *Poor Richard's Almanac*. It could be a motto for corn growers everywhere.

Corn Palaces

In the early years of the twentieth century a craze known as the Corn Show swept the country. Farmers competed to produce the biggest, the best, and the most mathematically perfect ear of corn, the hopefuls often judged in theatrical Corn Palaces especially constructed for this purpose. Only one such palace still survives, in Mitchell, South Dakota, a turreted extravaganza built in the days when the citizens of Mitchell decided to outshine the glamorous celebrations of the Grain Palace in the neighboring town of Plankinton.

CHAPTER EIGHT
In Which

CUCUMBERS IMITATE PIGEONS

plus

The Emperor Tiberius's Moveable Garden, Sparta's Beastly Broth, Cleopatra's Beauty Secret, New York's Electric Pickle, and A Burmese Cucumber King

A cucumber should be well sliced, and dressed
with pepper and vinegar, and then thrown out,
as good for nothing.
SAMUEL JOHNSON

cucumber

The lot of the parent of teenagers is often not a happy one. Virginia planter Landon Carter of Sabine Hill records in his diary on July 24, 1766, that he's worried about his daughter Judy. "She does bear ungovernable the whole summer through," he writes, "eating extravagantly and late at night of cucumbers and all sorts of bilious trash." Teenagers: they're moody; they keep awful hours; they eat junk food; and they form foolish attachments. The cucumber-gorging Judy eventually eloped, to her father's fury, with her cousin Reuben — though presumably he eventually forgave her, since in his will he left her 800 pounds sterling and a gold watch.

Judy Carter's cucumber, *Cucumis sativus*, comes to us by way of India, where it has been cultivated for at least three thousand years — and perhaps considerably longer, since excavations in 1970 at Spirit Cave on the Burma-Thailand border dredged up seeds of cucumbers, peas, beans, and water chestnuts, remains of meals eaten, according to radiocarbon dating, in 9750 BCE. The wild ancestor of our present-day edible cucumber has never been definitively identified, but one guess is *C. hardwickii*, an unappetizing native of the Himalayas, small and bitter, scattered with nasty little spines. It may have been *C. hardwickii* that the unfortunate Enkidu ate along with worms, figs, and caper buds in the ancient Sumerian epic *Gilgamesh*.

Time and human effort, however, eventually created a sweeter and less off-putting vegetable, and the result quickly spread. The ancient Egyptians supposedly ate them at every meal, dipped in bowls of brine, and used them to make a questionable drink called cucumber water. To do this, a hole was cut in a ripe cucumber, the inside stirred up with a small stick, the hole plugged, and the cucumber then buried in the ground for several days. When unearthed, boasts an ancient recipe, "the pulp will be found converted into an agreeable liquid," possibly the concoction the Israelites mourned as they slogged thirstily through the desert after Moses.

Nonetheless, not everybody liked cucumbers, and some thought them downright dangerous. Charles Estienne and Jean Liébault's *L'Agriculture et Maison Rustique*, translated in 1616 into English as *The Country Farm*, warns starkly that "The use of Cucumbers is altogether hurtfull," and contemporary medical authorities cautioned that cucumbers filled the body with "cold noughtie humors" and brought on ague. Samuel Pepys recorded in his diary on August 22, 1663: "This day Sir W. Batten tells me that Mr. Newhouse is dead of eating cowcumbers, of which the other day I heard of another, I think, Sir Nicholas Crisp's son."

If not fatal, they were nondescript. A quote from the biblical Apocrypha states, "A scarecrow in a garden of cucumbers keeps nothing," which certainly implies that the cucumber was not the top crop on the Middle Eastern block. Nutritionally, that "nothing" is literal. The average cucumber — like the average jellyfish — is 96 percent water, and contains little else other than a smidgen of vitamins A and C (1 percent and 2 percent of the Recommended Daily Allowance, respectively), all in the peel. At that rate, in terms of vitamin A, it takes 120 unpeeled cucumbers to equal one carrot. Food historian Waverley Root describes the cucumber as "as close to neutrality as a vegetable can get without ceasing to exist."

Still, all that water gave the characteristically cool cucumber a banner reputation as a refreshing thirst-quencher. Early caravans took them along as a sort of vegetable water bottle; overheated Greeks mashed them and mixed the pulp with honey and snow to make an ancient version of sherbet. The Romans were enthusiastic about them, occasionally eaten raw but more often boiled and served with oil, vinegar, and honey. The emperor Tiberius was mad for them, consuming, according to Pliny the Elder, ten a day, every day. To indulge his autocratic whims, Roman gardeners began growing cucumbers in earth-filled carts, which they trundled about from spot to spot to make the most of the sun. In the off-season, they grew them in cucumber frames, of the sort Peter Rabbit fell into so disastrously in Mr. McGregor's garden, glazed with transparent sheets of *specularia*, which was probably mica.

❀

Cucumber cultivation dwindled with the decline and fall of the Roman Empire, and only reappeared in force in the sixteenth century, a period of deprivation that chef and food writer Bert Greene refers to as the "cucumber black-out." Still, in the late eighth century, Pepin (the Wise) of France, possibly influenced by a classical belief that steeping seeds in cucumber juice

The Cucumber King

In the tenth century CE, a farmer became king of Burma because of a cucumber. The story goes that King Theinhko, after a recreational day galloping through the forest, was hungry, and so paused to pick and eat a cucumber from a farmer's field. The furious farmer killed him with a spade. The king's attendant then told the farmer — possibly making up the rule on the spot — that whoever killed a king then became a king in his stead.

The farmer was unwilling to leave his cucumbers, but was eventually persuaded by offers of gold, silver, elephants, and a new wardrobe. When he arrived at the palace, the queen — "fearing lest the country and villages be cast into turmoil" — accepted the situation, provided the farmer had a bath. He ruled Burma for 33 years as King Nyaung-u Sawrahan, popularly known as the Cucumber King.

protected them from insect predation, ordered rows of cucumbers planted around his vineyards to keep boll weevils, borers, and cutworms away from the valuable grapes; and Pepin's renowned son, Charlemagne, ordered them planted in the royal gardens. He even declared them his favorite fruit, and — though cucumbers are found on his plant list under "Salads" — he reportedly ate them for dessert, in custard tarts.

Cucumbers were being grown in England in the fourteenth century, but only became truly popular, the story goes, during the reign of Henry VIII, under the auspices of the first of his six queens, Catherine of Aragon, who liked them sliced in her Spanish salads. They lasted better than Henry's wives, and by the reign of Elizabeth I, according to John Gerard's *Great Herball* (1597), English gardens boasted five varieties: the Common, the Turkey, the Adder, the Pear Fashion, and a mysterious "rare &

beautiful cucumber" from Spain, a foot in length and streaked and spotted in "divers colours." John Parkinson, in his horticultural manual *Paradisi in Sole Paradisus Terrestris* (1629), mentioned seven varieties, including one that "bareth but small fruit (used in pickles)" and another the size and shape of a lemon.

❊

The medicinal cucumber dates to ancient times. Surprisingly, despite its phallic shape and size, the cucumber is one of the few vegetables in the Greek pharmacopoeia that is *not* an aphrodisiac. Sixteenth-century German herbalist Leonhart Fuchs quotes the Greek proverb "Let a woman weaving a cloak eat a cucumber," adding that "female weavers, if we believe Aristotle, are unchaste and eager for lovemaking. So to restrain and weaken their urge, the adage advises women weavers to eat cucumbers."

Sleeping on a bed of cucumbers was said to alleviate fever — hence the saying "cool as a cucumber"; cucumber leaves stamped in wine were said to be effective for treating dog bites; and women wishing for children were encouraged to wear a cucumber suggestively suspended from the waist. To dream of cucumbers was believed to indicate the imminence of falling in love. The Romans claimed that cucumbers scared away mice, and John Gerard claimed that cucumbers, eaten three times a day in oatmeal pottage, could cure swellings of the face, noses "red as roses," pimples, "pumples," and like disasters of the seventeenth-century complexion.

The horticultural cucumber was subject to an equal array of arcane beliefs. Cucumbers were said to be frightened of thunderstorms, so one expert gardener advised draping the plants in comforting "thin Coverlets" in the event of violently inclement weather. Estienne and Liébault, of the "hurtfull" cucumbers, claimed that cucumber seed more than three years old would yield (presumably nonhurtful) radishes when planted, but since they also suggested crushing flat parsley with a garden roller to make it curly, their advice should perhaps be taken with a grain of salt.

A number of growers who should have known better claimed that cucumbers waxed and waned along with the moon. It was customary to pick cucumbers at the full of the moon, in hopes of getting the very biggest, which were also considered the very best. Garden designer Batty Langley objected to this practice in his *New Principles of Gardening* (1728):

> " 'Tis a very great Custom amongst a great many People to make choice of the very largest Cucumbers, believing them to be the best, which are not, but instead thereof, are the very worst, except such as are quite yellow. Therefore in the Choice of Cucumbers, I recommend those that are about three Parts grown, or hardly so much, before those very large ones, whose Seed are generally large, and not fit to be eaten, excepting by such Persons whose stomachs are very hot."

The vitriolic Dr. Samuel Johnson objected to all cucumbers, of whatever size, saying "A cucumber should be well sliced, and dressed with pepper and vinegar, and then thrown out, as good for nothing." It's possible that he may have changed his mind given a chance at cucumbers prepared *à la* Elizabeth Rafald, who in *The Experienced English Housekeeper* (1769) recommended that large-sized cucumbers be stuffed with partly cooked pigeons, cleaned, but with heads and feathers left on, so that the heads appeared attached to the cucumber. These were cooked in broth and served garnished with barberries.

General Ulysses S. Grant, who had simpler tastes, loved cucumbers, and often made an entire meal on sliced cucumbers and a cup of coffee. Eliza Leslie includes two cucumber recipes in her *Directions for Cookery* (1840), one for raw cucumbers in vinegar and oil, and one for cucumbers sliced, sprinkled in flour, and fried in butter, which she recommends as a breakfast dish.

Cucumbers journeyed to the Western Hemisphere with Columbus, who planted them in his experimental garden on Haiti in 1494. They seem to have done well. By 1535, Jacques Cartier observed "very great cucumbers" in Canada near Montreal, and Hernando de Soto found "cucumbers better than those of Spain" in Florida in 1539. The colonists planted them, and by 1806 seedsman Bernard M'Mahon, author of the comprehensive *Gardener's Calendar*, listed eight standard varieties in American gardens, including the impressive Long Green Turkey, twenty inches long at maturity.

❊

Also grown in American gardens, according to M'Mahon, was the West Indian gherkin, *Cucumis anguria*, nicknamed the Jerusalem pickle. *C. anguria* was described in an eighteenth-century natural history of Jamaica as a walnut-sized pale green fruit, "far inferior" to the garden cucumber, but edible if soaked in vinegar. This fazed the American colonists not at all since, in the absence of alternative preservation techniques, it was standard practice to pickle practically everything, from walnuts and peaches to artichokes and eggs.

Amelia Simmons advised pickling cucumbers in white wine vinegar, with added cloves, mace, nutmeg, white peppercorns, "long pepper," and ginger. Harriott Pinckney Horry's 1770 *Recipt Book* has a similar recipe, "To Mango Muskmellons and Cucumbers and to pickle French Beans, firkins, etc.," also said good, with a little adaptation, for oranges.

Preservation by pickling works by immersing the food in an acid solution — most commonly vinegar — which prevents the growth of microorganisms and accompanying food spoilage. Vinegar is an invention of unspecified but considerable antiquity. The Babylonians made it from dates, the ancient Chinese from rice and barley, and the Spartans used it in their notorious black broth, a mix of pork stock, vinegar, and salt that sounds a bit like hot-and-sour soup. Apparently it wasn't. According to the Athenians, consumption of it explained the Spartans' legendary bravery in battle: black broth was so awful that anyone compelled to eat it was willing to die.

Everybody loved pickles. Pickles even prodded the ordinarily scientific Thomas Jefferson into poetry: "On a hot day in Virginia,

Sour Wine

Our word *vinegar* is derived from the French *vin aigre*, or "sour wine," reflecting its first major European source, as a by-product of the wine-making industry. Wine goes sour under the ministrations of a bacterium called *Acetobacter*, which consumes the existing alcohol, leaving behind a mixture of 4 percent acetic acid in water. A similar bacterial process sours beer to yield malt vinegar, and apple juice to yield the American specialty, cider vinegar. In the absence of any kind of vinegar, frontier families pickled their produce in the ever-available corn whiskey.

I know nothing more comforting than a fine spiced pickle, brought up trout-like from the sparkling depths of the aromatic jar below the stairs of Aunt Sally's cellar." Benjamin Franklin recommended pickles for "squeamish stomachs"; Cleopatra attributed her beauty to pickles; and Amerigo Vespucci — our nation's namesake — started life as a pickle seller.

Pickles were endlessly popular in the nineteenth century, often the only taste relief in a monotonous diet of meat and potatoes. "A dinner or lunch without pickles of some kind is incomplete," stated *Good Housekeeping* magazine in 1884. Today more than half the cucumbers grown in the United States are made into pickles, and Americans consume an annual nine pounds of pickles apiece — a national 26 billion pickles per year.

❂

The most famous pickle in American history is almost certainly the signature pickle of Pittsburgh's Henry J. Heinz. Heinz's biography is the quintessential Horatio Alger story: by the age of eight, Henry was selling surplus vegetables from the family garden; by twelve, he'd gone commercial, with his own 3½-acre plot of land. By the 1860s, he was selling bottled horseradish; in the 1870s, he started bottling pickles; and in 1876 — a landmark year for Heinz — he introduced the tomato ketchup that made both his fortune and his name.

By 1888, Henry had a 22-acre factory complex outside of Pittsburgh, complete with steam heat, electric lights, "equine palaces" for the 110 jet-black Heinz horses (who pulled cream-colored wagons trimmed in pickle green), and a 1,200-seat auditorium with a stained glass dome. The pickle became a national icon in 1893, when Henry passed out free pickle-shaped watch

Burpee's 1888 seed catalog carried the Serpent or Snake cucumber, which grew up to six feet in length, coiled like a snake.

charms (stamped with the name HEINZ) at Chicago's World's Columbian Exposition. By 1896, Henry had a forty-foot electric pickle dazzling the residents of New York City on Fifth Avenue.

Until the Heinz era, little effort had gone into the improvement of the cucumber. The first notably deliberate attempt at cucumber hybridization resulted in Tailby's Hybrid, a high-yield large-fruited cucumber introduced to gardens in 1872. It was carried in Burpee's 1888 catalog, along with 19 other cucumber varieties, including the Russian or Khiva Netted cucumber, oval with a white-netted brown skin, said to be "well adapted for cold, bleak situations," and the Serpent or Snake cucumber, which grew up to six feet in length, coiled like a snake. Seed purveyors Vilmorin-Andrieux describe this last in *The Vegetable Garden* (1885), adding that when ripe it exudes "a strong odour of Melons." Among their other twenty-seven listed cucumber cultivars is the Bonneuil Large White, a sweetly scented, papaya-shaped cucumber grown near Paris exclusively for use in perfumes.

Vilmorin-Andrieux suggests that growers straighten their market cucumbers ("as one good and straight Cucumber is worth nearly a dozen small and deformed ones") and describes a method for doing so, by forcing the young fruits into open-ended cylindrical glasses. More than a thousand workers were employed in this task in one English market garden, according to Vilmorin-Andrieux, which somehow brings to mind such horticultural oddities as Lewis Carroll's gardeners painting the roses red in Wonderland. Those cucumbers too far gone in deformity were brutally sent to the pickle factory.

The obsession with straightening the cucumber is an ancient one. Early Chinese growers suspended stones from the ends of fruits with a tendency to curl, and modern breeders have selected for straightness, along with such traits as size, yield, disease resistance, flavor, and that commercial bugbear, shelf life. Innumerable cultivars are available today including many time-honored heirloom breeds, among them the Lemon, which looks like one; the White Wonder, a dull ivory color; the tiny Crystal Apple; and the dirigible-shaped Zeppelin.

❀

Flavor in garden cucumbers has been plagued by bitterness, the occasional mouthful of which still gives a chilling reminder of what cucumber-eating was like in the bad old days of the prehistoric Himalayan wilds. The bitterness is due to a class of compounds called cucurbitacins, terpene derivatives that are as repulsive to certain insect pests as they are to human beings. Cucurbitacin-less mutants have been developed, enabling growers to produce crops of nonbitter cucumbers, but the tastier fruits, chemically disarmed, are consequently more susceptible to insect damage.

Bitterness varies from crop to crop and from year to year — even from cucumber to cucumber — with no real explanation to date as to just why. Some varieties are more prone to bitterness than others; but in all cases bitterness seems related to stress: too much chilly weather, for example, or not enough rain.

❀

In Jonathan Swift's *Gulliver's Travels* (1726), Lemuel Gulliver, on his post-Lilliput voyage to Laputa, ran into what

CHAPTER NINE
In Which

AN EGGPLANT CAUSES A HOLY MAN TO FAINT

plus

*A Trek along the Silk Road,
The Ashy Apples of Sodom, Dining at
Delmonico's, Thomas Say's Beetle,
A Pot of Magic Molasses, and
A Condiment for Cannibals*

*The man who sees on New Year's Day Mount Fuji,
a hawk, and an eggplant is forever blessed.*
JAPANESE PROVERB

eggplant

I n Daniel Pinkwater's *Borgel* (1990) — one of the most hilari-
ous kids' science-fiction books of all time — Melvin's mysterious space- and time-traveling Uncle Borgel tells his young
nephew the story of "The Rabbit and the Eggplant," in which
an eggplant challenges a rabbit to a footrace. The townspeople,
convinced that the eggplant has some clever trick up its sleeve,
bet all their money on it. On the day of the race, the rabbit
streaks out of sight and crosses the finish line, while the eggplant
just sits there. The infuriated spectators turn on it and eat it. The
moral of the story: "Don't bet on an eggplant."

For much of history, however, people in effect have been
doing just that, since transforming the eggplant from its unpleasant wild ancestor to the lush fat fruit of today must have looked
like a long shot. It certainly took a lot of blind faith, dedication,
and effort. The original eggplant, botanists believe, blossomed
somewhere in south central Asia, where its peculiar-looking
fruits, bitter taste, and nasty thorns did little to recommend it
to the primitive palate. Nonetheless, some hardy soul eventually
domesticated it.

Traditionally, this took place in India, where eggplant pops
up in Sanskrit documents as early as 300 BCE. An alternative,

or possibly simultaneous, site is China, where a recent survey of ancient Chinese plant literature identified eggplants under cultivation in the Chengdu (Sichuan) province in 59 BCE. Today China and India are the world's top eggplant producers, with the United States trailing far behind, in twentieth place.

❋

The original Chinese eggplant didn't taste good, and the best guess is that it was originally cultivated for use as a medicine. (A Chinese medical treatise of the sixteenth century describes eggplant-based preparations for everything from intestinal hemorrhage to toothache.) Perhaps for this reason, when eggplant finally made it to the table, it was eaten nervously. Like the notorious blowfish, it was thought safe only if prepared by trained cooks. Its Chinese name, *ch'ieh-pzu*, in most pessimistic translation, means poison.

As increasing numbers of diners cleaned their plates without lethal incident, the eggplant become more commonly acceptable, although it still retained a reputation for danger. It reached the Middle East by the sixth century, probably via traders on the Silk Road. Persian physicians were skittish about it, attributing to it a long list of harmful effects, among them pimples, leprosy, and elephantiasis.

The cooks, however, won out, and in the Middle East, the eggplant attained true culinary stardom. Persian chefs, who had already mastered such challenges as smoked camel's hump, zebra, and Arabian ostrich, were hardly people to balk at eggplant and soon devised hundreds of recipes. The later Turks, whose versatile cuisine featured raisins and olives, goats and pigeons, rose water, almonds, yogurt, and powdered pistachio nuts, were said to eat eggplant at every meal. One dish, eggplant stuffed with pine nuts, was reputedly so overwhelmingly scrumptious that it was known as *Imam Bayildi* ("The Holy Man Fainted") because such was its gustatory effect. (An alternative version of the story holds that the cleric fainted in horror, having discovered that his young bride had used up her entire dowry of olive oil in cooking eggplant.)

The eggplant traveled with the invading Moors through northern Africa and into Spain, where in the twelfth century a horticulturally accomplished Moorish Spaniard named Ibn-al-Awam described four cultivated varieties: white, violet, dark purple, and black. It arrived in northern Europe by the thirteenth century, where it was received squeamishly. Practically everybody except the dauntless Italians refused to eat it, though it did achieve some popularity in upper-class gardens as an exotic ornamental.

The lavishly illustrated *Tacuinum Sanitatis* — a series of medieval health manuals translated from the Arabic and much prized by fitness-conscious aristocratic fourteenth- and fifteenth-century Europeans — includes wonderful images of purple eggplants. The accompanying text warned that eggplant was an aphrodisiac: in one illustration a pair of lovers, presumably overcome by desire, embrace in front of a row of eggplants, while an eggplant-impervious chaperon shakes a scandalized finger at them.

Common in Renaissance Europe were small white-fruited varieties — hence the descriptive name "egg" plant — but other types were known. Leonhart Fuchs (1542) mentions purple and yellow eggplants; Rembert Dodoens (1580) — who calls them "unholsome" and claims they fill the body with evil humors — mentions purple and "pale"; and Jacques Dalechamp (1587) describes purple, yellow and "ash-colored" varieties in long, round, and pear shapes.

Master herbalist John Gerard, who lists white, yellow, and brown eggplants in his *Great Herball* (1597), adds that the Egyptians eat them boiled and roasted, with oil, vinegar, and pepper, and then warns that nobody else should do likewise: "I wish Englishmen to content themselves with meats and sauce of our owne country than with fruit eaten with apparent peril; for doubtless these Raging Apples have a mischevious qualitie, the use whereof is utterly to be forsaken." John Parkinson in *Paradisi in Sole* (1629), sounding disbelieving, writes that "in Italy and other hot countries . . . they do eate them [eggplants] with more desire and pleasure than we do Cowcumbers."

❀

The ominous nickname of raging, or mad, apple derived from eggplant's reputation for inducing instant insanity in the unwary eater. This originated, the story goes, with the first Occidental to sample the new vegetable. Tickled with its luscious appearance, he gulped one down raw and promptly fell into a fit (the result, one vegetable authority suggests, of acute gastritis). The incident was to haunt the eggplant for centuries. Sir John Mandeville, an inventive (and possibly invented) fourteenth-century traveler, added fuel to the fire when — along with mermaids, monsters, and a lot of wholly imaginary Asian geography — he described the eggplant-like Apples of Sodom, delectable-looking purple Levantine fruits that crumbled to ashes when picked. Milton, in *Paradise Lost*, fed these to Lucifer's hapless fallen angels.

Historically, it was clear that the eggplant was a vegetable to approach with trepidation. As well as insanity, it was liable to provoke fever, epilepsy, and unbridled lust. Also, the fruits dangerously resembled those of the demonic mandrake, which shrieked when dug out of the ground, a sound that promptly killed anyone who heard it.

This last, absent the shrieking, had at least an element of truth. The eggplant belongs to the Solanaceae or Nightshade family, along with the tomato, potato, pepper, and petunia, and such dark-sheep cousins as mandrake, tobacco, belladonna, and jimson weed. In 1753, Linnaeus, in his botanical taxonomic opus *Species Plantarum,* grudgingly listed the eggplant as edible, and assigned it for posterity the scientific name *Solanum insanum* — later revised to *Solanum melongena*, which means "soothing mad apple," a nice piece of scientific fence-sitting if there ever was one.

The Italian common name for eggplant, *melanzana*, comes directly from the older *mala insana*, or mad apple. The more tactful French *aubergine* and Spanish *berenjena* are derivations of the Indian word for eggplant, *brinjal.* The English word *eggplant*, according to the *Oxford English Dictionary* (*OED*), dates to the mid-1700s and referred initially to the small white egg-shaped eggplants, though the term was eventually expanded to refer to all eggplants, of any size, shape, or color. The Germans call it the *Eierfrucht* or eggfruit, and the Jamaicans, who originally got theirs from the conquistadors, refer to them cosily as garden eggs.

When the eggplant did show up on the early European table, it did so in style. A surviving record of an Italian banquet thrown by Pope Pius V in 1570 includes eggplant on the vast menu, in which the papal guests started out with marzipan balls, grapes, and prosciutto cooked in wine, then worked their way through spit-roasted skylarks, partridges, pigeons, and boiled calves' feet to a grand finale of quince pastries, pear tarts, cheese, and roasted chestnuts. The eggplant appeared in the second course, roasted and sliced, with quails.

In the next century, eggplant was championed by France's Louis XIV, who, for all his defects, had spectacular taste in food, mistresses, and gardens. The court — less enthusiastic about new foods — resisted, perhaps hoping that the king would be distracted by more appealing seventeenth-century culinary introductions, such as coffee, tea, chocolate, sherbet, turkey, and champagne.

※

It's not known when *S. melongena* made it to the American side of the Atlantic. Some say it arrived with the Spanish explorers; others credit Thomas Jefferson, who grew it, along with everything else he could lay his hands on, in the vast vegetable garden at Monticello. Others hypothesize that eggplant arrived in the slave ships from western Africa, and was first established along the southern coast of the United States, where it was known familiarly as Guinea squash. A final faction claims that eggplant was introduced to American diners by Delmonico's, the magnificent New York restaurant founded in 1831 by the Swiss Delmonico brothers, Peter and John.

Delmonico's was coupled with Yosemite Valley by a London newspaper of the 1880s as one of "the two most remarkable bits of scenery in the States." An endless succession of the rich and famous ate there, including Jenny Lind, Louis Napoleon, Abraham Lincoln, Charles Dickens — who routinely drank two bottles of champagne and a glass of brandy for lunch — and Samuel F. B. Morse, who dramatically dispatched the world's first telegram from his table. (A reply came back in forty minutes.) Delmonico's in the 1830s popularized eggplants and artichokes, both strangers to the relatively lackluster contemporary American cuisine. The restaurant also served up the first American avocadoes, watercress, and truffles, and invented Lobster Newburg, Eggs Benedict, Oysters Rockefeller, and Chicken à la King.

By the nineteenth century, eggplant appeared regularly in cookbooks, baked, stuffed, boiled, fried in butter, or, more exotically, stewed in wine and pepper or pickled in honey and vinegar. Mary Randolph, in *The Virginia Housewife* (1824), claims that the purple ones are best, and recommends parboiling them, then frying, dipped in egg yolk and grated bread. "They are very delicious," she says, "tasting much like soft crabs." Miss Eliza Leslie, in her *Directions for Cookery* (1840), included recipes for eggplant stewed, fried, and stuffed, adding unexpectedly that "Eggplant is sometimes eaten at dinner, but generally at breakfast." Sarah Rorer, in her *Philadelphia Cookbook* (1886), recommends that fried eggplant be served with tomato catsup.

Eliza Leslie's eggplants were doubtless fried in the very best butter — Miss Leslie came down hard on cooks who reserved their sour or spoiled butter for cooking purposes — and they even more certainly soaked up a lot of that butter during the cooking process. A notable characteristic of the eggplant is its spongy texture.

The Cannibal Eggplant

Solanum uporo — nicknamed the "cannibal tomato" — is actually a cannibal eggplant, native to Tahiti and the Fiji islands. According to Berthold Seeman, who made a somewhat nervous visit to Fiji (then known as the Cannibal Islands) in 1860, *S. uporo*, a two-inch tomato-red fruit, was a favored stomach-settling accompaniment to a meal of people. "It appears," Seeman noted, "that human flesh is extremely difficult to digest."

Like a sponge, eggplant tissue contains a large number of intercellular air pockets capable of holding a hefty amount of liquid. Unlike a sponge, however, eggplant reaches a point in the cooking process where it becomes self-squeezing: eventually the heat generated by frying causes the cellular structure to collapse, flattening the air pockets, and extruding the accumulated oil. Popular today for fried eggplant feasts is olive oil, the ingredient that caused the legendary imam to faint — but Middle Eastern gourmets traditionally used *alya*, an oil rendered from the overgrown tails of a special breed of fat-tailed sheep. (The valuable tails were sometimes supported on small two-wheeled wooden carts to protect them from the ordinary wear and tear of sheep life.) Oil-less eggplant possesses a mere 50 calories per cup; sautéed, over 300.

❀

By the nineteenth century, the eggplant was also firmly established as a denizen of the vegetable garden. Vilmorin-Andrieux list fifteen kinds — ten purple, two white, two green, and one striped in purple and white "lengthways" — but purple was the undisputed king. "The purple eggplant is almost the only color grown in our kitchen gardens," writes Edward Sturtevant in his late-nineteenth-century *Notes on Edible Plants*. The famous purple results from ring-shaped chemical compounds called anthocyanins, from the Greek for "blue flower." Unfortunately these biological blues, reds, and purples are both water-soluble and heat-sensitive, which bodes ill for their survival in the cooking pot and explains why boiled red cabbage and strawberry jam often go an unappetizing pinkish brown.

The loss of purple is seldom a consideration in eggplants, which are often peeled before cooking. Once peeled, however, eggplants, like apples, avocadoes, bananas, raw potatoes, and pears, have a tendency to turn an ugly brown. In these fruits, cell disruption by teeth or paring knife releases an enzyme called polyphenol oxidase, which reacts with phenolic compounds in the fruit tissue to form unappetizing brown polymers.

In some cases the browning reaction can be slowed down by chilling, though in others cold only makes matters worse: bananas, for example, natives of the balmy tropics, undergo rapid cell damage in the cold and release quantities of polyphenol oxidase, which is why banana peels turn black in the refrigerator. The browning enzyme is also inhibited by the chloride ions in salt, which is useful in the case of potatoes and eggplants, frequently served salted, but less so in the case of apples and pears. Polyphenol oxidase is most effectively blocked by acidic conditions, which is why a dash of citric-acid-rich lemon juice does wonders for preserving the green in guacamole. Browning is also inhibited by ascorbic acid, better known as vitamin C.

Phenolic compounds, however, are far more than potentially unsightly culinary nuisances. Phenolics are antioxidants, effective at sopping up reactive and cell-damaging free radicals, with reported benefits that include antiaging and anticancer effects and a reduction in LDL ("bad cholesterol"). In 2003, researchers John Stommel and Bruce Whitaker analyzed 115 different eggplant varieties from locations as far-flung as southeast Asia and Africa, plus popular cultivars grown in the United States, and found that eggplants are powerhouses of antioxidant activity. Eggplants contain some fourteen different phenolic compounds, most prominently the particularly potent chlorogenic acid.

❋

Stommel and Whitaker's eggplants came from stores at the National Plant Germplasm Center in Griffin, Georgia — a repository of seeds of cultivated crop plants and their wild relatives. They found an astonishing diversity of eggplants. While the most familiar in the United States today is the bulbous purple pear, eggplants also come in red, yellow, green, and orange, and in shapes that range from long and cucumberlike to tiny and round. There are narrow finger-shaped Oriental varieties, and slim foot-long curved cultivars called snake eggplants.

All, botanically, are fruits — specifically, giant berries developing from flowers that sprout, unusually, smack out of the plant stem rather than from a leaf axil. Even in cultivated varieties, the stems may still carry a few scattered spines, remnants of the days when the ancestral eggplant battled off herbivores with offputting inch-long thorns.

Purple pears possess green calyces and predominate on vegetable counters; the skinny Oriental types have purple calyces and, though curiously less popular, are tastier. The superiority of the flesh of the Oriental eggplant derives from its slow-developing seeds, which give the Oriental cultivars less of a tendency toward bitterness than their seedier American equivalents. Seediness, incidentally, is the root of all evil in over-the-hill eggplants: those past their prime, identifiable by their brownish tinge and telltale puckery look, are heavily seeded and inedibly bitter.

✳

One of the prime consumers of eggplant, however, is not all that picky. *Leptinotarsa decemlineata*, the Colorado potato beetle, is said to like eggplants even better than potatoes. The beetle was first described in 1823 by Thomas Say, a founder of the Entomological Society of America and the author of the much-respected three-volume *American Entomology* (1824–1828). Say served as chief entomologist at the Philadelphia Museum of Science, where, between bug-collecting expeditions, it was his custom to sleep under the skeleton of a horse in the museum collection.

At the time of his seminal description, the beetle, yet to discover the delights of potatoes and eggplants, was a fairly innocuous creature living off buffalo bur, a solanaceous weed of the Colorado River basin. It came across potatoes sometime in the mid-nineteenth century, when Western settlers started planting them, and moved ravenously eastward in search of them, encountering along the way such additional goodies as eggplants, peppers, and tomatoes. Steadily eating, it reached Illinois in 1864, Ohio in 1869, and the East Coast in 1874, and had managed to cross the Atlantic to Europe in 1876.

Adult potato beetles are about half an inch long, striped lengthwise in black and yellow. They're relatively lethargic creatures, enough so to qualify for the first set of one British gardener's anti-pest instructions: "If it moves slowly enough, step on it; if it doesn't, leave it — it'll probably kill something else."

Though effective, this method was impractical commercially, and farmers instead turned to the arsenic-based chemical pesticide Paris green — so named from its early use as a rat killer in the Paris sewers. Paris green, sounding pleasantly benign, appears in "Three Boys With Jugs of Molasses and Secret Ambitions," one of Carl Sandburg's *Rootabaga Stories* (1922). The three boys of the title step in a puddle of spilled molasses, which magically shrinks them to the size of beetles, and visit the Potato Bug Country. There they have marvelous adventures with spider villages and railroad trains until Mr. Sniggers, applying Paris green to his potato plants, splatters some onto their heads, which causes them to regain their normal size.

In real life, a splatter of Paris green on one's head was likely to have been lethal. Paris green slaughtered potato beetles for about thirty years, until it was replaced by the even more potent lead arsenate in 1892. Both compounds were necessarily used in immense quantities — ten to one hundred pounds per acre — and possessed dire side effects, killing off, along with the beetles, birds, household pets, and an occasional human being.

These days the latest in anti-beetle preparations is a "biological pesticide," a new strain of a toxin-producing microorganism, the soil bacterium *Bacillus thuringiensis*. The toxin, a digestive-tract poison, is highly specific, affecting only the target insect species, and thus sparing dogs, children, and other living things. The time-honored method for small-scale disposal of potato beetles, however, is still to pick them off the plants one by one and drop them into a coffee can of soapy water.

LETTUCE PUTS INSOMNIACS TO SLEEP

plus

An Emperor's Astonishing Recovery,
A Dish of Angel's Throat,
A Fashionable French Salad Maker,
Thomas Jefferson's Mondays, and
Socrates's Suicidal Spoon

Lettuce is divine, although I'm not sure it's really a food.

DIANA VREELAND

Lettuce

L ettuce consumption is steadily on the rise. Americans these days each munch their way through thirty-odd pounds of lettuce a year, a more than fivefold increase since the salad-stingy turn of the twentieth century. A recent Armed Forces food preferences poll ranked green salads above such traditional fighting foods as meat, potatoes, and ice cream.

Lettuce, everyone agrees, is healthfully thinning. At a wispy eight calories a cup, you can eat an entire bushel of the stuff for the caloric price of a slice of cheesecake. It also, historically, has a range of other health benefits. Pliny the Elder, after stating somewhat dauntingly that wild lettuce thrown in the sea immediately kills all the fish in sight, recommended lettuce as a mouthwash for toothache or as an ointment for wounds, scorpion stings, and spider bites. He also reported that lettuce preparations neutralize poisons (except, unfortunately, white lead), aid digestion, and cure burns, bladder infections, and insomnia. In any case, it seems to have done something: the Emperor Augustus, wasting away of some mysterious ailment, was saved by a lettuce diet and a regimen of cold baths.

The Roman emperor Tacitus, according to the *Historia Augusta*, a collection of biographies written in the second and third centuries CE, was another lettuce beneficiary. Tacitus was known for his exemplary ascetic lifestyle: he drank less than a pint of wine a day; he ate his bread dry; he eschewed gold and jewels (especially on wall coverings and his wife); and he never served pheasant except on his birthday. When it came to lettuce, however, he "would indulge himself without stint," claiming that the large quantities he consumed allowed him to get a good night's sleep.

❀

Lettuce, since ancient times, has been recommended as a soporific. Dogma held that a bowl before bedtime would put you out for the night. There's some truth to this, and it's all due to the distinctive milky juice (Pliny the Elder called it "phlegm") that can be seen oozing from the bottoms of cut lettuce stems. The scientific name for lettuce, *Lactuca*, is based on this lettuce juice, derived from the Latin *lac*, which means milk.

Technically, it's not a milk at all, but a latex, a water-based emulsion manufactured by such plants as the rubber tree, the dandelion, and the sapodilla tree, whose dried latex, chicle, was the basis of the first chewing gums. Latex contains numerous long-chain hydrocarbon polymers, some of which possess the desirable property of elasticity — that is, they snap back into shape after being stretched. During World War II, Russia, deprived of tropical rubber, made an acceptable substitute from dandelion latex; and lettuce latex, given a little chemical time and effort, could conceivably yield, if not a cost-effective bicycle tire, at least an occasional rubber band.

In wild lettuce, *Lactuca virosa*, the latex contains terpene-based alcohols potent enough to make people sleepy, and to generate the somewhat overblown nickname lettuce opium. Dried balls of lettuce latex were used as sleep inducers in medieval England, occasionally mixed with henbane and poppy for additional sedative oomph, and dried lettuce latex or lettuce teas were used similarly in colonial America. A mild sedative known as lactucarium, prepared from wild lettuce extracts, was used in hospitals up through the Second World War.

In the 1970s, there was a brief fad for smokable lettuce opium, packaged under such brand names as L'Opium and Lettucene, and promoted with the slogan "Buy your lettuce before they make it illegal!" They never did, and customer interest was short-lived, probably both for the same reason: nobody got a bang out of smoking lettuce because there wasn't actually much of anything in it.

❀

Still, lettuce's reputation for putting people to sleep may account in part for its reputation as an anti-aphrodisiac. Dioscorides, the first-century Greek naturalist who served as a surgeon to Emperor Nero's soldiers, wrote that lettuce would protect lonely enlisted men from dreams filled with "libidinous images." John Evelyn's *Acetaria* (1699) lists among the many admirable qualities of salad greens "beneficial influences on morals, temperance, and chastity." A dire Elizabethan anti-lettuce warning states:

> "The plentifull and dayly eating of the Lettuce by married persons is very incommodious and noisome to them, in that it not only doth diminish the fruitfulness of children, but the children often borne do become idle foolish and peevish persons."

The only naysayers in this litany of lettuce-dampened ardor seem to have been the ancient Egyptians, who viewed lettuce as Viagra and dedicated it to Min, the coal-black god of fertility, usually depicted with a crown of feathers and an immense erect penis. The discrepancy — why the same plant turned Europeans off and Egyptians on — has been the subject of research by Italian ethnobotanist Giorgio Samorini. After studying depictions of lettuce in Egyptian bas-reliefs, Samorini determined that Min's lettuce was *Lactuca serriola*, a bitter biennial believed to be the ancestor of modern cultivated lettuce, now found growing wild over most of the temperate world.

Tough and spiny — its common name is prickly lettuce — *L. serriola* is a pest in pastureland, since cattle who misguidedly eat it develop emphysema. Its latex, however, is rich in phytochemicals, and Samorini argues that the sexual effect (or lack of) is a matter of dosage. At low lettuce doses, according to Samorini, the effects of lettuce lactones — lactucin and lactucopicrin — predominate. These are the compounds that give lettuce its bitter taste, protect the growing plants from leaf-munching insects, and, in people, have a sedative effect. At higher doses, however, latex's component of cocaine-like tropane alkaloids kicks in, eliciting euphoria, excitement, and arousal. The Europeans, Samorini argues, simply didn't eat *enough* lettuce.

❋

Lettuce, taxonomically, belongs to Asteraceae, the Daisy or Sunflower family, a collection of some 1,600 genera and over 22,000 species, among them such garden favorites as marigolds, chrysanthemums, zinnias, Jerusalem artichokes, dandelions, and *Artemisia absinthium* (wormwood), from which is distilled the green alcoholic drink absinthe. The ancestral lettuce, *L. serriola*, according to genetic and population-diversity analyses, probably originated in eastern Turkey and Armenia, and was domesticated slowly over a long period, perhaps first being grown not as a salad herb, but for the oil contained in its seeds.

According to Herodotus's gossipy *Histories*, cultivated lettuce, *Lactuca sativa*, less bitter, less prickly, and leafier than its wild ancestor, was being served at the royal tables of Persia by 550 BCE. The ancient Greeks served it up flavored with saffron and olive oil, and carried green pots of it through the streets during the springtime Festival of Adonis. The Romans — who disseminated lettuce throughout their empire — preceded their gargantuan banquets with refreshing lettuce salads, in the belief that lettuce enhanced the appetite and relaxed the alimentary canal in preparation for an onslaught of camels' heels, flamingo tongues, stuffed warblers, and sea anemones smothered in fermented fish sauce. Lettuce was also occasionally eaten cooked or pickled. The Roman cookbook *Apicius* includes recipes for a "Field Salad" of lettuce dressed in vinegar and brine and a "Harmless Salad" in an infusion of ginger, rue, "meaty dates," pepper, honey, and cumin.

❀

The medicinal reputation of lettuce may have enabled it to survive the Roman departure from northern Europe, when many other Roman-introduced plants were abandoned and lost. Lettuce is included in the early fifteenth-century *Tacuinum Sanitatis*, accompanied by an illustration of a blonde in a blue gown clutching a clump of leaf lettuce; an appended note warns that lettuce is harmful "to coitus and the eyesight," but adds that its dangers can be alleviated by mixing it with celery. The early English were hardly salad fans: Queen Elizabeth ate beef, mutton, and rabbit pie for breakfast, and a perfectly acceptable Tudor company dinner consisted of meats, fish, bread, and beer, with a few "Orenges" for dessert.

Contemporary vegetables did include lettuce, cabbage, spinach, and radishes, though "rude herbs and roots" were generally considered fit only for the starving and the poor, or, worse, "more meet for hogs and savage beast to feed upon, than mankind." Lettuce's persistent reputation as a sex suppressant also did it little good. Still, the seventeenth-century French courageously consumed it — lettuce hearts, candied, were eaten in a sweet dish called *gorge d'ange*, or "angel's throat" — and the domineering Louis XIV (father of seven) liked lettuce salads seasoned with tarragon, pimpernel, basil, and violets. John Evelyn, in *Acetaria*, calls lettuce a "Noble Plant" and lists popular contemporary cultivars, among them the familiar-sounding cabbage, cos, curled, and oak-leaf lettuces, plus a variety called Passion, a peculiar moniker in the context of the times.

According to famed gastronome Joan Anthelme Brillat-Savarin in *The Physiology of Taste* (1825), at least one destitute young Frenchman became very rich serving salads to the English. M. d'Albignac's career began when he mixed a salad dressing for a group of young men at a restaurant in London, a performance so impressive and delicious that he was next invited "to dress a Salad" at a mansion in Grosvenor Square. More invitations followed and soon, nicknamed "the fashionable Salad-maker," d'Albignac had purchased a carriage in which he traveled from dinner party to dinner party, toting a fitted mahogany case filled with salad-dressing ingredients. By the time he returned to France, he had amassed a fortune, with which he purchased an estate "on which, for aught I know," Brillant-Savarin concludes fairy-tale-fashion, he lived happily ever after.

❀

L. sativa came to America with Columbus, who planted some in the West Indies in 1493. A quick crop, it was favored by greens-hungry early explorers. Samuel de Champlain and company planted some on an island in the St. Croix River in Maine in 1619, and Captain John Smith's crew followed suit some years later, planting an island garden that "served us for sallets in June and July." The first European colonists arrived equipped for salad planting. Three ounces of "lettice" seed appeared on John Winthrop, Jr.'s 1631 bill of garden seeds.

Lettuce was routinely planted in kitchen gardens of the seventeenth and eighteenth centuries. At George Washington's Mount Vernon, 16 of the 61 plots in his near-acre-sized kitchen garden were devoted to lettuce. A visitor notes that dinner with the General was "very good, a small roasted pig, boiled leg of lamb, roasted fowles, beef, peas, lettuce, cucumbers, artichokes, puddings, tarts, etc." Another, less grateful, recorded snarkily that the Washington salads lacked olive oil.

In 1806, according to Bernard M'Mahon's *Gardener's Calendar*, Americans were choosing among a mere six cultivars of lettuce. By 1828, New York's Grant Thorburn had upped the count to thirteen, and by the 1880s, there were well over a hundred. Early catalogs and listings featured all four of the lettuce types available today: head or cabbage, butterhead, loose-leaf, and cos or romaine. Heading lettuce, *L. sativa* var. *capitata*, became the universally preferred lettuce in the late nineteenth century, as reflected by its availability in seed catalogs. Burpee's 1888 *Farm Annual*, for example, listed twenty-four head lettuce varieties, four cos cultivars, and three looseleafs. Vilmorin-Andrieux's *The Vegetable Garden* (1885) described fifty-six head lettuces, seventeen cos types, and four looseleafs (under the name "small or cutting" lettuces).

✳

Heading lettuce appeared on the vegetable scene in medieval times — and perhaps only with difficulty then, since a surviving horticultural hint from the 1570s suggests trampling on young seedlings to encourage proper head formation. Advice of the same ilk outlined a means of producing "Odiferous Lettice" by embedding the seed in the seed of a citron, and more flavorful lettuce by watering nightly with sweet wine. This last technique must not have worked, since the dense-packed heads of leaves seem to have been relatively tasteless almost from their inception.

A Treatise on Gardening (1765) written by "A Citizen of Virginia" — believed to be Thomas Jefferson's cousin John Randolph — says of them: "This sort of Lettuce is the worst of all kinds in my opinion. It is the most watery and flashy, does not grow to the size that many of the other sorts will do, and very soon runs to seed." It seems to have been used mostly for soups, like the solid-headed cabbages it so closely resembled.

Tasteless or no, head lettuces continue to dominate the American market, pale cannonball-like vegetables relentlessly shipped east from the lettuce fields of California. (California produces some 70 percent of this country's lettuce, the bulk of it in head varieties.) An earlier and more lettucelike form of var. *capitata* is butterhead lettuce, which forms soft, loose, floppy-eared heads around hearts of such tender consistency that early eaters were reminded of butter. Most familiar of butterhead lettuces are the Boston lettuce and Bibb, or Kentucky limestone, lettuce, developed by Kentuckian John J. Bibb in the late 1800s and served by the dedicated at Kentucky Derby breakfasts.

❄

Cos or romaine lettuce, *L. sativa* var. *longifolia*, also forms an upright "head" around a central bud or heart, but the romaine heads are loose, long, and cylindrical. The individual leaves are elongated ovals, reminiscent of kitchen tasting spoons, and one story holds that Socrates drank his lethal dose of hemlock from such a "spoon" of romaine.

The common name *romaine* is a corruption of *Roman*; the even older name *cos* is taken from the Greek island of Cos, where the Romans originally obtained these mildly tangy leaves. It arrived in France in the 1300s, when the papacy, after much ill-advised meddling in earthly politics, abruptly relocated from Italy to French Avignon, bringing their garden vegetables with them. In France, the Roman lettuce came to be known as the frenchified Romaine, and became so popular that outside the country it was called Paris lettuce. An heirloom cultivar called Paris White Cos is still available today.

Romaine lettuce is said to have reached China in the seventeenth century, when the ruling emperor demanded as tribute the choicest vegetable grown in each of his subject domains. He received, among other offerings, beets, scallions, spinach, and romaine lettuce, known in the Far East as the wine vegetable because reportedly it tasted like wine. Appropriately, today the erstwhile Roman lettuce is the main ingredient of Caesar salads.

Tastier yet are the looseleaf lettuces, *L. sativa* var. *crispa*, a mixed bag of nonheading greens whose flat, frilled, or double-ruffled leaves in bright green, dark red, and bronze are ornamental as well as delectable in the salad bowl. These are known as cut-and-come-again lettuces because, if consistently picked, new leaves will continue to sprout throughout the summer growing season.

Prominent among these is the perennially popular Black-Seeded Simpson, a direct descendant of the Early Curled Simpson introduced by grower A. M. Simpson in 1864. Older are Oak Leaf lettuce, named for its lobed oak-leaf-shaped leaves, and an entrancing breed called Deer Tongue, whose pointy leaves reminded somebody of the tongues of deer. In 1973 a looseleaf lettuce made legal history when it was awarded the first patent — strictly speaking, a Plant Variety Protection Certificate — ever granted by the federal government to a plant seed product. The recipient was Burpee's Green Ice, a deep green, crinoline-like lettuce of "outstanding taste and looks."

❀

While salad lettuce appears in colors ranging from ruby red to pearl white, the shade we most associate with it is leaf green — the color of dollar bills, which is why "lettuce" has been a slang term for money since 1929. Green, in plants, is due to the pigment chlorophyll, a complex ring compound with a central magnesium ion, chemically similar to the iron-toting heme molecule of human and animal red blood cells. There are five known kinds of chlorophyll — a, b, c, d, and f — each of which absorbs light of a slightly different range of wavelengths.

Chlorophyll f, for example, only discovered in 2010, is most active at a wavelength of 706 nanometers (nm), at the far-red end of the visible spectrum, which, for chlorophyll, is off the beaten track. The most common form of chlorophyll in higher plants is chlorophyll a, an attractive bright bluish green pigment that absorbs in the mid-red region of the spectrum, most efficiently at a wavelength of 662 nm. Substitution of an oxygen molecule for a crucial pair of hydrogens converts chlorophyll a to olive-green chlorophyll b, present to about half the amount of a. It prefers blue light, preferably at a wavelength of 453 nm.

Along with assorted carotenoid pigments, chlorophyll uses the energy absorbed from sunlight to convert unprepossessing carbon dioxide and water into sugar, a process known as

The chlorophyll craze began with chlorophyll-based toothpaste — marketed by Pepsodent in 1950 as the green Chlorodent — followed by a chlorophyll-flavored dogfood.

photosynthesis. Leaves, such as those of lettuce, are specialized for this purpose, large flat surfaces crammed with chlorophyll molecules, the better to soak up the sun.

In the 1950s, chlorophyll perversely received what was probably its biggest publicity boost, and not from the fact that it provides our planet with food, but from its purported ability to eliminate smells. The chlorophyll craze started with Benjamin Gruskin, a respectable Finnish-born doctor at Temple University, who in the 1930s developed a semisynthetic water-soluble form of chlorophyll, now known as chlorophyllin. Gruskin had high hopes for his chlorophyll derivative as an all-purpose treatment for infection. Initial studies indicated that it was effective against everything from peritonitis and brain abscesses to burns, ulcers, and the common cold. Results from subsequent investigations, however — some by the U.S. Army — were much less promising, and drug manufacturers chose instead to pursue antibiotics.

Soluble chlorophyll did, however, interest a double-barreled Irishman named O'Neill Ryan, Jr., who took out a "use" patent on Gruskin's discovery in 1945. The first of Ryan's brainchildren was a chlorophyll-based toothpaste — marketed by Pepsodent in 1950 as the green Chlorodent — followed by a chlorophyll-flavored dogfood. Over the next two years, spurred on by growing ranks of chlorophyll consumers, diverse businesses entered the marketplace with chlorophyll chewing gum, mouthwash, deodorant, cigarettes, soap, shampoo, skin lotion, bubble bath, popcorn, diapers, sheets, and socks. A chlorophyll-based pipe tobacco was said to keep pipes as "fresh as an alfalfa leaf." Schiaparelli invented a chlorophyll cologne.

Plans were in the works for chlorophyll salami and chlorophyll beer when the Food and Drug Administration rained all over the green parade, announcing that there was "no conclusive evidence" that chlorophyll had any deodorizing effect on anything whatsoever. The *Journal of the American Medical Association* caustically pointed out that goats, which practically live on chlorophyll, smell dreadful; and in 1953 the *British Medical Journal* published the work of a Glasgow University chemist who had systematically tested the effects of chlorophyll on such undesirable effluvia as skunk, onion, garlic, and human body odor, and found it a flop. Chlorophyll products subsequently petered out, and chlorophyll returned to its everyday function.

❀

The more sunlight leaves receive, the more chlorophyll and carotenoid pigments accumulate to cope with the energy input, and the darker in color the leaves become. The outer leaves of head lettuces are thus the darkest and greenest, while the inner light-deprived leaves are pigmentless and pale. The darker leaves are the most nutritious, since they are most heavily packed with the carotenoid beta-carotene, a precursor of vitamin A. Green leaves usually contain one carotenoid molecule for every four to five molecules of chlorophyll, a ratio that supplies looseleaf lettuce with a substantial 1,900 International Units of vitamin A per one hundred grams (about ten leaves). Butterhead lettuce contains only half that, and the largely light-shielded crisphead lettuce only one-sixth as much. Lettuces, in similarly decreasing order, are also sources of calcium and vitamin C.

Other than that, the lettuce leaf consists mostly of water, about 95 percent by weight. This water is what makes lettuce crisp: cells high in water bulge turgidly against each other, producing the crunchy texture so desirable in fresh lettuce leaves. Conversely, since lettuce is so internally waterlogged, it is particularly subject to water loss and wilting. To prevent this sad happening, modern lettuce eaters often store their leaves in refrigerator crispers, confined compartments that maintain an atmosphere of high humidity.

Best, of course, is to pick it, fresh and crisp, straight out of the garden, an occupation that has improved in status since the seventeenth century, when "to pick a salad" meant to indulge in a meaningless and trivial task. Luckily salad picking today ranks with ambitiously making hay while the sun shines, rather than with slothfully letting the grass grow under one's feet.

MELONS UNDERMINE MARK TWAIN'S MORALS

plus

*Marco Polo's Fruit Leathers,
Dr. Livingstone's African Discovery,
Mrs. Trollope's Annoyance, and
Queen Anne's Pomander Ball*

It was not a Southern watermelon that
Eve took; we know it because she repented.
MARK TWAIN

Melon

You're thinking perhaps that melons aren't vegetables, and what on earth are they doing here. And you're right, of course: they're not vegetables, but fruits, both botanically speaking and in the foodie sense of the word. They're the only things in the vegetable garden that we ordinarily eat straight off the vine for dessert. On the other hand, the Chinese, who raise cooking melons, treat them like vegetables.

It's a tricky distinction. Oklahoma, whose official state fruit (since 2005) is the strawberry, declared the watermelon its official state vegetable in 2007. The Oklahoma watermelon bill was sponsored by Senator Don Barrington (R-Rush Springs) — one-time winner of a hometown watermelon-seed-spitting contest — who held that the watermelon is a vegetable by virtue of its relationship to the obviously vegetable (non-dessert) cucumber and gourd. Nineteen state senators and the National Watermelon Promotion Board disagreed. Among the dissenters was Nancy Riley (D-Tulsa), who stubbornly insisted that her dictionary called watermelon a fruit, which most of them do.

A fruit, to a botanist, develops from the fertilized ovary of a flower, which means that tomatoes, squash, pumpkins, cucumbers, bean and pea pods, peppers, eggplants, and corn kernels are all fruits. A botanical vegetable, on the other hand, is any edible part of a plant that doesn't happen to be a fruit, such as roots (beets, carrots, and turnips), leaves (spinach, cabbage, and lettuce), flower clusters (cauliflower and broccoli), stems (asparagus), tubers (potatoes), and bulbs (onions). In the popular sense, however, fruit is a treat, which is why teachers get apples instead of eggplants, and why Hades chose a pomegranate to tempt Persephone.

The very word fruit comes from the Latin *fructus* or *frui*, meaning to enjoy. Fruits generally have the edge over vegetables because they appeal to the sweet tooth — a sense actually located at the tip of the tongue and active from infancy. Babies, no fools, repeatedly opt for applesauce over strained peas, and the sweetness preference persists undeterred into adulthood. Most temperate-zone fruits contain about 10 to 15 percent sugar by weight; tropical-zone fruits are even sweeter at 20 to 26 percent. In the annual vegetable garden, the melons are a bit on the low side: muskmelons, when ripe, contain 6 to 8 percent sugar, about half as much as the average apple or pear. Watermelons — described by Mark Twain as "chief of the world's luxuries . . . when one has tasted it, he knows what angels eat" — contain 12 percent sugar, max.

❁

Melons, classification-wise, are a mess. Historically, they were thought to be funny-looking cucumbers. Pliny the Elder describes a "new form of cucumber" peculiarly "shaped like a quince." "Cucumbers of this kind," he continues, "do not hang from the plant but grow of a round shape laying on the ground;

they have a golden color." His quincelike cucumber also spontaneously separated from its stalk when ripe, which sounds suspiciously like a melon.

Thomas Hill's *Gardener's Labyrinth* (1577), intended as a comprehensive guidebook for gardeners, including "instructions for the choice of seedes, apt times for sowing, setting, planting, and watering, and the vessels and instrumentes serving to that use and purpose," explained that the ancients considered pumpkins and melons to be "a kinde of Cucumbers," which made sense, according to Hill, because cucumbers in the garden sometimes spontaneously turn into melons or pumpkins. This spurious scrap of information survived well into the eighteenth century in gardening manuals that warned against planting melons and cucumbers in close proximity for fear that crossbreeding would produce cucumber-flavored melons.

Melons and cucumbers are both members of Cucurbitaceae, variously known, depending on one's major interest, as the Melon, Cucumber, Gourd, Squash, or Pumpkin family. Both belong to the genus *Cucumis*, but are separate species — respectively *C. melo* (melons) and *C. sativus* (cucumbers) — and so do not interbreed. An exception is the sinuous Armenian cucumber (*C. melo* var. *flexuosus*) — also called the yard-long or snake cucumber — which will cross with the melon because, despite its cucumberish name and appearance, it actually is a melon.

❊

Taxonomists organize melons into three major groups, which unfortunately correspond only vaguely to common garden melonspeak. The melon known to most of us as the cantaloupe is botanically a muskmelon, *C. melo* var. *reticulatus*, the word *reticulatus* referring to the netted shell or rind. The fashion-conscious French call these embroidered melons. They are heavily fragrant, green- or orange-fleshed, and usually weigh two to four pounds apiece.

The true cantaloupe, *C. melo* var. *cantalupensis*, is primarily grown in Europe. Most of these are segmented, with hard (but not netted) shells and orange or green flesh. The name comes from Cantalupo ("wolf howl") in Italy, site of a palatial papal vacation home outside Rome, where the melons were reputedly first cultivated in Europe in the sixteenth century. Casaba and honeydew melons are winter melons, scientifically known as *C. melo* var. *inodorus* because they lack the intense fragrance of other melons. All three of the melon groups — muskmelons, cantaloupes, and winter melons — are closely related and given a sporting chance will promiscuously interbreed.

Recent phylogenetic analyses, undertaken to investigate the complex genetic and geographical scrambling among *Cucumis* species, indicate that the common ancestor of both cucumber and melon originated in Asia. Today, though, the closest living wild relative of the melon is indigenous to Australia.

❀

The ancient Greeks ate melons. One story recounted by food historian Waverley Root tells of a melon half pitched by a heckler at the orator Demosthenes in the course of a political debate. Demosthenes, never at a loss, is said to have promptly clapped the melon on his head and thanked the thrower for finding him a helmet to wear while fighting Philip of Macedon. Melons, temptingly cut in half as if for eating raw, appear in a painting on a wall in Herculaneum, the next-door neighbor of Pompeii.

The Roman cookbook *Apicius* includes a recipe for "Melon-Gourds and Melons," at least the first of which — most likely the Chinese bottle gourd, *Lagenaria siceraria* — must have been boiled before coming to the table. The author recommends a dressing of pepper, pennyroyal, honey, broth, and vinegar, with perhaps the addition of silphium, or giant fennel.

The melon faded from Europe with the decline of the Roman Empire. It reappeared sporadically, following contacts with the Near East — Charlemagne is said to have acquired some in the course of his altercations with the Spanish Moors, and the Crusaders may have brought a few home from their debilitating struggles with the Saracens. Marco Polo noted melons in the course of his epic thirteenth-century journey to Cathay, growing near the city of Sapurgan (possibly Shibarghan in Afghanistan). The Sapurganians grew "the very best melons in the world. They preserve them by paring them round and round into strips, and drying them in the sun," at which point — presumably turned into fruit leathers — they tasted "sweeter than honey."

The melon was finally cultivated again in quantity in fifteenth-century France, where it enjoyed a popularity craze of the sort that these days surrounds rock musicians. By 1583, the dean of the College of Doctors of Lyons, Professor Jacques Pons, had solemnly produced a *Succinct Treatise on Melons*, which listed fifty different methods of melon preparation, and in 1699 John Evelyn, in superlatives he usually reserved for salad greens, deemed melons "the noblest production of the garden." Even Montaigne, who generally preferred salted beef to sweets, fell for the melon, announcing in the course of his celebrated *Essays* (1580), "I am not excessively fond of salads nor of fruits, except melons." Out-of-season melons were eagerly cultivated in hot-beds and greenhouses, and Louis XIV, never one to stint himself, had seven varieties cultivated at Versailles, all under glass.

Despite a number of spurious sightings, there were no melons in North America until the European colonists brought them here. Early records of Indian "pompions" almost certainly refer to less luscious pumpkins or squash. One of the earliest accounts of the colonial melon comes from Adrien Van der Donck, a Dutch administrator who arrived in the New Netherlands in 1642 with the doubtful assignment of keeping an eye out for the interests of the financial bigwigs back home. Van der Donck, who had the distinction of being both the only lawyer and the only university graduate in the Dutch colonies, was an avid observer and note-taker, and in 1653 published the result of both activities in his comprehensive *Description of the New Netherlands*. In it, he describes the colonial muskmelons, which were nicknamed "Spanish pork" and grew "luxuriantly."

Thomas Jefferson grew melons at Monticello, including eighteen hills of "Zatte di Massa," a cantaloupe, and eleven hills of muskmelons. He also grew "citron" melons, primarily used for pickling, and, in 1824, experimented with the "Serpentine cucumber."

The earliest muskmelons and associates were, to the critical modern eye, hopelessly tiny. The Romans, who imported melons from Armenia, were dealing in fruits the size of oranges, and even the green-fleshed Nutmeg melon, so popular in America in the early nineteenth century, started out not much bigger than a softball. None of the early melons was as sweet as their latter-day descendants either, though the beleaguered South during the Civil War boiled melons down as a source of sugar and molasses.

By the mid-nineteenth century, green-fleshed melons were being replaced in the popular favor by orange-fleshed melons, which were both gaudier and higher in vitamin A. By the late 1800s, there was also increasing interest in so-called "novelty" melons.

One such, the Banana melon or Banana cantaloupe, was introduced in 1883, a smoothly elongated pale yellow fruit with salmon-pink flesh. "When ripe," commented Massachusetts seedsman J. J. H. Gregory, "it reminds one of a large overgrown banana and, what is a singular coincidence, it smells like one." It doesn't seem to have tasted particularly good, and W. Atlee Burpee, who states significantly that they grow it in New Jersey, damns it as "poor quality." Burpee, generally critical of foreign novelty melons, nonetheless offers a selection of them in very small and undescriptive print, repressively reminding the buyer that "our American sorts are best adapted for market purposes."

The casaba melon (named for Kasaba, Turkey) arrived in this country in the 1850s under the auspices of the U.S. Patent Office, which distributed packets of free seeds to potential growers. However, no one seems to have liked it much — the casaba was green, amid the prevailing preference for orange — and it only became popular in the 1920s. The honeydew melon, also green, appeared in the early 1900s, discovered, the story goes, by a gentleman named Gauger who squirreled away the seeds

Dr. Livingstone, before his whereabouts were discovered by the persistent Henry Stanley, observed vast tracts of watermelons in the Kalahari Desert.

of the melon served him for breakfast at his New York City hotel. The melon was subsequently identified as a French winter melon called White Antibes.

❀

The watermelon, though a distant cousin of *C. melo*, is an entirely different kettle of fish, prevented by genetic distance from cross-pollinating with other garden melons. Watermelons are natives of tropical Africa. Dr. Livingstone, before his whereabouts were discovered by the persistent Henry Stanley, observed vast tracts of them growing wild in the Kalahari Desert in 1854. Their seeds, he noted, were dispersed by antelopes.

Watermelons were cultivated in the Nile River Valley by 2000 BCE — an unmistakable immense striped watermelon appears in an Old Kingdom (2600–2100 BCE) tomb painting, posed on a platter. They seem to have been introduced to Europe in the eighth century CE with the Moorish invasion of Portugal and Spain, though the climate at points further north was too cool to suit them — or indeed any melon. A bill of 1612 mentions "earthen pans for the coverage of the Mellons," and John Parkinson notes in *Paradisi in Sol* (1629) that when it came to melons, "this country hath not had until of late yeares the skill to nourse them up kindly," and mentions that melons were "only eaten by great personages," presumably those who had greenhouses.

The watermelon was wildly successful in the New World. It was introduced by the Spaniards, and promptly outran them, the seeds rapidly passing "from tribe to tribe like smoke signals." Expeditions of exploration found watermelons in Georgia, Florida, the Rio Grande Valley, and throughout the American

Southwest, and Père Marquette noted watermelons growing along the Mississippi River in 1673. He found them "excellent, especially those with red seeds."

Dutch settlers also had watermelons, called citrulls or water-citrons, which the observant Adriaen Van der Donck referred to in 1655 as "a fruit only known before to us from its being brought occasionally from Portugal." The colonial versions were sometimes crushed for juice, a popular beverage — and the singleminded English fermented it, to make watermelon wine. John Josselyn, in *New England's Rarities* (1674), mentioned its use as an antidote for fever: "Watermelon is often given to those sick of Feavers and other hot diseases with good success." (Failing that, home medics advised cranberry conserve or sassafras chips boiled in beer.) Josselyn thought the watermelon "proper to the countrie," which it wasn't.

The colonial watermelon was at the small to middling end of the scale by present standards, though the travel diary of Hugh Grove, who toured Virginia in 1732, mentions watermelons "green and bigg as a Pumpin." Modern cultivars range in weight from a tiny five to a Sunday-school-picnic-sized hundred pounds, though the general trend today is toward the smallish. Particularly popular are the cannonball-shaped "icebox melons," so nicknamed because — at an average of 10 to 15 pounds apiece — they fit nicely in the family refrigerator.

⚛

Despite the lurid pink associated with the word watermelon, watermelon flesh can be red, orange, yellow, or white, and the fruit itself can be round, ovoid, oblong, or practically cylindrical, with rinds of pale green to almost black. Late nineteenth-century

catalogs routinely offered twenty to thirty watermelon cultivars, among them the mouthwatering Golden Honey (yellow-
fleshed), the Jersey Blue (dark blue rind), and the Moon and
Stars (deep green rind sprinkled with bright yellow spots). Low-
sugar varieties — citrons — were grown specifically for pickling, and judging by Amelia Simmons, watermelon "rine" pickles
were common by at least 1796.

Watermelon, a historical thirst-quencher, is 92 percent
water, but the remaining 8 percent is surprisingly high in nutrients. Red-fleshed watermelon contains lycopene — the same
lush pigment that puts the red in tomatoes and red grapefruit —
but has 40 percent more of it, ounce for ounce, than the tomato,
previously believed to be the dietary leader in lycopene. A highly
effective antioxidant, lycopene consumption has been shown to
reduce the incidences of certain forms of cancer and to cut the
risk of heart disease.

Even better, depending on one's medical priorities, may be
watermelon's content of citrulline, which — converted to the
amino acid arginine via biochemical pathways in the body —
lowers blood pressure and bolsters the circulatory and immune
systems. Furthermore, via elevation of nitric oxide, it exerts a
Viagra-like effect on the body's blood vessels, though researchers
hasten to caution that, unlike Viagra, it is not "organ-specific."

❄

The major watermelon event of the twentieth century was
the development of the seedless melon, a Japanese innovation
that bids fair to eliminate the old-fashioned summer seed-
spitting orgies on the back porch. The seedless watermelon, first
introduced to this country in 1948, is triploid, which means that

instead of the ordinary two sets of chromosomes per cell, these variants have three — which explains all the *tri*s and *triple*s that pop up in seedless watermelon varietal names. The flesh, extra-solid and sweet, is generally thought superior to that of the seeded melons, but seedless melons are generally pricier than their diploid relatives, due to poor germination rates and low yields. Seedless watermelons, being seedless, can't make more melons, and are the vegetable equivalent of mules.

Some people, of course, *like* the seeds. Watermelon seeds are a traditional snack food in Asia and the Middle East, where they are roasted, spiced, and sometimes sold in bags like popcorn. But most of us apparently don't. According to the National Watermelon Promotion Board, only 16 percent of the watermelons sold in American grocery stores now have seeds — down from 42 percent in 2003.

Emphatically not among watermelon seed lovers was the impossible-to-please Frances Trollope, author of the American-damning *Domestic Manners of the Americans* (1832). Mrs. Trollope encountered watermelons in Cincinnati, where wagon loads were brought to the market every day, after which "I was sure to see groups of men, women, and children seated on the pavement round the spot where they were sold, sucking in prodigious quantities of this water fruit. Their manner of devouring them is extremely unpleasant; the huge fruit is cut into half a

The major watermelon event of the twentieth century was the development of the seedless melon, which may eliminate the old-fashioned summer seed-spitting orgies on the back porch.

dozen sections, of about a foot long, and then, dripping as it is with water, applied to the mouth . . . while, ever and anon, a mouthful of the hard black seeds are shot out in all directions, to the great annoyance of all within reach." She tried some melon and found it "vile stuff," though eventually learned to like it, at least when taken with claret and sugar.

❄

Professional melon breeding took off at the end of the nineteenth century, with some fifty new melon varieties appearing on the market between 1880 and 1900. Recent research has concentrated on the development of disease-resistant varieties, though modern science has done little about one of the foremost melon pests, the human being.

Even Gilbert White, the mild-mannered English clergyman who authored the famous *Natural History of Selborne* in the mid-eighteenth century, had his share of such melon troubles. His gardening diary of the 1760s is a chronicle of woes, beginning with his French beans "strangely devoured" by snails; his grapes, attacked by wasps (White attempted to divert them by hanging up bottles of treacle and beer); his cabbages, gnawed by hares; and his turnips and celery, withered by drought. The night of September 18, 1764, was the final straw: his cucumbers and melons — and his horse block — were pulled to pieces by persons unknown.

To Reverend White's credit, he never resorted to drastic measures, of which there were many available. In *The Encyclopedia of Gardening* (1822), John Loudon lists under "Machines for destroying Vermin and for Defense against the Enemies of the Garden" two "engine traps for man," the common and the humane, both of which in more or less merciful fashion broke the legs of unauthorized intruders.

Luckily for American literature, such were not employed by the farmers of Hannibal, Missouri, back in the days when Samuel Clemens — not yet Mark Twain — was filching watermelons. The first watermelon that Sam stole ("retired" is the word he preferred, as in "retired from circulation") he took to a nearby lumberyard, broke open with a rock, and found to be green.

"What should a high-minded young man do after retiring a green watermelon?" Twain asked in "The Watermelon" (1907). "What would George Washington do? Now was the time for all the lessons inculcated at Sunday School to act.

"And they did act. The word that came to me was 'restitution.'" Young Clemens took his green watermelon back to the farmer who owned it and conned him into apologizing and handing over a ripe one.

❅

This morally reprehensible course is about the best available to the possessors of green melons, since a melon, once picked, is as sweet as it is ever going to get. The sugar content of melons, like that of oranges and pineapples, depends on the length of time spend attached to the stem and the photosynthesizing leaves. Melons do not accumulate starch, which means that there is no comfortable backlog of potential sugar in storage available for release after picking. The melon itself is programmed to self-pick once sugar content reaches optimal levels.

At this point, a separation, or abscission, layer forms across the stem, blocking the further downward passage of nutrients,

> *"What should a high-minded young man do after retiring a green watermelon?" Twain asked.*

and effectively booting the mature melon out of the parental nest. The mature melon literally falls off the vine into the hand of the properly patient gardener. If wrenched off prematurely, as is often the case with the commercial muskmelon, which ships poorly when fully ripe, there's not much that man or nature can do. Ethylene gas has little effect on the stubborn muskmelon; experiments have shown that it can induce softening of the unripe flesh, but no increase in sugar or flavor components. (See Chapter Nineteen for more on ethylene gas.)

Not all melons appeal to growers on the grounds of sugar content. *C. melo* var. *chito*, for example, the mango melon or vine peach, has a hard yellow shell and pale unscented flesh and was grown in the nineteenth century as a pickling melon. A recipe of the 1890s recommends it as a dinner dish, stuffed with cabbage and baked. Even less edible is *C. melo* var. *dudaim*, nicknamed Queen Anne's pocket melon or the pomegranate melon. Grown solely as an ornamental, this ball-sized yellow-and-orange pomegranate melon, a relative of the luscious cantaloupe, is so fragrant that it was once carried by upper-class ladies as a pomander ball.

CHAPTER TWELVE
In Which

ONIONS OFFEND
DON QUIXOTE

plus

The Seedy Side of Pompeii,
King Cadwallader Carries the Day,
An Odoriferous Constellation,
Demons, Tigers, and Evil Eyes,
The King of Poland's Soup,
and A Tulip Tragedy

> *It's hard to imagine civilization without onions.*
> **JULIA CHILD**

onion

Since the 1930s, "to know one's onions" has meant to be well informed, on top of things, competent, and equal to the odd emergency. Taken literally, however, knowing one's onions is much easier said than done. Clearly it has driven taxonomists wild: the common onion, scientifically *Allium cepa*, is a member of a genus said variously to belong to the Lily family (Liliaceae), the Amaryllis family (Amaryllidaceae), or possibly to the Alliceae, a separate family all its own. At a guess there are around 700 species of alliums, many of them edible, including shallots and potato onions (*A. cepa aggregatum*), Egyptian or tree onions (*A. cepa proliferum*), Welsh bunching onions (*A. fistulosum*), chives (*A. schoenoprasum*), garlic chives (*A. tuberosum*), rakkyo (*A. chinense*), leeks (*A. porrum*), kurrats (*A. kurrat*), and garlic (*A. sativum*).

There are also ornamental alliums or "flowering onions," grown solely for their looks, among them *A. moly*, the lily leek or golden garlic, the plant that kept Circe from turning Odysseus into a pig, and the spectacular *A. giganteum*, which bears lavender flowers the size of small grapefruits on towering four-foot stems. The flower cluster (inflorescence) is umbellate, meaning that the stalk or stem terminates in multiple flowers all born from a common point, a structure that resembles a Koosh ball.

Umbellate comes from the Latin *umbella*, which means parasol, since the individual flowers are often parasol-shaped.

In the common vegetable garden, the common onion rarely reaches the point of flowering. *A. cepa* is biennial: the tasty bulb that gardeners seasonally yank was intended by the onion plant as food for the following year's flowers and seeds. Onion bulbs — like ogres, as pointed out in the 2001 animated film *Shrek* — have layers. Like their possible relatives, the lily and the amaryllis, onions form true bulbs, each composed of a series of tightly overlapping fleshy leaf bases, or scales, surrounding a central bud. "The onion and its satin wrappings," wrote Charles Dudley Warner, "is among the most beautiful of vegetables and is the only one that represents the essence of things. It can be said to have a soul."

The scales are crammed with water and starch and held together by a basal plate of stem tissue, from which roots will develop if the onion bulb is planted rather than eaten. The crackly skin (officially known as the tunic) protects the scales from drying out. Because the bulb is a single united entity rather than a conglomeration of separate cloves as in garlic, it was referred to by the Romans as *unio*, meaning united. From *unio* came the medieval French *oignon*, the Anglo-Saxon *onyon*, and the modern *onion*.

❀

Onions were among the earliest of cultivated foods and probably among the first vegetables routinely nabbed by primitive hunter-gatherers, who could have easily identified them by their distinctive smell. They are believed to have originated in central Asia and have been domesticated for at least 6,000 years.

Moslem legend imprecisely dates them to the exit from the Garden of Eden: as Satan hastily departed, the angel with the flaming sword hot on his heels, onions are said to have sprung from his right footprint and garlic from his left.

The earliest known written reference to the onion is a Sumerian cuneiform tablet from about 2400 BCE, in which the onion appears as an innocent bystander in a complaint against the city governor, who had illegally co-opted the temple oxen to plow his onion and cucumber patches. Culinary onions are featured in the Yale Babylonian Tablets, which date to 1700–1600 BCE and constitute what may be the world's first cookbook. The tablets are a collection of caramel-colored clay slabs listing forty recipes for such Babylonian specialties as gazelle, pigeon, partridge, and goat, all heavily supplemented with onions, leeks, and garlic.

According to Herodotus, sixteen thousand talents (960,000 pounds of silver) were spent on onions, radishes, and garlic to feed the laborers for the twenty years it took to build the Great Pyramid at Giza, completed in 2650 BCE and the oldest of the Seven Wonders of the Ancient World. Onions appear on a wall painting in the pyramid of Pepi II (circa 2200 BCE), and Ramses IV, who died in 1160 BCE, went to his rest with onions placed in his eye sockets.

The Greeks and the Romans ate onions, though in both societies onions were generally viewed as fare for the lower classes. The first-century Roman cookbook *Apicius* shuns onions and garlic but does include four recipes for leeks, variously stewed in oil, wrapped in cabbage leaves, cooked with laurel berries, or boiled with string beans. No matter what one's personal opinion, it would have been politically inexpedient in the first century CE to sneer at the leek: the volatile emperor Nero, who fancied himself a vocalist, consumed them in such quantities to sweeten his singing voice that he was nicknamed Porrophagus, or "Leek Eater." Nero, who murdered his mother and stepbrother and tossed multitudes of Christians to the lions, was not an emperor to cross in the matter of vegetables.

The largely lower-class Roman military, unashamedly fond of onions, garlic, and leeks, distributed them across Europe in the wake of their conquests. Alliums were portable, adaptable, and easy to plant; one authority points out that the expanding boundaries of the Roman Empire can be tracked by plotting range maps for garlic. The legions' passion for alliums likely derived at least in part from the plants' time-honored reputation for promoting strength and courage. The fitness food of the day, onions were fed to Greek athletes in training for the Olympics, and gladiators were massaged with onion juice before entering the arena. In Aristophanes's play "The Knights," warriors stuff themselves on garlic in preparation for battle ("Well-primed with garlic, you will have greater mettle for the fight!"). Fighting cocks and warhorses were fed garlic; and in Rome, garlic was dedicated to Mars, the god of war.

Onions were strengthening in other senses too. Archaeologists uncovered a basket of onions in the ruins of Pompeii in the biggest and best of the town brothels — appropriate, since onions were said to "serve for no other thing but to provoke and stirre folke to the act of carnal copulation." Pliny the Elder mentions that garlic is an aphrodisiac (when pounded with fresh coriander and taken with neat wine); he also lists over a hundred and twenty medicinal uses for various alliums, and claims that leek skins make a nice dye for graying hair. In the Talmud — written around 500 CE — Ezra directs that garlic be eaten on Fridays to encourage Jewish husbands in the performance of their marital duty.

❀

Onions, along with beans and cabbages, were the prime vegetables of the Middle Ages. They were staples of monastery gardens, and Charlemagne, in his detailed *Capitularies*, listed six kinds to be grown on his imperial estates, including onions, shallots, leeks, and garlic. Chaucer's Summoner in the fourteenth-century *Canterbury Tales* was an onion lover: "Wel loved he garleek, oynons, and lekes, and for to drynken strong wyn, reed as blood."

The Forme of Cury (1390), compiled by the cooks of Richard II, includes a recipe for garlic, boiled whole and served as a vegetable, spiced with cinnamon and saffron; and describes a "Salat" of onion, leek, garlic, and herbs, all torn into little pieces and mixed with oil and vinegar. Chopped and mixed with violets, onions comprised a favorite savory; plain, they were recommended for dog bites, cystitis, and the stings of "venomous worms"; and mixed with honey and hen grease, they were said to remove "red and blue spots" from the skin.

By Elizabethan times, uses of the onion had multiplied. Medicinal uses ranged from the soothing of hemorrhoids to the healing of blisters, and Queen Elizabeth's surgeon, William Clowes, used onion juice to treat gunpowder burns. John Gerard, who must never have tried it, claimed that "the juice of an onion anointed upon a bald head in the sun bringeth the haire again

In the Sky, with Onions

According to Indian legend, it's onions that we have to thank for the star cluster called the Pleiades. A group of seven young Indian wives, the story goes, were fond of eating onions, but their husbands, disliking the smell of onion breath, became angry and forbade the practice. The wives, after thinking it over, decided that they preferred their onions to their husbands, so they used magical ropes made of eagle down to float up into the sky, where they remain to this day as the Pleiades, presumably eating onions to their hearts' content.

very speedily," but warned that overindulgence in cooked onions could bring on headaches and dimness of vision.

John Evelyn, in *Acetaria* (1629), says of onions: "The best are such as are brought us out of Spain, and some that have weighed eight Pounds. Choose therefore the large, sound, white, and thin skinned. Being eaten crude and alone with Oil, Vinegar, and Pepper, we use them in Sallet, not so hot as Garlic, nor at all so rank. In Italy they frequently make a Sallet of Scallions, Chives, and Chibols [a type of leek] only seasoned with Oil and Pepper, and an honest laborious Country-man, with good Bread, Salt, and a little Parsley, will make a contented Meal with a roasted Onion." To dream of such a contented meal, however was an ill omen, said to warn of impending domestic disaster.

❄

The problem with onions, almost all agree, is that they smell. Onion breath has been bedeviling the socially sensitive since the first hunter-gatherer ate the first wild onion bulb. Once you've eaten an onion, everybody knows it, which is why Don Quixote cautioned Sancho Panza to "Eat not garlic nor onions, lest they find out thy boorish origin by the smell." The American cow-boys called onions "skunk eggs."

One source suggests that smell made the leek the national emblem of Wales. The story goes that when the Welsh under King Cadwallader set out to fight the Saxons in the seventh-century Battle of Heathfield, their patron Saint David directed them to wear leeks in their caps. The usual explanation is that the identifying leeks allowed the combatants to tell friend from foe. An alternative holds that the Saxons were vanquished not only by Welsh military prowess, but by the "horrible odor" of leeks as well.

Occasionally we've even gone so far as to ban the horrible odor by law. In Hartsburg, Illinois, for example, it's illegal to snack on onions in a movie theatre; in West Virginia, children

Demons, Tigers, and Mosquitoes

The dynamic duo of smell and sting have given the onion and its rela-tives a reputation as a powerful all-purpose repellent, thought since ancient times to be capable of fending off devils, demons, vampires, witches, serpents, and the common cold. The ancient Greeks hung out strings of garlic to deter witches. The Koreans ate garlic before traveling through the mountains to protect themselves from tigers.

In medieval England, a mix of garlic and holy water drunk from a church bell was said to divest the possessed of demons; and in the thir-teenth century, garlic was used to ward off the Black Plague. An onion, thrown after a new bride, was said to protect her from the Evil Eye, and in Bram Stoker's famous novel, Professor van Helsing drapes Lucy in garlic to fend off the vampiric Count Dracula.

What garlic *does* appear to fend off — at least somewhat — are mosquitoes and ticks. Garlic preparations are used in natural anti-insect sprays.

are forbidden to come to school smelling of "wild onions"; and in Alexandria, Minnesota, husbands are forbidden to make love to their wives if their breath smells of garlic, onions, or sardines. Proposed remedies for onion eaters include post-onion mouthfuls of parsley, celery tops, coffee beans, cardamom seeds, and cloves; and Pliny the Elder swore by roasted beetroots.

Nothing, unfortunately, does much good. Onion, digested, generates an array of odoriferous volatile oils that enter the lungs where, exhaled, they create onion breath. The only truly effective solution, unacceptable to most of us, is not to eat onions.

The molecules that bring about this social stigma are sulfur-containing compounds that ordinarily function in the onion plant as an anti-pest defense. When an onion is sliced, chopped, bitten, stabbed, or otherwise attacked, cell disruption activates a chemical booby trap, bringing an up-until-then stolid and quiescent molecule called propenyl cysteine sulfoxide in contact with the enzyme allinase. The resultant rapid reaction spews out dozens of volatile, smelly, and eye-stinging substances that serve as the equivalent of Mace for threatened vegetables. Foremost among these in the onion is the sulfurous n-propyl-thiol; and the prime mover in garlic — one of the three most disliked odors in America, according to the *San Francisco Chronicle* — is diallyl disulfide.

As well as the odoriferous sulfur-based volatiles, onions exude pungent fumes that make the eyes water. The tear-inducing compound, powerful enough, said Benjamin Franklin, to "make even heirs and widows weep," is formally called the lachrymator, from the Latin *lacrima*, "tear." Its chemical structure, dickered over in laboratories since the 1950s, was definitively identified in 1979 by Eric Block and Robert Penn at the University of Missouri as a specific conformation of propanethiol S-oxide.

Propanethiol S-oxide is so volatile that it barely hangs around long enough to study and is accordingly difficult to isolate and purify. It very rapidly hydrolyzes in water, such as that present in the human eye, breaking down to produce hydrogen sulfide, sulfur dioxide, and sulfuric acid, which in turn irritate the eye and cause tearing. Onion peelers can avoid a bout of weeping by chilling the onions prior to applying the knife — low temperature reduces the volatility of the lachrymator — or by peeling under cold running water, which dissolves the lachrymator before it reaches the eyeball.

❄

In O. Henry's short story "The Third Ingredient," the recently unemployed Hetty Pepper sets out to track down an onion for her stew, because "A stew without an onion is worse'n a matinee without candy." Onions — eaten on every continent except Antarctica, to the tune of 105 billion pounds worldwide per year — are essential components of any number of creative cuisines. They figured prominently, for example, in the sixteenth-century French *restaurants*, which originally were not food-based business establishments but restorative soups, flavored with onions and herbs. By the eighteenth century, the name had acquired its modern meaning, spreading from the soup to the place in which it was eaten.

"A stew without an onion is worse'n a matinee without candy."

Classic French onion soup is said to have been created by the dethroned King Stanislaw I of Poland, father-in-law of Louis XV, who had time on his hands during his necessarily prolonged sojourn at his daughter's court. (Stanislaw is also noted for traveling across Europe disguised as a coachman and for inventing *baba au rhum*.) The culinary versatility of the onion is perhaps best illustrated, however, by the story of an eighteenth-century French caterer who, faced with hungry customers and no entrée, served up a pair of old water-buffalo leather gloves, shredded and simmered with onions, mustard, and vinegar. The recipients reported them delicious.

❀

Onions came to the New World with the first European colonists. Alexander Whitaker — the clergyman who baptized Pocahontas — wrote in his descriptive *Good Newes from Virginia* (1613) that "Our English seeds thrive very well here, as Pease, Onions, Turnips, Cabbages." Yellow storage onions — still the most common kind found today in supermarkets — traveled to America belowdecks on the *Mayflower* and were planted in the first Pilgrim gardens.

Wild onions, the new settlers soon found, had preceded them: over seventy species of *Allium* are indigenous to North America, among them wild garlic, ramp, prairie onion, and tree onion. Such wild onions reportedly saved Jesuit explorer Père Marquette and company from starvation on the way from Green Bay to the site of modern Chicago in 1674. The name Chicago, aptly, comes from the Indian *Cicaga-Wunj*, "Place of Wild Garlic."

Ubiquitous in later colonial gardens, the onion was a great favorite of George Washington, who referred to it besottedly as "the most favored food that grows." Colonial onions were eaten roasted, boiled, or pickled. An interesting, if somewhat vague, pickling recipe survives from Harriott Pinckney Horry's *Receipt Book* of 1770: it involves soaking the onions in brine in the sun for two days, then immersing them in "strong Vinegar with a good deal of spice."

Onions were used to treat insomnia (two or three, raw, eaten daily), pneumonia, diabetes, and rheumatism in human beings, and mange in animals. Onion juice was considered an effective antiseptic well into the nineteenth century. During the Civil War, doctors in the Union Army routinely used it to clean gunshot wounds, and General Grant, deprived of it, sent a testy memo to the War Department: "I will not move my troops without onions." They sent him three cartloads.

❁

A Misguided Munch

The most expensive onion ever eaten turned out not to be an onion at all. It was offhandedly consumed by a nameless sailor in the 1630s on board a ship transporting, among other items of cargo, a load of tulip bulbs.

The bulbs were headed for the gardens of the filthy rich: Europe at the time was in the throes of tulipomania, a craze that sent the price of individual tulip bulbs, newly introduced from the seraglios of Turkey, to astronomical heights. The sailor, who afterward remarked only that he thought it remarkably insipid-tasting for an onion, had snacked on a *Semper Augustus* tulip bulb worth fifteen hundred dollars on the open market.

Onions are loosely divided into two categories: storage onions, which are generally stronger tasting and more pungent, and sweet onions, including Spanish, Vidalia, Walla-Walla, and Bermuda varieties, these last a favorite of Ernest Hemingway. Collectively, they come in a wide range of sizes, shapes, and colors. Bulbs may be flat, round, pear-shaped, or elongated, as in the foot-long onions of Japan. Colors include white (*Sturtevant's Edible Plants of the World* (1919) lists four grades of onion whites: plain, dull, silvery, and pearly), yellow-green, copper, salmon-pink, blood-red, and purple.

And all are stunningly good for you. Avoided by Elizabethans, who liked their ladies plump, on the grounds that it encouraged weight loss, the onion at 38 calories a bulb is a godsend for the struggling twenty-first-century dieter. It also contains useful quantities of potassium, phosphorus, and vitamin C, and the yellow varieties are good sources of vitamin D.

More than that, however, the onion is now touted as a nutraceutical, a portmanteau word cobbled together from "nutrient" and "pharmaceutical," meaning a food with medicinal, health-promoting qualities. The onion — so yummy on pizza, so tasty in salad — is also a vegetable medicine chest. Onions are excellent sources of flavonoids, powerful antioxidants that have been shown effective in protecting people from a range of chronic diseases.

Red onions, for example, contain more than twice as much of the flavonoid quercetin as kale, more than thirty times as much as broccoli, and forty times as much as green tea. Regular consumption of onions reduces the incidence of stomach and colon cancers, and the risk of cardiovascular disease. The onion's smelly sulfur-rich compounds have antiasthmatic properties, and its fiber content, primarily in the form of a polysaccharide called inulin, is not only good for the bowel, but has also been shown to reduce blood sugar levels in diabetics. Onions may even be good for your bones: in animal studies at least, an onion peptide has been shown to inhibit osteoporosis, a condition that affects some 44 million Americans.

❋

Unlike the ordinary bulbous onion — where the rule is one seed, one onion — shallots and potato onions are multipliers, and accordingly much more generous with their returns. Shallots are named for the ancient city of Ascalon (now Ashkelon) in Israel, where they were once intensively cultivated. They produce loose clusters of bulbs or cloves, milder-tasting than onions and, unless homegrown, much more expensive. The related potato onions first arrived in the United States in the early nineteenth century: New York seedsman Grant Thorburn offered them as a new introduction in 1828. Larger than shallots, these produce seven or eight deep-yellow-skinned lateral bulbs per plant. Their number and underground location apparently reminded some early grower of potatoes.

Egyptian onions, also called top or tree onions, were unknown in Egypt, but grow wild throughout temperate North America. These peculiar perennials bear their bulbs at the tips of the leaf stalks, hence "top" onion. Both bulbs and leaves are edible. Similarly perennial are chives and garlic-flavored Chinese chives, grown for their tangy leaf stalks, and Welsh bunching onions, which originated not in Wales, but in eastern Asia. The "Welsh" is believed to be a corruption of the German *welsch*, meaning foreign.

Leeks, sometimes called the poor man's asparagus, look at first glance like obese scallions. They do not form bulbs, but are grown for their enlarged leaf bases, as are the related Mediterranean kurrats. Rocambole, also called sand leek or serpent garlic, produces both underground bulbs and aboveground bulbils (edible) at the tips of twisted snakelike stalks.

True garlic, multicloved and potent, is beloved of herbal medics and Italian cooks and anathema to vampires and cabbage worms. The name comes from the Anglo-Saxon *gar-leac*, *gar* meaning spear because of the vaguely spear-shaped cloves, and *leac* meaning plant or herb. There are two major subspecies of garlic, colloquially known as hardneck and softneck. Hardneck, *A. sativum* ssp. *ophioscorodon*, produces six to eleven cloves around a central woody stalk; softneck, *A. sativum* ssp. *sativum*, up to twenty-four cloves around a soft middle stem. Silverskin, the most common garlic in grocery stores, is a softneck.

Thomas Jefferson planted and ate it, but Amelia Simmons of *American Cookery* (1796) held that "Garlick, tho' used by the French, are better adapted to the uses of medicine than cookery."

CHAPTER THIRTEEN
In Which

PEAS ALMOST POISON GENERAL WASHINGTON

plus

*Robin Hood's Revenge,
Thor's Dragons, An Early American
Pea Contest, Thomas Knight's
Pocket-Knife Plant, and
Winston Churchill's
Bare Necessities*

How luscious lies the pea within the pod.
EMILY DICKINSON

King John of England, the uncongenial monarch under whom Robin Hood wreaked so much havoc on the rich, died on October 19, 1216. According to the encyclopedia, death was due to dysentery and fever, but according to food historians, it was due to overindulgence in peas, seven bowlfuls at a single sitting. (Alternatively, the fatal dish was lampreys, unripe peaches, or toad's blood in the royal ale.)

If peas, King John could have done better for himself in the way of last meals. The thirteenth-century pea was tough, starchy, and unpalatable compared to the sweet tender varieties grown today. Even under a heap of feather mattresses, it would have given the sensitive heroine of Hans Christian Andersen's *The Princess and the Pea* (1835) a lousy night's sleep and turned her black and blue.

According to Norse legend, peas arrived on earth as a punishment sent by the god Thor who, in a fit of pique, dispatched a flight of dragons with peas in their talons to fill up the wells of his unsatisfactory worshippers. Some of the peas missed the mark and fell on the ground, where they sprouted and developed into pea plants. The new vegetable was placatingly dedicated to Thor and thereafter eaten only on his day, Thursday — and from then on, Thor, when peeved, sent dwarves to pick the pea vines clean. The Chinese claimed that peas were found on journeys through the countryside by the (probably mythological) Emperor Shen Nung, known as the "Divine Farmer," who also taught the Chinese people to grow wheat and rice, invented the rake and the plow, and discovered tea.

Actually the origin of the pea is a mystery. It's a food plant so ancient that nobody knows, botanically or geographically, just where it came from. Hedging their bets, plant scientists propose somewhere in a broad swath from the Near East to central Asia — possibly Afghanistan or northern India. Annoyingly, the oldest pea to date turned up outside the hypothetical primal pea zone. Excavated at the Spirit Cave site on the Myanmar (Burma)-Thailand border, the world's oldest peas — probably gathered wild rather than cultivated — were radiocarbon-dated to 9750 BCE.

Ancient pea remains, however, are ubiquitous. Peas have been recovered from Swiss lake dwellings and from Neolithic farming villages scattered across Europe, and carbonized leftovers from Near Eastern pea feasts — likely domesticated peas — have been dated to 7000 BCE. All these early peas, archaeologists guess, were far tougher propositions than *Pisum sativum*, the edible peas of today. In order to choke them down, our ancestors probably roasted them and then peeled them like chestnuts.

❄

Peas, both wild and tame, are legumes, members of the family Fabaceae, which bear their fleshy proteinaceous seeds in a protective pod. The third largest of the flowering plant families, trailing only Orchids (Orchidaceae) and Daisies (Asteraceae), the legumes include some 700 genera and 20,000 species world-wide, popping up everywhere from rain forests to deserts. Pea relatives range from minuscule herbs to massive trees, and include lentils, broad beans, chickpeas, soybeans, peanuts, lima beans, kidney beans, carob, licorice, clover, wisteria, mimosa, rosewood, indigo, and kudzu.

The Greeks and Romans grew peas. Hot pea soup was peddled in the streets of Athens; fried peas — or perhaps fried chickpeas or garbanzo beans (*Cicer arietinum*) — were sold to spectators in lieu of popcorn at the Roman circus and in theaters. *Apicius* lists fourteen recipes for peas, including basic peas (with leeks and herbs), peas "Supreme Style" (with thrushes, Lucanian sausage, bacon, and white sauce), and peas *à la* Vitellius (with hard-boiled eggs and honey). According to the fourth-century *Historia Augusta*, the extravagant teenaged emperor Elagabalus, whose brief reign ended in an assassination arranged by his grandmother, served peas with gold pieces at his banquets, as well as lentils with onyx, beans with amber, and rice with pearls.

Most peas in the ancient world were consumed dried, the drying process being considered essential to cure the pea of its "noxious and stomach-destroying" qualities. Uncured peas were occasionally left on the vines by farmers, with the intention of poisoning pestiferous rabbits, who thus may have gotten the most out of the classical pea. For the next several centuries dried peas remained the rule, convenient because peas thus treated could be stored almost indefinitely for winter use, as ships' stores, or as a bulwark against famine.

Dried peas were used to piece out wheat flour, or were boiled to make the ubiquitous pease porridge that, as an ever-present staple on the medieval hearth, was served daily, hot, cold, and in the pot nine days old. Not always a simple dish, one recipe of the early eighteenth century began with beef broth in which was boiled a chunk of bacon and a sheep's head, then added nutmeg, cloves, ginger root, pepper, mint, marjoram, thyme, leeks, spinach, lettuce, beets, onions, old Cheshire cheese (grated), "sallery," turnips, and "a good quantity" of peas. To obtain a "high taste," the cook recommended tossing an old pigeon in with the bacon.

Garden peas — grown in kitchen gardens and eaten fresh and green — began to make a hesitant debut in the fourteenth century; and by the fifteenth, English pea fanciers were growing the Hastings, the first English pea thought worthy of a proper name. They were popular enough to be hawked through the streets of London as "Fresh gathered peas, young Hastings!"

The even more popular — perhaps sweeter — Rouncival pea seems to have been developed sometime in the late fifteenth century in the London gardens of the Hospital of St. Mary of Rouncevalles. (Both names come from Roncevaux, the famous pass in the French Pyrenees where Roland trounced the Saracens.) Thomas Tusser, the English farmer-poet who wrote *500 Pointes of Good Husbandrie* (1557) — an agricultural instruction manual in which activities for each month of the year are described in rhyming couplets — mentions Rouncival peas in the tasks allotted to January: "Dig garden, stroy mallow, now may at ease / And set (as a dainte) thy runcivall pease."

That it was grown "as a dainte" indicates that the Rouncival was eaten green, rather than dried and stored. The Rouncival may also have been the first white-flowered garden pea — field pea flowers were a gaudier pink and purple.

By the seventeenth century, the garden or "greene" pea was the pea of choice for the dinner table; the field pea, now designated as "mean," was the stuff of porridge, pig feed, and the poor. The French were famed for their passion for green peas, a habit they may have picked up from Italy, when Catherine de Medici, who married France's future King Henry II in 1533, introduced "pisella novelli" from Florence.

By the next century, green pea eating was an obsession at the court of Louis XIV. A May 1695 letter of Madame de Maintenon, last and most successful of the king's many mistresses (he married her) reads:

> "The subject of peas is being treated at great length: impatience to eat them, the pleasure of having eaten them, and the longing to eat them again are the three points about which our princes have been talking for four days. There are some ladies who, after having supped with the king, and well supped too, help themselves to peas at home before going to bed at the risk of indigestion. It is a fad, a fury."

The peas were dunked, pod and all, into a dish of sauce, and then eaten out of the shell. The king himself frequently overdid it in the matter of peas; the royal doctors recommended billiards to alleviate his subsequent digestive woes.

❁

The pea arrived in the Caribbean with Christopher Columbus, who planted some in 1493 in a garden on Hispaniola. It first reached New England in 1602 when Captain Bartholomew

Gosnold paused to put in a few rows on the Maine island of Cuttyhunk. The first colonists arrived well equipped with peas. The Pilgrim crop failed the first year (as did the barley, optimistically intended for English beer), but by 1629 the governor's garden at Massachusetts Bay, according to the Reverend Francis Higginson, was growing green peas "as good as I ever eat in England." John Smith gloated over the pea crop at Jamestown ("Pease dry everywhere"), and peas figured routinely in the lists of supplies recommended for newcomers by seasoned settlers. One such, dated 1635, calls for "three paire of Stockings, six paire of Shooes, one gallon of Aquavitae, one bushel of Pease."

Peas were a favorite of Thomas Jefferson, who planted some thirty different kinds in the Monticello gardens. Jefferson was a convivial gardener, known for sharing seeds and plants and delighting in dialogue about the triumphs and tragedies of gardening. Jefferson family history holds that he originated the Charlottesville neighborhood pea contest, a competition among local gardeners to see who could produce the very first peas of the year. The winner hosted a community dinner in which a featured dish was a serving — or at least a teaspoonful — of the season's new peas. Jefferson's peas rarely came in first; the invariable winner seems to have been George Divers of Farmington, a close personal friend, to whom the defeated Jefferson wrote cheerfully and challengingly in 1807: "We had strawberries yesterday — when had you them?"

George Washington noted the appearance of the first peas at Mount Vernon — "Had Peas for the first time in the season at Dinner," he writes on May 25, 1785 — and, at least according to legend, narrowly escaped death by pea in the Revolutionary

> *"The cooking of pease with mint," wrote Mary Henderson in 1882, "is a good way of utterly destroying the delicious natural flavor of the pea."*

War. The story goes that in 1776 Thomas Hickey, a Loyalist sympathizer, had conspired to kill Washington by putting poison in a dish of peas, to be served to him while dining with his fellow officers at New York's popular Fraunces Tavern. Luckily Fraunces's young daughter Phoebe learned of the plot and intercepted the fatal dish in time. Hickey was arrested and executed by hanging before an audience of 20,000 outraged patriots.

To have peas "in perfection," Mary Randolph writes in *The Virginia Housewife* (1824), "they must be quite young, gathered early in the morning, kept in a cool place, and not shelled until they are to be dressed" — after which she recommends boiling for half an hour and serving them up with chopped mint and butter. Actually better yet is to pick them just before popping in the pot, since peas, like corn, deteriorate rapidly after picking. The modern pea, 25 percent sucrose by weight, once picked loses nearly half of its sugar in six hours at room temperature.

❈

The practice of cooking peas with mint may have originated to disguise the starchy taste of early varieties of peas. Hannah Glasse's Peas-Porridge recipe in *The Art of Cooking Made Plain and Easy, Which far Exceeds any thing of the Kind ever yet Published* (1747) calls for "a bunch of dry'd Mint," and Amelia Simmons's instructions "To boil green Peas" (1796) recommend adding to the water a few leaves of mint, salt, and a chunk of butter the size of a walnut.

The mint custom became so entrenched that it persisted, despite the development of newer, sweeter, and less starchy cultivars of peas. By the nineteenth century progressive pea cooks were urging that it be abandoned. Instead, they suggested, peas should be prepared in the "American mode" — that is, boiled in plain mintless water. "The cooking of pease with mint," wrote Mary Henderson in *Practical Dinner Giving* (1882) "is a good way of utterly destroying the delicious natural flavor of the pea."

The nineteenth-century garden pea was delicious and rapidly becoming more so. Perhaps more than any other vegetable, the pea is a study in obsolescence: as breeders developed increasingly sweeter peas, older and less satisfactory varieties vanished. The Hastings pea seems to have disappeared by the early eighteenth century; the Rouncival was all but gone by the early nineteenth. The 1807 edition of Philip Miller's *Gardener's Dictionary* reports dismally that "Rose, Rouncival, sickle, tufted and hotspur peas are lost."

❁

The culling of the starch-heavy, smooth-seeded, old-time peas was largely the fault of Thomas Andrew Knight, who, sometime prior to 1787, discovered a peculiar wrinkle-seeded pea. Knight, who served as president of the Royal Horticultural Society from 1811 until his death in 1838, is arguably the father of horticultural science. One story holds that he became fascinated with plants as a small boy, watching a gardener plant what he thought were sticks and being told that they'd grow up to be beans. They did, upon which the awed young Knight planted his pocketknife, hoping to grow a tree of knives. When the knife tree failed to materialize, Knight there and then determined to figure out why. He was to spend his life elucidating the mysteries of plant growth and development.

At the age of 29, upon the death of his older brother, Knight inherited a castle, a substantial bank balance, and a 10,000-acre estate, upon which he was able to pursue his wide-ranging interests in plant physiology and breeding. His true love seems to have been the apple, although he investigated and improved upon a wide range of plants, among them strawberries, pears, cabbages, and potatoes, as well as peas. Knight crossed his serendipitous wrinkle-seeded pea to produce a series of wrinkled cultivars known as "marrowfats" for their superlative tastiness. By 1787, "Knight's wrinkled Marrow peas" were a prime pick for British gardens.

Knight's experiments with wrinkle- and smooth- (or round-) seeded peas preceded the famous pea-plant experiments of Gregor Mendel by some fifty years and established some of the same principles, although Knight never made the intellectual leap that allowed Mendel to formulate the laws of inheritance and infer the existence of the gene. Both studied pea crosses using the same reliably reproducible characteristics in peas — height (tall or dwarf), flower color (white or red), seed color (green or yellow), and seed shape (round or wrinkled) — and both achieved the same results. Mendel, however, had the better interpretation of the evidence, which is why today we speak of Mendelian rather than Knightian genetics.

Only in the 1990s, however, did geneticists discover just what makes Knight's wrinkled-seeded peas pucker up. As the round pea matures it converts its youthful sugar into starch, a more durable and stable storage form of carbohydrate. It does so by means of a starch-branching enzyme — SBE1 or starch-branching enzyme 1 — essential in the synthesis of the snarly branched-chain starch molecule called amylopectin. The wrinkled pea, on the other hand, has a mutant nonfunctional SBE1 and therefore is sugar-heavy and starch-deprived. High-sugar peas accumulate more water during development, due to osmosis — ripe, they're generally fatter than starchy peas — but upon drying, they've got more water to lose, which causes them to wrinkle like deflated balloons.

❊

By the latter half of the nineteenth century, dozens of garden pea varieties were available. William Cobbett, peevish author of *The English Gardener* (1833), lists seven, adding somewhat snappily, "There are several others, but here are quite enough for any garden in the world." By 1885, Vilmon-Andrieux's *The Vegetable Garden* described 170 different varieties, categorized as either shelling peas or sugar peas.

Shelling peas, which can be either smooth- or wrinkle-seeded, develop within inedible pods, rendered unchewably indigestible by their fibrous parchment lining. Parchment-less edible-podded peas of the sort commonly known as Chinese or snow peas seem to have been developed not by the Chinese, but by the Dutch. The earliest European mention dates to 1536. It is likely that these are the peas, expensively imported from Holland, that were considered such a treat at the court of Elizabeth I, and that were eaten as *mange-tout*, meaning "eat all," in sixteenth- and seventeenth-century France.

The classic snow pea must be picked on cue, at what breeders call the "slab-pod" stage, before the inner peas begin to bulge out and stringiness develops. A snow pea past its prime tends to twist arthritically due to the lack of supportive parchment — the "bones" of the pod — and concomitantly develops an unpleasant taste. The eighteenth-century "sickle" pea was likely an edible-podded pea.

❅

These problems have been eliminated for spoiled modern gardeners by the advent of the Sugar Snap pea, a hybrid developed in the 1950s by breeder Calvin Lamborn of the Gallatin Valley Seed Company in Twin Falls, Idaho. Lamborn's pea is the result of a cross between a variant of a tough-podded processing pea called Dark Skilled Perfection and a conventional snow pea. His original intent was to solve the snow-pea twisting problem by adding genetic material from the strong-podded mutant strain; the unexpected outcome, a tasty sugar pea with a round (not flat, like the snow pea) pod, juicily edible into full maturity, is now touted as a serendipitous triumph for pea breeding. The "snap" designation comes from the pea's breaking characteristics: it cracks neatly in two, like a green bean.

Sugar Snap peas, though best fresh off the vine, are also suitable for freezing, a fate that has overtaken 90 percent of the national pea crop since Clarence Birdseye came up with his commercial freezing procedure in 1929. Birdseye, who began his commercial career selling frogs to the Bronx Zoo, reputedly developed his fast-freeze process while working as a field naturalist for the U.S. government in Labrador, where he observed the local Eskimos' technique for freezing fish. Prior to Birdseye's rapidly "frosted foods," green peas didn't keep all that well. Amelia Simmons claimed that peas, drained and stored in bottles sealed with mutton fat, would last "till Christmas," but frankly it sounds iffy to me.

A reliable bottling technique for preserving food was devised in 1809 by French confectioner Nicholas Appert, who was attempting to win the 12,000 franc prize offered by Napoleon — known for his canny insistence that an army marches on its stomach — for the better provisioning of his troops. Appert's fragile glass bottles, the forerunner of today's ubiquitous Mason jars, were replaced in 1810 by tin canisters (soon abbreviated to cans), pioneered by British merchant Peter Durand. Peas can be canned, but not prettily: the necessary heating process destroys the chlorophyll that gives peas their characteristic pea green, and turns them instead a dispiriting military olive shade.

Better by far to pick them from the garden. "All the essentials of life," according to Winston Churchill, are a mere four: hot baths, cold champagne, old brandy, and new peas.

CHAPTER FOURTEEN
In Which

PEPPERS WIN THE NOBEL PRIZE

plus

A Recipe for Guinea Pig,
Opposing Angry Elephants,
How a Pepper Is Like a Tarantula,
A Perspicacious Pirate,
and A Deathbed Bowl of
Son-of-a-Bitch Stew

There's a confrontation with destiny awaiting you. Somewhere, there is a chile you cannot eat.

DANIEL PINKWATER

Montezuma, in best Aztec tradition, drank his cocoa cold, unsweetened, and laced with vanilla and chile pepper. The Spaniards, who shortsightedly described the Aztec *chocolatl* as "food fit only for pigs," were more enthusiastic about the fiery red spice, pegging it as a substitute for the outrageously expensive black pepper, *Piper nigrum*.

Black pepper, imported since ancient times from the Spice Islands via India and Persia, had served Europe for some 2,000 years as both a taste-tingling spice and a legitimate medium of exchange. Rome paid off the marauding Visigoths with pepper (3,000 pounds of it, by one account), and pepper featured heavily in medieval wills and dowries. Rents were paid in peppercorns, and in feudal France, if a serf could come up with a pound of black pepper he/she could buy his/her freedom.

By the late fifteenth century, black pepper was literally worth its weight in gold: the rise of the Ottoman Empire, followed by the fall of Constantinople to the Turks in 1453, had disrupted trade routes and sent pepper prices through the roof. The appalling cost of pepper played no small part in the decision of Ferdinand and Isabella to fund Christopher Columbus's long-shot spice-seeking voyage west.

On January 15, 1493, Columbus entered in his log the first written mention of New World pepper: "There is also much *aji* which is their pepper and is worth more than our pepper, no one eats without it because it is very wholesome." New World pepper — the name comes from the Hindi for pepper, *pippali* — was no more pepper than the New World natives were Indians, but the name, once bestowed, stuck. The new peppers — unlike such suspicious American introductions as tomatoes and potatoes — were wildly successful, adopted rapidly and enthusiastically by cultures across the globe.

The Portuguese brought them to India in the early fifteenth century, where they became a prime constituent of curry, and from whence they were conveyed further east. Within fifty years of Columbus's pepper-discovering voyage, New World peppers were growing in China and Japan. The northern Europeans seem to have gotten theirs on the rebound from India, which led to confusion about where they came from in the first place. German herbalist Leonhart Fuchs refers to the American peppers in 1542 as "Calicut peppers;" and John Gerard in 1597 calls them "Ginnie Peppers," adding that they were "verie well known in shoppes at Billingsgate." The new peppers arrived in the Balkans with the conquering Turks in the first half of the sixteenth century, where they were called *peperke* or *paparka* — and the Hungarians, by a short linguistic jump, had acquired their famed *paprika* by 1569.

❁

The New World peppers belong to Solanaceae, the Nightshade family, specifically to the genus *Capsicum*, which includes some twenty-five species, five of which are cultivated by human gardeners. The term "capsicum" — used by the precise when they want to talk about American peppers — was coined in 1700 by Joseph Pitton de Tournefort, early plant taxonomist and plant hunter for the gardens of Louis XIV. Supposedly he came up with it either from the Latin *capsa* ("box"), for the (at least in some cases) boxlike shape of the fruit, or the Greek *kapto* ("to bite"), for the pepper's tongue-searing pungency.

Columbus's *aji* (pronounced ah-hee), the Arawak name for pepper, is still used in Spain today, along with the near-universal *chile*, from the Nahuatl (Aztec) *chilli*, also meaning pepper. (We

The Pirate and the Pepper

Bell peppers were grown by the Indians of Central America well before the arrival of Columbus. When the name *bell,* presumably referring to the pepper's shape, was first adopted is a mystery, but the earliest written use of the term seems to have been by Lionel Wafer in *A New Voyage and Description of the Isthmus of America* (1699).

Wafer, a ship's surgeon, had thrown in his lot in 1679 in Jamaica with a band of buccaneers, eventually linking up with the brilliant William Dampier, who managed to combine piracy with literature, cartography, and natural history. Wounded in a gunpowder explosion in 1680, Wafer was marooned in Panama for many months, during which he lived with the local Cuna Indians and noticed the local peppers. By the time he was retrieved, his erstwhile shipmates failed to recognize him, since he was wearing face paint, a breechclout, and a ring in his nose.

Eight years later, with a chest full of pieces of eight, he decided to retire and settle in Jamestown, Virginia, where he was promptly arrested for piracy. He was eventually acquitted, although a portion of his loot was confiscated and used to fund the new College of William and Mary. His account of his life with the Panamanian Indians was later translated into French, German, Swedish, and Spanish.

speak more Aztec than you might think: also from the Nahuatl we get *avocado, chocolate, coyote, guacamole, mesquite, tamale,* and *tomato*) Most researchers agree that the capsicums originated in the mountains of central Bolivia; and recent studies by archaeo-biologists from the Smithsonian Institute and the University of Calgary indicate that they have been domesticated for upwards of 6,000 years.

The latest tool for probing the pepper's distant past is the microscopic analysis of starch grains, tiny particles left behind on ancient stone grinding tools and cooking vessels. The semi-crystalline starch grains are distinctive enough that researchers can distinguish capsicum grains from those of corn, beans, and squash, and differentiate between grains from wild and domesticated peppers. The oldest identified so far, dating to 6,100 years ago, came from a pair of archaeological sites in southwestern Ecuador, where the inhabitants, based on their microscopic leavings, ate a varied diet of peppers, corn, squash, beans, yucca, arrowroot, and palm fruit.

Dozens of varieties of today's five domesticated pepper species were grown by pre-Columbian Indians. Perhaps our best window on early pepper cuisine is the *General History of the Things of New Spain,* also known as the Florentine Codex, completed in 1569 by the astute and observant Franciscan friar Bernardino de Sahagún. Father Bernardino — who lived to the age of ninety — spent more than sixty years in Aztec Mexico, during which he learned to speak fluent Nahuatl and compiled the detailed twelve-volume work on Aztec society touted by some as the first work of modern ethnography.

In the matter of food, he notes that the Aztecs had more than twenty different varieties of chile peppers, among them "hot green chiles, smoked chiles, water chiles, tree chiles, beetle chiles, and sharp-pointed red chiles," variously used in a range of dishes such as "frog with green pepper, newt with yellow pepper, tadpoles with small peppers, maguey grubs with a sauce of small chillis [and] lobster with red chilli, tomatoes, and ground squash seeds." Bernabé Cobo, who traveled through Central and South America in the late sixteenth and early seventeenth centuries, observed some 40 different pepper varieties, some as small as pine nuts, others the size of plums.

Most common in gardens today are breeds of *Capsicum annuum*, a versatile crew that includes sweet bell peppers, red paprika peppers, pimiento peppers (used primarily to stuff olives), and an array of hot peppers, among them the familiar jalapeño and cayenne and the tiny chiltepin or bird pepper. The first description of the mild bell pepper is generally attributed to Lionel Wafer, a surgeon's mate turned buccaneer, who observed them in the 1680s while marooned on the Isthmus of Panama. Visiting Swedish naturalist Peter Kalm, observing the plants of Philadelphia in 1748, noted "Capsicum annuum or Guinea pepper" growing in gardens, used "strewed" over roasted meat or fried fish, or pickled with cucumbers.

Thomas Jefferson grew cayenne, "Bull Nose" (a form of bell), and bird peppers. Seeds of these last were the gift of a Captain Samuel Brown, who sent them from San Antonio, Texas, in 1813; Jefferson planted them both in his kitchen garden and in pots. He worried that the plant might be "too tender" for the Virginia climate, and in a subsequent letter to Brown reported that "the Capsicum I am anxious to see up; but it does not show itself . . . I do not yet however despair of them." Eventually it seems that he did, since there is no further mention of bird peppers in his Garden Book.

Capsicum baccatum and *C. pubescens,* cultivated by the Incas of Peru, both were among the gifts with which Atahualpa attempted to buy off the invading Spaniards under Pizarro. *C. baccatum* was reputedly a favored flavoring for accompanying broiled guinea pig, while *C. pubescens*, commonly called the rocoto pepper, is a thick-fleshed stuffing pepper, described by latter-day Peruvians as "hot enough to kill a gringo." *C. frutescens* is known to most of us as the prime ingredient of Tabasco sauce, and *C. chinense* includes the bright yellow-orange habañero pepper and the Scotch Bonnet pepper, so named for its resemblance to a tam-o-shanter. Like all capsicums, *C. chinense* is American, not Chinese: the name is a goof perpetrated by Dutch plant collector Nikolaus von Jacquin in 1776, who may have obtained some pepper seeds from China.

❀

C. chinense is blisteringly hot, which — although not all peppers are — is the capsicums' major claim to fame. Historian Peter Martyr, writing in 1493, barely after American capsicums had touched down on European soil, mentions that the fruits were "hotter than the pepper of the Caucasus" (that is, black pepper). By the 1550s, botanist-physician Rembert Dodoens announced that the new peppers were strong enough to kill dogs; and in 1772 the botanically minded Dominican priest Francisco Ximénez wrote of a Cuban pepper so inflammatory that a single pod could render "a bull unable to eat."

Pepper-generated heat (specialists prefer the term "pungency") is due to a family of flavorless, odorless but explosively obvious chemical compounds known as capsaicinoids. Officially known as vanillyl amides, at least six of these have been identified to date — the first, capsaicin, crystallized and named in 1876 by John Clough Thresh, an Englishman working in India, where the dominant seasoning, curry, teems with capsaicinoids. The various capsaicin compounds have somewhat different effects on the human mouth: three give what are described as "rapid bite sensations" in the back of the palate and throat; two produce a low-intensity slow burn on the tongue and mid-palate. Different combinations of these produce the different hotness characteristics of individual pepper strains.

Pepper hotness rating — though now objectively analyzed using high-performance liquid chromatography (HPLC) — was in the past solely a function of the professional human tongue. The technique traditionally used is the Scoville Organoleptic Test, devised in 1912 by Wilbur Scoville of the Parke-Davis

Liquid Lava

The website www.peppers.com, which claims to feature the "World's Largest Collection of Hot Sauces," lists more than 2,000 fearsome pepper preparations, with descriptors that include "agony," "venomous," "hellfire," "sudden death," "liquid lava," "berserker," and "Krakatoa." In season 8 of the popular TV show "The Simpsons," Homer falls victim to the Merciless Peppers of Quetzlzacatenango ("grown deep in the jungle primeval by the inmates of a Guatemalan insane asylum"), a pepper so scorching that it brings on hallucinations, including an interlude with a talking coyote voiced by Johnny Cash. Collectively, such hot peppers have become a staple of popular culture, spawning mouth-scorching hot-pepper-eating contests nationwide.

The hottest pepper known to date is the recently identified bhut jolokia, *or "ghost chili," grown in northeastern India, evaluated at just over a million SHUs.*

pharmaceutical company. In Scoville's process, pepper samples are steeped in ethanol, and the extracts diluted in a sucrose solution to yield a "cordial." Samples of these cordials are sipped by trained tasters, who determine the weakest dilution at which the hotness sensation is detectable.

Pepper pungency is expressed in Scoville Heat Units (SHU), with the sweet bell pepper — dead bottom when it comes to pepper hotness — scoring 0 SHU. The feisty jalapeño usually ranges from 2,500 to 4,000 SHU, which means that jalapeño extract has to be diluted by a factor of 2,500 to 4,000 before it loses its zing. The Tabasco rates 60,000 to 80,000 SHU; and the unspeakable habañero, depending on the cultivar, packs a punch of 150,000 to 575,000. The hottest pepper known to date is the recently identified *bhut jolokia* or "ghost chili," a *C. chinense* grown in northeastern India, evaluated at just over a million SHUs.

From pepper to pepper, capsaicin content is affected by climatic conditions, geographic location, and age of the fruit. As a general rule, warm-weather peppers are higher in capsaicin than their cool-weather relatives, which explains why those crops raised in the United States are usually calmer than those raised south of the border. The weather factor can be felt on even a short-term basis. According to the late Jean Andrews, Texas pepper expert and author of *Peppers: The Domesticated Capsicums* (1995),

New York City Transit officials dusted hot pepper on subway token slots to prevent unprincipled teenagers from sucking tokens out of the turnstiles.

a summer heat wave will spice up the capsicums of every garden in its path. Particularly effective are sweltering nights: a high night temperature appears closely correlated to capsaicin level. Hotness also increases with age of the fruit. Infant peppers are universally harmless; in most, pungency only begins to develop around four weeks of age, then increases steadily with advancing maturity.

Capsaicin can be off-putting. It's the major ingredient in the anti-dog-and-mugger aerosols toted by mail carriers and joggers; ranchers smear it on their sheep to discourage wolves and coyotes; gardeners spray it on their flower bulbs to ward off squirrels and (in Texas) sprinkle it around their vegetable gardens to fend off armadillos. Experiments conducted in Alaska indicate that pepper spray is effective in deterring bears (except when it's windy) and Indian researchers hope to use extracts of *bhut jolokia* both as a counterinsurgency weapon and as a defense against marauding elephants.

In a brief surge of creativity in 1983, New York City Transit officials dusted hot pepper on subway token slots to prevent unprincipled teenagers from sucking tokens out of the turnstiles. In what can only be hoped was an even briefer surge in the eighteenth century, entertainment-minded Londoners sneakily poured hot pepper into snuffboxes as a practical joke.

Capsaicin is also the main component of modern and historical organic insect sprays. In the mid-1800s, a Dr. Barton of

Philadelphia boasted of successfully defeating cucumber beetles with his personal fumigatory mix of ground red pepper and tobacco. A rose lover of the same era advised those with insect-infested rosebushes to "take a shovel of live coals of fire, split open a red pepper and lay on the coals, and hold so that the smoke will go through the bush."

※

But what does capsaicin do for the pepper? What's all this hot stuff for? Although it's clear that evolutionarily, plants do nothing without a good reason, until recently the biological benefits of capsaicin to its parent pepper have been less than obvious. Now, however, research by Joshua Tewksbury and colleagues from the University of Washington indicates that capsaicin functions in "directed deterrence" — that is, it wards off some pepper-eating animals but not others.

In the wild, pepper seeds are usually dispersed by birds, which is why wild peppers tend to have gaudy-colored and jauntily erect fruits. Attached in an upright position to the parent plant, the fruit sticks suggestively up out of the foliage, the better to attract the attention of birds. (In the hands of early pepper growers, who were anti-bird, plants were selected for pendant fruits, dangling downward and sneakily hidden in the leaves, which is standard for the modern cultivated pepper.) Pepper seeds pass undamaged through avian digestive tracts, to be scattered far and wide in the aftermath of bird dinners.

Seeds eaten by masticating mammals, however, are for the most part crunched up and destroyed. Hence the purpose of tongue-searing capsaicin: it doesn't bother helpful, seed-distributing birds, but puts off seed-munching mammals. Backyard birdwatchers sometimes spritz birdseed with capsaicin-containing pepper to keep squirrels out of their feeders.

❈

The obvious mammal that capsaicin does not protect the pepper against is us. No matter how scorching the pepper, people persist in eating them. Psychology professor Paul Rozin of the University of Pennsylvania, who studies people's relationships to food, believes that our passion for peppers is an example of "constrained risk": we like hot peppers for the same reason that we enjoy scary movies and roller-coaster rides, because they give us an exciting and adrenalin-laden thrill of danger, without actually being dangerous.

Alternatively, consuming hot peppers may give us a natural high. Capsaicins bind to sensory neurons in the mouth and throat that specialize in sensing heat and pain. Activation of pain receptors on the cell surfaces releases substance P, a neuropeptide that transmits pain signals to the brain and central nervous system, and triggers the release of endorphins, endogenous morphine-like compounds that reduce pain and stress, and — if you're lucky — induce euphoria. Pepper eating, in other words, may invoke the lazy person's equivalent of the runner's high.

The sensation of heat that accompanies pepper eating is also the result of a molecular interaction. A protein called the

Ow! Try Yogurt

To get rid of the burn of a hot pepper, forget water or beer. Capsaicinoids are not water-soluble, but will dissolve in fats and oils. The best bet is a mouthful of yogurt, cheese, or ice cream.

If you've eaten a hot pepper, you know how a tarantula bite feels.

TRPV1 receptor on the surface of sensory cells is activated by heat at temperatures above 109 degrees F — these are the cells, for example, that tell you when you're being scalded in the shower. Similarly, TRPV1 is activated by capsaicin, but (deceptively) at normal body temperature (98.6 degrees F) or below, which gives you the sensation of being scorched without actually being burned. Peculiarly, capsaicin seems to share this mechanism of action with tarantula venom. Pain-inducing chemicals in spider venom bind to the same receptor on the sensory cell surface, creating the same painful, burning effect. If you've eaten a hot pepper, in other words, you know how a tarantula bite feels.

❋

As well as harmlessly hot and painful, peppers are flavorful, and these days most growers and diners aim for a more positive gustatory effect than a screech followed by a gulp of milk. Flavor appears closely associated with carotenoid compounds, colorful molecules that turn the capsicums their gaudy reds, oranges, and yellows. The deeper the color, according to Jean Andrews, the more flavorful the pepper.

The major red in red peppers is capsanthin, a carotenoid that constitutes some 35 percent of pepper pigments. This powerful and safely natural coloring agent is used these days to color sausages, cheeses, fruit gelatins, drugs, and cosmetics. Included in chicken feed, it turns chicken skin yellow and attractively darkens the color of egg yolks; fed to dairy cows, less successfully, it produces pinkish milks and butters. It spruces up plumage color in cage birds and, in zoos, improves the look of dingy flamingoes.

Red peppers also contain at least five other carotenoid pigments and, in some varieties, as many as thirty. The yellow and orange capsicums get their color from beta-carotene, also a major pigment of carrots. Green peppers are capsanthin-less; brown peppers, such as the "chocolate-colored" Mexican pasilla pepper (or *chile negro*), contain both chlorophyll and capsanthin,

Son-of-a-Bitch Stew

Kit Carson's last words may have been *"Adios, compadres"* — or, favored by chili fans, he may have said in his last gasp, "Wish I had time for just one more bowl of chili."

The origin of Carson's favorite chili is also up for grabs. Various theories attribute its source to the chile-laden pemmican of the Plains Indians, to the Canary Islanders who introduced cumin seed to San Antonio in the 1730s, or to the chuckwagon cooks on the cattle trails. Or possibly to the *lavanderas*, or laundresses, who accompanied the Mexican army during the border battles of the 1830s and 1840s, and who, along with scrubbing shirts, stuffed the soldiers with a mix of goat meat, wild marjoram, and red chiles known as son-of-a-bitch stew.

From any or all of the above, chili has evolved into a meal for all regions. Maine chili is made with shell beans, California chili with avocados and olives, Alaska chili with moosemeat, and Texas chili (which originated, claims a vociferous Ohio faction, in Cincinnati) with goat, skunk, or snake. Teddy Roosevelt's Rough Riders made chili with beefsteak and may have consumed a pot or two before taking part in their famous charge up San Juan Hill.

Famous chili fanciers include Will Rogers, who routinely judged a town by the quality of its chili, and Jesse James, who passed up the bank in McKinney, Texas, because the town harbored his favorite chili parlor.

a mix of red and green that produces a biological brown. (The pasilla, dried, resembles a raisin; hence its name, from the Spanish *pasa*, "raisin.")

❈

The pepper is a repository of nutritional goodies. Peppers bulge with vitamins C, A, E, thiamine (B_1), riboflavin (B_2), and niacin (B_3). Vitamin C — now touted as a preventive for the common cold — was first purified in 1928 by Hungarian biochemist Albert Szent-Györgyi from a rejected supper dish of sweet paprika peppers. The sweet pepper concoction may be the most fortunate failed recipe in history. Szent-Györgyi, who had been struggling unsuccessfully with extracts of bovine adrenal glands, described it as a "treasure trove" of the new vitamin, for which discovery he was to win the Nobel Prize for Physiology and Medicine nine years later in 1937.

Peppers can contain six times as much vitamin C as oranges and, as early as the seventeenth century, were taken to sea by Spanish sailors, who may or may not have recognized their usefulness as a scurvy cure. The green fruit has the highest levels of vitamin C. Levels decrease with maturity, and one researcher has found that as capsaicin goes up, C drops off, which argues that the hottest peppers aren't necessarily the healthiest. Raw fresh fruits are the best C sources; content diminishes about 30 percent in canned or cooked peppers and essentially vanishes

Szent-Györgyi's peppers may be the most fortunate failed recipe in history, leading as it did to the discovery of vitamin C.

altogether from dried peppers. One three-ounce sweet pepper is enough to provide an adult with his or her U.S. Recommended Daily Allowance of vitamin C with a bit left over.

Historically, the capsicums have also been valued medicinally, dating back at least to the ancient Mayas, who used them to treat asthma, coughs, and sore throats. The sixteenth-century Spanish priest José de Acosta noted that moderate consumption of peppers "helps and comforts the stomach for digestion," which it may indeed have done: recent research has shown that capsaicin boosts secretion of saliva and stomach acids, and increases peristaltic movements. On the other hand, too much pepper "is prejudicial to the health of young folks, chiefly to the soul, for it provokes to lust."

Henry Phillips, in his *History of Cultivated Garden Vegetables* (1822), recommends preparations of "Guinea Pepper" for yellow fever, influenza, and toothache, and various contemporaries pitched peppers for everything from acne and apoplexy to vertigo and venereal disease. Capsaicin does seem effective in deep-heat rubdown liniments for achy muscles and arthritis, and a dash of powdered pepper in your socks is said to warm up cold feet.

There's also some evidence that capsaicin may be effective as an anticancer drug. Preliminary studies have shown that capsaicin effectively kills tumors in mice suffering from pancreatic or prostate cancer. In the latter study, mice were given capsaicin in amounts equivalent to a human consuming ten habañero peppers three times a week; results showed that 80 percent of the cancer cells in the treated mice had died and the remaining tumors were just one-fifth the size of those in the untreated

A dash of powdered pepper in your socks is said to warm up cold feet.

controls. On the other hand, other results indicate that capsaicin may actually exacerbate stomach and skin cancers, so plunging into a weekly gorge on peppers may be premature.

These days Americans eat on average 16 pounds of bell peppers and 6 pounds of hot peppers a year. California is the leading bell-pepper producer in the United States, while New Mexico — whose state vegetable is the chile pepper — leads the nation in chiles. America's most popular chile pepper is the jalapeño, and of all peppers it has probably had the most exciting career. In November 1982, when astronaut Bill Lenoir took a few on board the spaceship *Columbia*, the jalapeño became the first capsicum in space.

CHAPTER FIFTEEN
In Which

POTATOES BAFFLE THE CONQUISTADORS

plus

*A Victorian Dr. Spock, Weeping
Peruvian Brides, Rafting to Polynesia,
Marie Antoinette's Coiffeur,
The Reverend Berkeley's Microscope,
and A Weapon of Mass Destruction*

What I say is that if a fellow really likes potatoes, he must be a pretty decent sort of fellow.

A. A. MILNE

potato

Pye Henry Chavasse, the Dr. Spock of the Victorian era, was a fan of potatoes. In his 1844 bestseller, *Advice to a Mother on the Management of Her Children*, he avers that "old potatoes, well cooked and mealy" are the best vegetable a child can possibly eat — provided they were very well mashed, since lumps, warns Chavasse, have been known to send the young into convulsions. He was doubtful about the benefits of greens, though reluctantly permitted an occasional serving of asparagus, broccoli, cauliflower, or turnip, and he absolutely forbade onions and garlic.

Thanks to Chavasse, students at Eton were fed nothing but mutton and potatoes for lunch and dinner all three hundred and sixty-five days of the year, the dietary monotony only alleviated by plum pudding on Sundays, a bequest of Lord Godolphin in 1785. Charles Dickens wrote that "the inmates of a workhouse or gaol were better fed and lodged than the scholars of Eton."

The unfortunate Etonians were not alone in their distaste for potatoes. Eighteenth-century French Enlightenment philosopher Denis Diderot, chief editor of the famous *Encyclopédie* (which eventually ran to thirty-five volumes, published from 1751 to 1772), stated sourly that the potato "cannot pass for an agreeable food." No matter how one prepared it, the result was "tasteless and floury," although it just might possibly have "some value in the colonies," where presumably people were hungry enough to eat it. French naturalist Raoul Combs in 1749 pronounced it "the worst of all vegetables," and William Cobbett, English farmer, journalist, and social activist, who called it "the villanous root," simply loathed it. Even drinking the water in which potatoes were boiled, according to Cobbett, could induce irreversible moral damage; and he bemoaned the fact that Sir Walter Raleigh was not beheaded earlier, before he had had the chance to introduce the British to the insidious potato.

Actually, the potato may not have been Sir Walter's fault. Potatoes were domesticated about 10,000 years ago in the Andes of Peru by high-altitude-dwelling ancestors of the Incas. To the original planters, the potato must have been a godsend, since not much else grows readily in the Andean high sierra. While corn wimpishly peters out around 11,000 feet, potatoes proliferate undaunted up to 15,000, which means, should you be so inclined, you could establish a productive potato patch halfway up Mount Everest.

The original potatoes were small by modern standards — plum- or even peanut-sized. The original growers ate them with llama, guinea pig, squash, and beans or, closer to sea level, tomatoes, peppers, and avocadoes. Ancient Andean potato cuisine was dominated, however, by *chuño*, an unappetizing form of processed potato made by freezing, thawing, and stamping repeatedly on the unfortunate tubers until they were reduced to a blackened, desiccated mass. This preparation had to be reconstituted with water before eating and thus was a sort of primeval instant mashed potatoes. Like its instant descendant, chuño was noted for its superb keeping qualities.

❊

The first Europeans to encounter potatoes were the Spaniards in the early sixteenth century, when Francisco Pizarro and company — out after gold and emeralds — stumbled upon them near Quito, Ecuador. One of their company, Pedro Cieza de Leon, who apparently joined the expedition at the tender age of fourteen, is sometimes credited with the first description of the potato, in his 1553 history of his experiences, *The Chronicle of the Incas, or the Seventeen-Year Travel of Pedro Cieza de Leon Throughout the Mighty Kingdom of Peru.* The potato, Cieza de Leon writes, is one of the principal foods of the Indians, along with maize: "a kind of earth nut which, after it is boiled, is as tender as cooked chestnuts."

Alternatively the first to get the potato into print was Juan de Castellanos, who saw some in 1537 and described them somewhat condescendingly as "white and purple and yellow, floury

The One That Makes the New Bride Weep

The Peruvians immortalized their potatoes in pottery: archaeologists have unearthed potato-shaped funeral urns, potato-decorated cooking pots, and, for junior potato eaters, potato-shaped whistles. The Quechuas, the indigenous people of South America, amassed over one thousand different names for potatoes, linguistic evidence of the crop's immense regional importance. Varietal names, based on size, shape, and behavior, included "cow's-tongue," "guinea-pig fetus," "red cucumber," and "the one that makes the new bride weep," a potato notoriously difficult to peel.

roots of good flavor, a delicacy to the Indians and a dainty dish even for Spaniards." He said they were the size of an egg and referred to them as truffles.

⚜

The English, despite much loose talk about the "Virginia" potato, acquired theirs from Cartagena, Colombia, where Sir Francis Drake, after a profitable season of picking off Spanish treasure ships in the Caribbean, paused to lay in supplies for the long sea voyage home. His potato-stocked vessel then stopped off in Virginia to collect a handful of hungry and discouraged colonists from Roanoke Island, a colony financed, but never visited by, Walter Raleigh. All returned to Mother England in 1586. (A second round of colonists had worse luck, vanishing in naggingly mysterious fashion, leaving behind only a baby's shoe and the word *Croatan* carved on a tree trunk.)

Samples of Drake's Colombian potatoes were passed on to Raleigh, who reportedly planted them at Youghal in County Cork, his estate in Ireland, and to herbalist John Gerard, who never quite sorted out where they came from. Gerard thought them "mighty and nourishing," especially if their regrettable tendency toward "windinesse" was eliminated by eating them sopped in wine. By the 1633 edition of his *Great Herball*, potatoes rated a whole chapter of their own, titled "Of Potato's of Virginia." The "Virginia" potatoes were designated Common, or Bastard, Potatoes, presumably to distinguish them from the genuine article, the sweet potato.

⚜

The common potato, scientifically *Solanum tuberosum*, belongs to the family Solanaceae, along with the tomato and the eggplant. Of the 2,000 or so species in the bulging genus *Solanum*, about 170 are tuber bearers, and of the tuber bearers, only eight are routinely cultivated and eaten by people. Most of these have stuck pretty much close to home in the Andes of Peru; only *S. tuberosum* has attained fame worldwide. Perversely, it has done so under a misnomer: our word *potato* derives from a completely unrelated plant, the Caribbean *batata*, or sweet potato.

The sweet potato was discovered by Columbus on his second trip to the New World and sent back to Spain in 1494 along with a number of unhappy Indians, sixty parrots, and three gold nuggets. Taxonomically, the sweet potato, *Ipomoea batata*, belongs to Convolvulaceae, the Morning Glory or Bindweed family. The scientific name comes from the Greek *ips* ("worm") and *homoios* ("like"), since Carolus Linnaeus — the eighteenth-century Swedish botanist, famed for his system of plant classification — thought the twining vines looked unpleasantly like worms.

Beneath these wormish vines, the roots accumulate stored food and swell to form sweet potatoes. (The sweet potato, no matter what American Southerners may call it, is not a yam. The yam belongs to the family Dioscoreaceae and comes from Africa.) Unlike the sweet potato, the common potato, for all its suggestive underground location, is not a root vegetable, but a tuber, the outgrowth of an underground stem, or stolon. With

The question of how the sweet potato made it to Easter Island, New Zealand, and Hawaii is a mystery worthy of The X-Files.

both potatoes, however, the result is the same: if you want to eat them, you have to dig them up.

❋

Sweet potatoes were referred to in sixteenth- and seventeenth-century literature as "Spanish potatoes," an indication of who in Europe planted them first, though John Gerard, still struggling with potato geography, called them "Skyrrets of Peru." He planted some in his garden, where they died as soon as it got cold. They did well, however, in the steamy American South: Robert Beverley, in his *History and Present State of Virginia* (1705), described them with uncomfortable imagery as "about as long as a Boy's Leg, and sometimes as long and big as both the Leg and Thigh of a young Child, and very much resembling it in Shape. I take these Kinds to be the same with those, which are represented in the Herbals, to be Spanish Potatoes." He thought they were native to Virginia, which they weren't.

Neither are they native to Polynesia, where archaeological research shows they were growing by 1000 CE, a good 500 years before Europeans made it to the Pacific. In the potato world, the question of how the sweet potato made it to Easter Island, New Zealand, and Hawaii is a mystery worthy of *The X-Files*. Thor Heyerdahl, the Norwegian ethnographer and ocean adventurer, was chasing sweet potatoes when he crossed the Pacific from Peru on a balsa-wood raft, the *Kon-Tiki*, in 1947. His theory was that Polynesia was first settled by seafaring South Americans.

An equal and directionally opposing theory holds that the early Polynesians traveled to South America by canoe and collected sweet potatoes while there, and another not particularly well-received long shot suggests that early Chinese traders, after touching down in California and South America, dropped potatoes off in Polynesia on their way home. Or sweet potatoes may have managed the voyage on their own: some evidence suggests that drifting seed capsules could have survived in salt water long enough to wash up intact on a Polynesian beach.

In Europe, sweet potatoes were considered delicacies through the sixteenth and early seventeenth centuries, on a par with such exotic goodies as oranges and dates. They were particular favorites of Henry VIII, and in quantity, judging by his hefty later portraits. Henry preferred his potatoes baked in pies, and a surviving Tudor era recipe describes a pie filling of mashed sweet potatoes combined with quinces, dates, egg yolks, the brains of three or four cock sparrows, sugar, rose water, spices, and a quart of wine. The sweet potato was considered an aphrodisiac as well as a taste treat: when Shakespeare's Falstaff shouts "Let the sky rain potatoes!" in *The Merry Wives of Windsor*, he was hoping for *Ipomoea batata*.

❁

The common potato might have had better luck if English cooks had stuck to pie cuisine. However, it seems that they didn't, and the upsetting result did little for the potato's popular reputation. Sir Walter Raleigh, the story goes, gallantly made a gift of potatoes grown in his Irish garden to Queen Elizabeth I. The queen's cooks, uneducated in the matter of potatoes, tossed out the lumpy-looking tubers and brought to the royal table a dish of boiled stems and leaves, which made all who ate them deathly ill. Potatoes, understandably, were banned from court and it was some centuries before they managed to wholly live down their toxic public image.

Forbidden Fruit

Presbyterian ministers in Scotland forbade potato eating on the grounds that nobody mentioned potatoes in the Bible. Some even suggested that the potato may have been the Forbidden Fruit that caused all the trouble in the Garden of Eden, which leaves us with an appealing vision of Eve and the snake grubbing about with a spade.

Rickets, scrofula, leprosy, tuberculosis, and syphilis were variously blamed on potatoes. William Cobbett, the potato-hating British journalist, blamed them for sloth. In the late nineteenth century, Reverend Richard Sewall accused them of leading to wantonness in housewives, since their preparation required so little time and effort that female hands were left idle and primed to do the Devil's work.

The culprits in the royal banquet disaster were the poisonous potato alkaloids solanine and chaconine, manufactured by the plant to fend off insect pests. These are present in highest quantity in the stems and leaves, which ordinarily people don't eat. Tiny amounts are also present in the tubers where, under normal circumstances, they contribute harmlessly and positively to the potato's overall taste. Under certain conditions, however, they can accumulate to the point of toxicity. Alkaloid production in tubers is turned on by exposure to light or to extremely cold or hot storage temperatures. Luckily for the unwary, light also stimulates the production of chlorophyll, which means that dangerous tubers are green.

✼

The Dutch introduced the potato to Japan in the early seventeenth century, where it was relegated to use as cattle fodder until Commodore Perry talked the Emperor into trying a few in 1854. Peter the Great acquired potatoes on a visit to Holland in 1697 and brought them home to Russia as a treat for imperial banquets; in the next century, his ungrateful peasants spurned them as "the Devil's apples." Apprentices in colonial America refused to eat them, claiming that potato-eating might shorten their lives, and as late as the mid-nineteenth century, many thought potatoes fit only for livestock. A contemporary *Farmer's Manual* suggested they be planted near the hog pens, the better for convenient feeding.

Despite the fact that the Germans have the distinction of publishing the first known potato recipes, in *Ein neu Kochbuch* (1581), printed on the august press of Johannes Gutenberg, potato acceptance by the average German was not without a struggle either. Potatoes became a staple in Germany only at the insistence of the Emperor Frederick II (the Great), who, after a series of disastrous Prussian crop failures, distributed free seed potatoes throughout his realm. The ungrateful recipients wanted nothing to do with them, complaining that the potatoes had no taste or smell ("not even dogs will eat them"), at which point the fed-up Frederick thundered that anyone refusing to plant his potatoes would have his or her nose and ears cut off. An alternative story holds that he won over the recalcitrant by publicly eating potatoes on the balcony of the imperial palace.

Whether due to carrot or stick, by the 1750s the Prussian potato fields were well enough established to feed the populace during the lean years of the Seven Years' War; and two decades later the crop was so substantial that by 1778, when Frederick plunged Prussia into the War of the Bavarian Succession, the conflict was nicknamed *Kartoffelkrieg* — the Potato War — since the opposing forces spent so much time raiding each other's potato fields.

One beneficiary of Frederick's potatoes was Antoine-Augustin Parmentier, a young French soldier who had spent a good part of the Seven Years' War in a Prussian prison, being fed exclusively on Frederick's potatoes. He emerged a champion of the potato, convinced that the nutritious tubers — to date neglected in France — had unplumbed possibilities. In 1771 he finally got a chance to present his potato to the public. In that year, following a severe crop failure, the Academy of Besançon offered a cash prize to whoever could come up with the best "study of food substances capable of reducing the calamities of famine." Parmentier won hands down with his comprehensive "Inquiry into Nourishing Vegetables That in Times of Necessity Could Be Substituted for Ordinary Food." Foremost among his proposed Nourishing Vegetables was the potato, weakly followed by the acorn, the horse chestnut, and the roots of irises and gladioli.

Even with Academy backup, the potato did not immediately leap to prominence, and Parmentier was to spend the next decades promoting his chosen vegetable. The problem almost certainly was misplaced emphasis, since he appears to have spent less time touting the potato as a vegetable, baked, boiled, mashed, or fried, than as a source of potato starch to be used as a substitute for wheat flour in baking. This never worked very well, though Voltaire experimented with it and managed to turn out "a very savorous bread." Annoyingly, from Parmentier's point of view, the only real popularity of potato starch seems to have been as a wig whitener.

Success came on the King's thirty-first birthday, August 23, 1785, when Parmentier foxily presented Louis XVI with a complimentary bouquet of potato flowers. The King tucked a flower in his lapel, Marie Antoinette stuck one in her coiffeur, and the potato, socially, was made. During his time in the royal sun, Parmentier supervised the preparation of a totally tuberous banquet, featuring some twenty potato dishes, from potato soup to postprandial potato liqueur, at which polymath Benjamin Franklin and chemist Antoine Lavoisier were said to have been among the guests.

By the end of the century, the potato was established in France as a useful and reputable field crop. By then Parmentier's name was so synonymous with potato that a move was made to rename the tuber *parmentière* in his honor, which never got off the ground. Instead he is preserved for posterity in *potage Parmentier*, potato soup.

There are few references to potatoes in the early days of the American colonies. Among them, Irish potatoes are said to have been served as a "rare delicacy" at a Harvard dinner celebrating the installation of a new president in 1707, although they seem to have played second fiddle to the brandy, beer, Madeira, and wine. Most sources agree, however, that the first credible record of colonial potatoes dates to 1719, when a patch was planted near Londonderry (now Derry), New Hampshire, by a newly arrived batch of Scotch-Irish settlers. The New Hampshire potato flourished and soon spread to adjacent settlements, reaching Connecticut in 1720 and Rhode Island in 1735.

"Had Irish potatoes from the garden," Thomas Jefferson records in his *Garden Book* on July 31, 1772. Still, the eighteenth-century potato was often viewed as something you ate only when everything else was exhausted. Potato consumption increased during the lean years of the Revolutionary War, and John Adams, who viewed this as a hardship, wrote in a bolstering patriotic letter home to Abigail: "Let us eat potatoes and drink water . . . rather than submit." She responded feistily that they could probably do as well on whortleberries and cow's milk.

By the end of the eighteenth century, however, the potato was a popular staple. Amelia Simmons, in *American Cookery* (1796), is upbeat about potatoes, writing that they supersede all other vegetables for "universal use, profit, and easy acquirement." She lists five varieties, of which the best, according to Amelia, is the smooth-skinned How's Potato ("most mealy and richest flavor'd"), followed by the yellow rusticoat (rusty-coated), the red, the red rusticoat, and the yellow Spanish. She recommends that potatoes be served roasted with "Beef, a Steake, a Chop, or Fricassee," and includes a dessert recipe for a sweet Potato Pudding that calls for a pound of mashed potatoes, a pound of sugar, cream, lemon, and nutmeg.

Named potato cultivars first began to appear in the mid-1700s; before that, varieties were vaguely differentiated on the basis of color and shape. Thomas Jefferson planted "round" potatoes, and contemporary lists of potato types allude vaguely to round, long, flat, rough, smooth, red, yellow, pink, purple, and kidney-shaped varieties. Bernard M'Mahon's 1806 *American Gardener's Calendar* mentions only one variety of potato in his list of sixty-seven "Esculent Vegetables"; by midcentury at least one hundred varieties were available, among them English Whites and Biscuits (both round), the La Plata (a long red), the purple-fleshed Chenango, and the Pennsylvania Blue.

Whatever one's personal opinion of the potato, almost everyone agreed that it was a good idea to feed them to somebody else. Filling and cheap, potatoes were an obvious solution to the perennial food problems of the poor, the army, the jails, the orphanages, and the insane asylums. The Royal Society of London, which had established a committee devoted to potatoes by 1662, advocated them as a famine relief crop. In 1664, John Forster, Gent., plugged potatoes in his long-windedly titled magnum opus, *Englands Happiness Increased, or a Sure and Easie Remedie against all succeeding Dear Years; by a Plantation of the Roots called Potatoes . . . Invented and Published for the Good of the Poorer Sort.* Seventeenth-century agriculturalist Arthur Young — a pen pal of George Washington — deemed the potato a "root of plenty" and wrote excitedly "Vive la pomme de Terre!"

Nutritionally, they were right: the potato is a dietary gold mine. One medium-sized tuber contains 3 grams of protein, 2.7 grams of dietary fiber, and 23 grams of carbohydrate. Each potato also contains about half the adult Recommended Daily Allowance of vitamin C — the Spaniards used potatoes as antiscorbutics on board the treasure galleons; and in Richard Henry Dana's *Two Years Before the Mast* (1834), the debilitated and scurvy-ridden crew is saved by encountering a brig provisioned with onions and potatoes. One man, "lying helpless and almost hopeless in his berth," was so revived by raw potatoes that in no time he was once again "at the mast-head, furling a royal."

Efficient and easy to grow, potatoes are usually propagated using "seed potatoes" — chunks of parent potato containing an

"One man, "lying helpless and almost hopeless in his berth," was so revived by raw potatoes that in no time he was once again "at the mast-head, furling a royal."

"eye." This is actually a cluster of minuscule buds from which stems and roots will sprout once the potato is planted. Potatoes produced in this fashion are clones, all genetically identical to their parent plant.

Potatoes do make seeds, which are contained in the potato berry, a small green tomatolike fruit that usually gets tossed unappreciatively on the compost heap. The seeds are tiny. There are perhaps fifty thousand in an ounce, enough to plant an acre's worth of potatoes, as opposed to a bulky sixteen hundred pounds of seed potatoes. Potato seed is also relatively disease-free compared to the tubers, which are notorious carriers of viruses, and it's solely through potato seed that genetic diversity is introduced into the largely uniform national potato crop.

Such diversity is a two-sided coin: since potato seed is a genetically mixed bag, developing potato varieties that breed true is no Sunday picnic. Most potatoes are tetraploid — containing quadruple sets of twelve chromosomes each — and such complex hybrids are difficult to sort out in even the most dedicated laboratory.

Seed potatoes, as in pieces of tuber, on the other hand, are reproducible, faster-growing, and produce more infant potatoes. In general, potatoes generate four times the calories contained in an identical area of land planted in grain. A mere acre's worth can feed a family of six for a year. In the eighteenth and nineteenth centuries, the nutritious and comparatively effortless potato ignited a pan-European baby boom. The unprecedented availability of food caused populations to double and double again. The Industrial Revolution was largely fueled by potatoes, which provided a wave of well-fed workers for factories, soldiers for armies, and immigrants for colonies overseas. A lot of us are around these days because of an influential potato in our pasts.

❊

Nowhere were the benefits of the potato more obvious than in Ireland. By the early 1800s, the Irish had been living off potatoes — and pretty much nothing but potatoes — for over two hundred years. Potatoes first reached Ireland, according to one story, in barrels washed ashore from the wreck of the Armada. Others credit Sir Walter Raleigh, and according to historian William McNeill, the most likely source was visiting Basque fishermen, who originally got their potatoes from Spain. In any case, by the early 1700s, nourished by potatoes, the population of Ireland had doubled to 2 million; by 1800, it had reached 5 million; and, by 1843, 8.5 million.

Outside observers were of two minds about the prolific potato and its prolific effects. The fiery William Cobbett — who wrote that "the Irish people are brave, generous, hospitable, laborious, and full of genius" — fumed that the "ever-damned potato" had reduced them to the "state of hogs, and worse than that of hogs . . . poor, ragged, half-naked creatures" living in mud huts and burning peat. Sir Walter Scott, on the other hand, touring Ireland in 1825, remarked on the gaiety and lightheartedness of the peasants, who were fond of fiddling and dancing, and were always willing to share their simple bowls of potatoes with passing tourists. Arthur Young, visiting in the late 1770s, praised the fine physiques of the Irish men and the good looks of the women.

❊

Cobbett's assessment of the potato proved closest to the truth. Dependence on a single subsistence crop is a recipe for disaster, and nowhere has this proved more tragically true than in Ireland. Potato crop failure and famine had struck Ireland at least twenty-four times between 1728 and 1845, the kick-off year of what we now know as the Great Hunger, but never before were the results so devastating. The Irish Potato Famine of the late 1840s has been cited as Europe's worst disaster since the passage of the Black Death in 1348-50. A million and a half Irish died, and a million and a half more fled overseas. Ireland, in one fell swoop, lost over a quarter of its population.

By the 1840s, the bulk of Irish fields were planted with a single variety of potato, a large, ugly, but notably fertile tuber descriptively known as the Lumper. In August of 1845, when the potato harvest began, the tubers, to universal horror, were found to have turned to black slime in the ground. The potato failure was not just an Irish but a global catastrophe — potatoes disintegrated worldwide across Europe and America, from the Andes to the Himalayas — but the Irish, wholly dependent upon potatoes, were by far the worst afflicted.

By the 1840s, the bulk of Irish fields were planted with a single variety of potato, a large, ugly, but notably fertile tuber descriptively known as the Lumper.

"Rotten potatoes have done it all!" raged the conservative Duke of Wellington.

Left to cope with the Irish situation was British Prime Minister Sir Robert Peel, nicknamed "Orange Peel" for his notorious nonsupport of the Irish. (Irish activist Daniel O'Connell once described him as having a chilly smile "like the silver plate on a coffin.") Actually he seems to have been a pleasant man in private life, with an adoring wife, seven children, and a massive manor in Staffordshire known for its magnificent gardens and flock of peacocks. Today he is best remembered for founding the Metropolitan Police, still known, in Sir Robert's honor, as bobbies.

To his credit, the chilly Sir Robert did his best, attempting to alleviate the catastrophic situation in Ireland by importing half a million dollars' worth of Indian corn from the United States. To do so he was forced to put his political reputation on the line. The purchase of food for Ireland necessitated the repeal of the disputed Corn Laws — tariffs that since the turn of century had restricted the import of foreign cereal grains. The Corn Laws had been a bone of vicious contention for decades: rich landowners, who supported them, wanted to ban cheap imported grain that might reduce their incomes; hopeful industrialists, who opposed them, argued that cheaper grain prices would drive down the price of food, thus freeing up more income for consumers to spend on manufactured goods.

The potato, by self-destructing, tipped the balance, forcing the British government, confronted with an island of starving Irish, to give way. The demise of the Corn Laws changed the political face of England and paved the way for a range of liberal reforms. "Rotten potatoes have done it all!" raged the conservative Duke of Wellington. Peel, in the wake of the potatoes, resigned his post as prime minister and never held government office again.

In the short term, cheap imported American corn did no good. The Irish, who had no mills and thus lacked the means to process, cook, or eat it, referred to the British offering as "Peel's brimstone," and continued to starve. Visitors to Ireland described a land in ruins: land untilled, cottages empty, the people "famished and ghastly," "tattered skeletons."

For many, the better part of valor was to flee: in the wake of the famine, over a million Irish immigrants came to the United States. Despite awful past experience, they brought with them their predilection for potatoes, which in their adopted country were soon nicknamed mickeys or murphys in honor of their prime consumers. The Irish and their potatoes were so closely linked in the popular mind that by the latter half of the nineteenth century the predominantly Irish Boston police were known as the Blue Potatoes.

✻

The 1846–48 potato failures were blamed on everything from steam locomotives to volcanic eruptions, gases from the newly invented sulfur matches, an elusive "aerial taint" from outer space, wet weather, and (from Charles Trevelyan, director of Britain's famine relief program) God's will. From whatever source, the blight was seemingly inexorable. Botanist John Lindley, editor of the *Gardener's Chronicle*, wrote despairingly "As to cure for this distemper — there is none." Queen Victoria called for a national day of prayer.

The evil genius behind the Great Hunger was eventually run to earth by a handful of amateur mycologists scattered across Belgium, France, and England — most effectively by an unprepossessing country clergyman, the Reverend Miles Joseph Berkeley of King's Cliffe in Northamptonshire, who, since his college days, had had a passion for fungi. When the blight appeared in the potato fields of King's Cliffe, the Reverend ("a tall well-built man of singularly noble appearance") rushed samples to his microscope and emerged with an illustrated 35-page report declaring the perpetrator of the blight to be a fungus.

Eventually designated *Phytophthora infestans* (the genus name means "plant destroyer"), the fatal fungus usually infects the plant leaves first, then spores wash into the soil to infiltrate and destroy the underground tubers. So rapid and devastating is the result that in the past the United States, the Soviet Union, and Germany have all conducted research on *P. infestans* as a possible biological weapon.

In Event of Disaster

The Irish Potato Famine led to a frenzy of potato breeding and diversification, to the point where potato cultivars now number in the thousands. The International Potato Center in Peru — home of the ancestral potato — has a collection of 5,500, plus a stash of 1,500 samples of germplasm from 100 wild species. The theory is that if potato disaster strikes again, we can eventually recover. E. O. Wilson said, "We should preserve every scrap of biodiversity while we learn to use it and come to understand what it means to humanity."

The catastrophic passage of *Phytophthora infestans* had a substantial impact on the types of potatoes grown, and breeders were egged on by such incentives as the offering of a ten-thousand-dollar prize from the Commonwealth of Massachusetts to the person to discover "a sure and practical remedy for the Potato Rot." The best of the proposed remedies was a new potato known as the Garnet Chili, developed in 1853 by Reverend Chauncey Goodrich of Utica, New York, from a wild South American variety.

From the Garnet Chili, Albert Bresee of Hubbardton, Vermont, produced the Early Rose, an introduction of the 1860s that rapidly became America's top potato. The Early Rose gave way in the 1870s to the Burbank potato, developed in 1873 by twenty-three-year-old Luther Burbank from a seedball stumbled across in his mother's Massachusetts garden. Burbank sold his landmark potato for $150 to nurseryman J. J. H. Gregory and used the proceeds to move to California. There he settled down in Santa Rosa and went on to create a white blackberry, a stoneless cherry, and a spineless cactus, plus a grand total of seventy-eight new fruits, nine new vegetables, eight new nuts, and several hundred new varieties of ornamentals, including the Shasta daisy. His potato is the ancestor of the Russet Burbank, the potato that made Idaho famous.

P. infestans, however, is still around. The killer mold — which can also doom tomatoes — still wipes out crops to the tune of over $6 billion a year worldwide. The reason, according to the international team of scientists who mapped the *P. infestans* genome in 2009, is the fungus's enormous and versatile complement of DNA. *P. infestans* has over twice as much DNA as its feebler and less invasive relatives, and it appears to be able to juggle its genes to adapt rapidly to varying conditions. With a little genetic adjustment, it evades chemical pesticides and demonstrates an uncanny persistence in overcoming the defense mechanisms of resistant potatoes.

Scientists continue to produce fungus-fighting potatoes. Best known in the United States is the defiantly named Defender potato, which came on the market in 2004, offspring of a cultivar called Ranger Russet and a blight-resistant Polish potato. Most recently geneticists at the Agricultural Research Service in Madison, Wisconsin, are attempting to cross cultivated potatoes with *Solanum verrucosum*, a highly blight-resistant wild potato species, and potatoes genetically engineered for blight resistance are being tested in Ireland, where a new and meaner strain of *P. infestans* popped up in 2009.

❀

By the early twentieth century, potato varieties numbered in the thousands. The seed house of Vilmorin-Andrieux, announcing despairingly that "the number of the varieties of the Potato is prodigious," listed a mere 135, including 31 French varieties, 18 German, 19 American (including the Jumbo White Elephant), and 25 English, among them the quintessentially British Rector of Woodstock and Vicar of Laleham.

Production of potatoes today tops 325 million tons a year, putting the potato fourth on the list of the world's staple crops,

Jefferson encountered "French" fried potatoes in Paris while American ambassador to France in the 1780s and become fond enough of them to offer fries to guests at Monticello.

Mr. Potato Head

When George Lerner invented the Mr. Potato Head toy in the late 1940s, it consisted of an assortment of plastic features — eyes, nose, mouth, ears, and a wardrobe of silly little hats -- intended to be jabbed into a real potato. Toy manufacturers didn't think much of it; the industry buzz was that the public would hate the frivolous waste of perfectly good food.

Nevertheless, a tiny Rhode Island business named Hasbro, Inc. consented to take it on. It was a brilliant call on Hasbro's part. In 1952, the year Mr. Potato Head hit the toy stores, he earned the company $4 million. He also had the distinction of being the first toy ever to be advertised on the then brand-new television.

By 1953, in a spirit of potato gender equality, Mrs. Potato Head came on the market, followed by a pair of Potato Head offspring, Spud and Yam. A plastic potato was substituted for the genuine vegetable in 1964.

behind wheat, rice, and maize. China is the world's top potato producer, turning out about a quarter of the total crop, most of which goes into vodka or livestock feed. Next in line are Russia, India, and the United States. (Ireland no longer even makes it into the top ten.) The U.S. accounts for about 20 million tons of potatoes a year, the lion's share from Idaho, whose modest state license plate reads "Famous Potatoes."

Americans eat about 117 pounds of potatoes a year, which averages out to about a potato a day apiece. About a third of these are fresh potatoes; the rest are processed, that is, frozen, dehydrated, French-fried, or chipped. Processing results in unavoidable vitamin loss, but that doesn't seem to hold American consumers back any. In this country, five billion pounds of potatoes a year go to make French fries.

We owe French fries to the Francophilic Thomas Jefferson. Jefferson encountered "French" fried potatoes in Paris while serving as American ambassador to France in the 1780s and become fond enough of them to offer fries to guests at Monticello once he returned home. The recipe "To fry Sliced Potatoes" that appears in Mary Randolph's *Virginia Housewife* (1824) is most likely Jefferson's, possibly by way of his French chef at the President's House in Philadelphia, Etienne Lemaire.

Despite this elite introduction, French fries didn't catch the public fancy until the 1870s and weren't really common until the twentieth century. They were known quite formally as "French fried potatoes" until the 1920s, when the name was shortened to "French frieds"; then a decade later it was truncated even further to the now-familiar "French fries." Most French fries today are Russet Burbanks, vaguely rectangular potatoes eminently suitable for dissection into squared-off strips.

In Great Britain, French fries are known as chips, as in "fish and chips," while potato chips are known as crisps, presumably because they are. Like ice-cream cones, Hula-Hoops, and Frisbees, potato chips are an American invention. The story goes

No Small Potatoes

The term "small potatoes" — meaning insignificant things or people — has been an insult since 1831. It's a terrible misnomer. Potatoes are productive, nutritious, and easy to grow. Over the last few decades, potato consumption has steadily increased in Asia, Africa, and Latin America — which means that potatoes are now providing food for a lot of previously empty tables. There's nothing small about potatoes.

Dehydrated potatoes date at least to the Civil War, when they were included — along with salt pork and hardtack — in the unappetizing rations of the Army of the Potomac.

that they first came to light in the late 1800s at the Moon's Lake House in Saratoga Springs, a then-fashionable upstate New York spa. The chef, an American Indian named George Crum, ran afoul of a cantankerous customer — embellished versions claim it was Cornelius Vanderbilt — who kept sending his fried potatoes back to the kitchen, complaining that they were too thick. Driven to the wall, Crum finally sliced his potatoes paper-thin and served up the fried result. The crispy potatoes were a wild success, and for years afterward, dubbed "Saratoga chips," were a specialty of the Moon's Lake House, stuffed into paper cornucopias made by the owner's wife.

❀

Dehydrated potatoes date at least to the Civil War, when they were included — along with salt pork and hardtack — in the unappetizing rations of the Army of the Potomac. They first made it big, however, in World War II, when they were merci-lessly fed to the U.S. troops. Civilians voluntarily ate 12 pounds apiece of these in 2009. Instant-potato proponents claim nutri-tional advantages, citing the average 20 percent nutritional loss that results from the amateur peeling of fresh potatoes in the home or institutional kitchen. That's easy to do, since one-third of the potato's nutrients are squeezed into a thin band called the cortex, located just beneath the peel. (It shows up as a darker border around the rim of potato chips.)

Instant potatoes are also said to be cheaper than genuine mashed potatoes. My personal feeling, however, is that potatoes should not have the consistency of Cream of Wheat, and that the best use of dehydrated potatoes is by the assorted filmmakers who have used the flakes in Christmas movies to imitate snow.

Even more inedible is the Amflora potato, a genetically modified spud designed for purely industrial use. The ordinary potato contains about 25 grams of carbohydrate per medium-sized tuber, most of it in the form of starch. The quickie test for starch, as you might remember from Biology 101, is to dunk the questionable material in iodine; if it turns black, it's starch. Perhaps the most creative use of the starch test in history was that of master criminal John Dillinger, who carved a pistol out of a potato, stained it with iodine, and used it to escape from jail. (To be fair, an alternative story claims he whittled the pistol from a piece of a wooden washboard and painted it with shoe polish.)

Starch is a complex carbohydrate, consisting of long chains of linked sugar molecules, which may be branched and bushy, forming amylopectin, or long and linear, making amylose. Potatoes contain both, usually in a ratio of about 4:1. In a potato-eating dietary sense, both are good: diets high in complex carbohydrates reduce the risks of heart disease and colon cancer. For industrial purposes, the preferred starch by far is amylopectin — and to reduce the prohibitive cost of separating desirable amylopectin from not-so-desirable amylose, the German Fraunhofer Institute for Molecular Biology and Applied Ecology came up with the all-amylopectin Amflora potato.

Potato starch is big business. Today it's a major component of paper, construction materials, adhesives, packing chips, emulsifiers for soups and gravies, and biodegradable plastics, which in turn are used for everything from picnic forks to golf tees. Potato starch was used as the adhesive on the backs of the first lickable postage stamps — the famous "penny black," bearing the profile of 15-year-old Princess (not yet Queen) Victoria, was pasted onto postcards with potatoes — and Autochrome, a photography process devised by Auguste and Louis Lumière in 1903, used potato-starch-coated glass plates to produce early color photographs.

Marilyn Monroe once posed in a potato sack, looking delectable and doubtless giving new meaning to the term hot potato, which since the 1920s has meant a spectacular girl. For those lucky enough to have one, the National Potato Promotion Board, based in Denver, Colorado, has decreed that February is National Potato Lover's Month, nicely timed to overlap with Valentine's Day.

If you'd really like to make points, there's a potato cultivar called Diamond, and another called Red Rose.

CHAPTER SIXTEEN
In Which

PUMPKINS ATTEND THE WORLD'S FAIR

plus

*Unexpected Explosions,
Renaissance Water Wings,
Captain Smith's Disappointment,
A Remedy for Freckles,
Montezuma's Hors d'Oeuvres,
and A Bargain with the Devil*

I'd like to coin a new term: Cucurbitacean *(kyoo-kur-bit-a-se-en) n. A person who regards pumpkins and squashes with deep, often rapturous love.*
AMY GOLDMAN

pumpkin

In 1699, Paul Dudley, Massachusetts judge and long-distance member of the British Royal Society, came upon a stray pumpkin vine in his pasture. Left to itself, he noted in a letter to the Society's *Philosophical Transactions*, the pumpkin grew until it "ran along over several fences and spread over a large piece of ground far and wide," generating in the process 260 pumpkins, not counting the small ones, or the unripe.

It's not recorded what Mr. Dudley did with his serendipitous pumpkins, but he doubtless put them to good use, since colonial New Englanders are said to have used more pumpkins in more ways than anyone else before or since. Boston, before it was Beantown, was Pumpkinshire, and New England VIPs, by the mid-nineteenth century, were boastfully known as big pumpkins. It just goes to show what a pumpkin can do.

The prolific Dudley pumpkin and offspring were cucurbits, members of the large and nightmarishly complex Cucurbitaceae family. Prominent pumpkin relatives include squash, cucumbers, melons, and gourds, plus a few off-the-wall distant cousins, such as *Benincasa hispida*, the wax gourd, the waxy cuticle of which can be scraped off and used to make candles, and *Luffa cylindrica*, from whose dried fruits trendy bathers acquire their luffa (or loofah) sponges. Pumpkins and squashes, so closely interconnected that many promiscuously interbreed to form misshapen but usually edible "squumpkins," have bewildered botanists for centuries.

❊

Common garden classification, which inconveniently bears little resemblance to accepted botanical order, divides the multitudinous squashes into summer and winter varieties. Summer squashes ripen in summer, have delicate edible shells and seeds, and should be eaten hot off the vine, since they have generally poor keeping qualities. Examples are the yellow crookneck, the bush scallop or pattypan, and the ubiquitous zucchini. Winter squashes ripen in the fall, have tough inedible shells and large hard seeds, and store well for periods of several months. Examples are the acorn, butternut, and Hubbard squashes, the spaghetti squash, and the orange-topknotted turban squash.

Pumpkins, botanically lumped with the summer squashes, behave persistently like winter squashes, and many early naturalists and travelers seem to have used the name "pumpkin" simply to indicate any fruit inordinately big and round. As late as 1885, French seed house Vilmorin-Andrieux listed a long string of vegetable behemoths in *The Vegetable Garden* under the heading "Pumpkins," stating: "Under this name, which does not correspond to any botanical division, are grouped a certain number of varieties of *Cucurbita maxima*, which are remarkable for the great size of their fruit." Included are the mammoth pumpkin; the huge Hubbard squash; the Valparaiso squash, shaped like an immense lemon; the chestnut squash, round and brick red; and the turban gourd.

More discriminating taxonomists these days sort the edible squashes into four basic species. *Cucurbita pepo*, noted for pentagonal stems with prickly spines, encompasses all the summer squashes, field pumpkins, acorn squashes, spaghetti squashes, and miscellaneous gourds. *C. maxima* (round stems) includes the banana, buttercup, Hubbard, mammoth, and turban squashes, and the giant pumpkins, now so popular in pumpkin-growing contests. *C. moschata* (pentagonal smooth stems) includes the butternut squash and the golden cushaw; and *C. mixta* (now often *argyrosperma*), the white and green cushaws and the Tennessee Sweet Potato squash.

❁

Amid all this variety — squashes come in an immense array of shapes (many bizarre) and in colors ranging from tan, cream and orange to blue, black and salmon pink — pumpkins distinguish themselves in the matter of sheer size. Joshua Hempstead, an eighteenth-century Connecticut colonist, noted in his diary for 1721: "Wednesd. 20th: saw a pumpkin 5 foot 11 inches Round." Like Joshua, few of us can resist the unusually enormous — or, apparently, keep ourselves from getting into fights over the precise enormity of it, which is why Sir Hugh Beaver in 1955 instituted the *Guinness Book of World Records*. He hoped by providing incontrovertible data to eliminate brawling in pubs.

Surprisingly, Thomas Jefferson, a man obsessed with size, seems never to have measured a pumpkin. Jefferson in the 1780s was engaged in the scientific equivalent of a pub brawl with Georges-Louis Leclerc, the Comte de Buffon, over — continentally speaking — whose was bigger than whose. Buffon, in his *Natural History*, published in forty-four volumes between 1749 and 1809, insisted that America was degenerate, its native inhabitants, animals, and plants all smaller, weaker, and generally punier than their European counterparts. Incensed, Jefferson countered with black bears, beavers, elk, and moose, all far larger than the next-best European equivalents, and dispatched Lewis and Clark on their cross-country expedition with instructions to find something huge to end the argument — ideally, a living mammoth.

The pumpkin, however — even though Jefferson planted eight acres of them on each of his plantations for feeding his livestock — seems never to have crossed his mind as a counter in the size debate. Perhaps the Jeffersonian pumpkins were just too small.

❀

The modern obsession with giant pumpkins has its roots in the competitive state agricultural fairs of the nineteenth century, where farmers and gardeners vied to win prizes for the biggest and the best. The giant pumpkin that first won America's fancy, according to Amy Goldman and Victor Schrager, authors of *The Compleat Squash* (2004), was an import from France, a variety of *C. maxima* known as the Jaune Gros de Paris or Large Yellow Paris. Among the first to grow these in the United States was Henry David Thoreau who, having obtained seeds from the U.S. Patent Office, managed to produce a 123½-pounder, with which he won a prize at the Middlesex Fair. He subsequently sold his "squash" to a buyer who planned to make a profit by selling the seeds for ten cents apiece.

Soon renamed the Mammoth, the Jaune Gros rapidly became ubiquitous in American gardens. In 1875 the delighted Mr. James Rister of Bethany, Missouri, wrote to seedsman J. J. H. Gregory, from whom he had purchased seeds of the "Mammoth French Squash": "I must brag a little, for I believe from the seed I had of you I raised the largest Squash in the world; it weighed over 300 pounds!"

In 1900, William Warnock, a carriage maker and hobby gardener from Goderich, Ontario, topped all previous records with a 400-pounder, a pumpkin so remarkable that it and Warnock were invited to the Paris World's Fair. Four years later, Warnock surpassed himself with a 403-pound pumpkin, exhibited in the Palace of Agriculture at the 1904 St. Louis World's Fair. (That same fair gave us the ice-cream cone, a re-enactment of the Boer War that included a horseman leaping from a height of 35 feet into a pool of water, and a lecture by fruit specialist J. T. Stinson in which attendees were first introduced to the maxim "An apple a day keeps the doctor away.") Warnock's 403-pound record was to stand for the next seventy-five years.

Mammoth cultivars proliferated in the interim, among them the Hundred Weight, the Mammoth Fifty Dollar, and Landreth's Yellow Monster. None, despite their hefty names, managed to outweigh Warnock's prize — until Howard Dill (thereafter nicknamed "Moby Dill") of Windsor, Nova Scotia, through a process of crossbreeding and selection, created the blimp-like Dill's Atlantic Giant. In 1980, an Atlantic Giant hit a record-breading 459 pounds; in 1981, one reached 493½.

Giant pumpkins today have passed the 500-, 1000-, and 1,500-pound marks, with apparently no end in sight. (The world

Great Pumpkins

The pumpkin is an American icon. It has been immortalized in prose and poetry by such literary greats as Mother Goose, Washington Irving, John Greenleaf Whittier, and L. Frank Baum, and few autumns pass without somebody quoting James Whitcomb Riley's colloquial tribute to the time "when the frost is on the punkin." Henry David Thoreau tossed it a left-handed compliment, reflecting on the solitary banks of Walden Pond that he would rather sit on a pumpkin and have it all to himself than on a velvet cushion and be crowded; and in 1697, master storyteller Charles Perrault provided his Cinderella with the best of both, transforming a solitary pumpkin into a velvet-cushioned coach to carry her in cucurbital elegance to the prince's ball.

Since 1959 we've been able to sympathize each Halloween with Charles Schultz's character Linus, patiently waiting for the Great Pumpkin to rise out of the pumpkin patch and fly through the air, delivering toys to all the good children in the world.

Best of all the pumpkin tales, however, may be one of Aesop's fables. It tells of a man who lay beneath an oak tree, criticizing the Creator for hanging a tiny acorn on a huge tree, but an enormous pumpkin on a slender vine. Then, the story goes, an acorn fell and hit him on the nose.

champion as of 2010 weighed in at 1,810½ pounds — approximately the weight of a Volkswagen Beetle.) According to horticulturists, the phenomenal size of recent cultivars results from a combination of genetic change and improved culture techniques. Size in pumpkins is ultimately determined at the cellular level. Large-fruited varieties have longer periods of cell division and thus more cells than smaller varieties; and those cells continue to expand in size after cell division comes to a halt. Between these two phenomena, *C. maxima* can pack on fifty pounds a day.

Giant pumpkins aren't pretty. Most have lost their bright pumpkin orange, due to a heavy influx of squash genes, and none are symmetrically round. The larger a pumpkin gets, the greater its tendency to suffer from a vegetable version of secretarial spread. Crushed by gravity, real behemoths slump, sag, and ooze "like Jabba the Hutt reclining on his divan," writes Susan Warren in *Backyard Giants* (2007).

❊

The very earliest cucurbits — probably originating in Central America — were small. They were also bitter, and were most likely valued by early eaters for their protein- and oil-rich seeds. Cultivation of squash and pumpkins dates back at least nine thousand years, judging by scattered remains of seeds and stems found in prehistoric caves in the Tamaulipas mountains of Mexico, and they are thought to have been the first domesticated of the "Indian triad" — squash, beans, and maize — that formed the basis of pre-Columbian Indian diet in both North and South America.

By the arrival of the Europeans, selection had produced squashes sizeable and succulent enough to attract notice. Hernando de Soto, cruising Tampa Bay in 1539, wrote that "beans and pumpkins were in great plenty; both were larger and better than those of Spain; the pumpkins when roasted had nearly the taste of chestnuts." Coronado saw "melons" (probably squash) on a gold-scouting expedition through the American Southwest, Cartier noted "*gros melons*" (probably pumpkins) in Canada in 1535, and Samuel de Champlain remarked on the "*citroules*" (squash?) of New England during his voyage of 1605. Columbus's account of his first voyage mentions Cuban fields

Exploding Pumpkins

Pumpkins, though you wouldn't think so to thump upon them, are amazingly malleable: a growing pumpkin encased in a box will obligingly turn itself into a cube. (Japanese growers have exploited this tendency to grow cuboidal watermelons in boxes, which stack efficiently for shipping.) They're not, however, infinitely plastic. The giant pumpkin, if it overreaches itself, can literally explode. Too much rain, for example, makes the growing pumpkin swell too fast, exerting pressure on weak spots in the rind, and causing it eventually and abruptly to crack open.

planted with "*calebazzas*," or gourds, which were more likely a hard-shelled winter squash.

❄

Botanical consensus is that the gourd grown in ancient and medieval Europe (*Lagenaria*) is of African origin and reached Asia and the Americas more than 10,000 years ago, most likely by simply floating across the ocean. Ancient Old World mentions of "squash" — those, for example, supposedly grown in the Hanging Gardens of Babylon — probably refer to *Lagenaria siceraria*, or bottle gourds. Some of these are edible, and it was likely a tasty *Lagenaria* that the Romans consumed, immature, doused with vinegar and mustard. Roman gardeners also grew gourds for show, in "grotesque forms" up to nine feet long, and Pliny the Elder mentions that gourd vines make a nice shade plant in gardens, when trained over roofs and trellises.

The uses of gourds were legion. Pliny mentions gourds as containers for turpentine, olive oil, honey, wine, and water; and Columella, in his first-century agricultural treatise *De Re*

Rustica, says gourds were used as floats for teaching boys how to swim. Gourds are popularly called "marine pumpkins," writes Giacomo Castelvetro in *The Fruits, Herbs, and Vegetables of Italy* (1614), "because they are used by inexperienced swimmers, scared of drowning, who strap a whole dried gourd under their chest to keep from sinking into the sea. Small children learn to swim in the rivers with them." In his *Dictionarium Botanicum, or a Botanical Dictionary for the Use of the Curious in Husbandry and Gardening* (1728), Richard Bradley describes the Fishermen's Gourd used in Italy to catch ducks: apparently these were large-size gourds, big enough to fit helmet-style over a man's head. They were fashioned with eyeholes; wearers submerged themselves sneakily in the water and grabbed ducks by the legs.

American natives similarly put *Lagenaria siceraria* to good use. John White, artist, sole surviving Roanoke colonist, and grandfather of Virginia Dare (the first English baby born in the New World), mentions in an account of 1585 that the local Indians used gourds as water buckets and as rattles (which they fastened on a stick and used to "make merri"). Adriaen van der Donck, in his *Description of the New Netherlands* (1655), describes gourds as "the common water-pail of the natives," some half a bushel in size. According to John Lawson, early eighteenth-century planters used these same gourds set on poles as purple-martin houses, since the martins, being "very warlike" birds, would scare away the crows.

❈

The American pumpkin and squash admittedly took a bit of getting used to. Some initial disappointments clearly arose from dashed expectations: many newcomers thought that the native

The New England settlers deemed the Narragansett askutasquash *"uncivilized to contemplate."*

cucurbits were a form of melon. Captain John Smith mentions a fruit like a muskmelon grown by the Virginia Indians, only "lesse and worse." It was almost certainly a squash, and "worse" is an understandable reaction if you bit a squash while hoping for melon. The New England settlers deemed the Narragansett *askutasquash* "uncivilized to contemplate," and the squash-and-seafood chowder offered them by hospitable Indian cooks they damned as "the meanest of God's blessings."

Edward Johnson, Massachusetts colonist and militia captain, wrote an early *History of New-England* in 1654 in which he refers to the new land as a "howling Desart" and points out how clever it was of the Lord "to hide from the Eyes of his people the difficulties they are to encounter . . . that they might not thereby be hindered from taking the worke in hand." Among these difficulties were wolves and bears, thickets, awful weather, earthquakes, and "Pomkins and Squashes," which is what the "poore people" had to eat instead of anything nice.

The genial Dutch of New Netherlands, on the other hand, found the local *quaasiens* "a delightful fruite," greatly favored by women because it was easy to cook. Traveller John Josselyn praised the squash in his *New England's Rarities Discovered* (1672), a volume that includes his "rude and undigested" observations of American topography, culture, and animal and plant life, chronological highlights of New England history, a "Description of an Indian Squa," and a note on a "pineapple" which, when picked, erupted into a horde of angry wasps. The squash, he says, is "a kind of Melon or rather Gourd for they oftentimes degenerate into gourds; some of these are green, some yellow, some longish like a gourd, others round like an apple; all of them pleasant food boyled and buttered, and seasoned with spice."

Native American gardens offered many varieties of squash. The Northeastern tribes grew pumpkins, yellow crooknecks, pattypans, Boston marrows — perhaps the oldest squash in America still in commercial production — and turban squashes; Southern tribes raised winter crooknecks, cushaws, and green-and-white-striped sweet potato squashes. The Indian name for the fruit, variously rendered as *askutasquash*, *isquotersquash*, or simply *askoot*, translated as "something to be eaten raw," probably the earliest, but least satisfactory, means of consumption.

❊

Porter and Pumperkin

Pumpkins, like practically everything else, can be turned into alcohol. The earliest American poem, written in 1630 by an anonymous Pilgrim, includes the verse: "If Barley be wanting to make into Malt / We must be contented and think it no Fault / For we can make liquor to sweeten our Lips / Of Pumpkins and Parsnips and Walnut-Tree Chips." The poem, titled "New England's Annoyances," is an exercise in sarcasm: the bottom line is that the Pilgrims missed real beer. The lousy substitute involved persimmons, hops, maple syrup, and pumpkin mash.

George Washington, who brewed his own beer, experimented with pumpkin porter, and Virginia planter Landon Carter invented an alcoholic pumpkin beverage that he seemed quite pleased with and christened "pumperkin."

Common practice by the time the *Mayflower* landed was to bake winter squashes and pumpkins whole in the ashes of the fire, then cut them open and serve them moistened with animal fat and maple syrup or honey. The earliest Pilgrim-invented pumpkin pie was a variation on this theme: the top was sliced off a pumpkin; the seeds scraped out; the cavity filled with apples, sugar, spices, and milk; the top popped back on, and the stuffed fruit baked whole. By the next century, the more classic Thanksgiving dinner version in a crust had appeared. The "Pumpkin Pie" recipe in Amelia Simmons's 1796 *American Cookery* calls for a pudding-like filling of milk, "pumpkin," eggs, molasses, allspice, and ginger baked in a "tart paste," or crust, of flour and butter.

Yankee culinary ingenuity also devised pumpkin stews and soups (with corn, peas, and beans), sauce (served on meat and fish), porridge, pancakes, bread, butter, and, with much effortful boiling, molasses. Pumpkin was cut in strips and dried to make a sort of pumpkin jerky.

The cucurbits also had a range of medicinal uses. As early as 1611, a Miss Elizabeth Skinner of Roanoke, Virginia, recommended squash seeds pounded with meal to remove freckles and other unsightly "spottes" from the face. The Indians ate squash and pumpkin seeds as a worm expellant, and whole squash (in quantity) for snakebite. The settlers drank pulverized squash and pumpkin seeds in water for bladder trouble and made tea of ground pumpkin stems to treat "female ills." The various pains of childbirth, toothache, and chilblains were thought to abate if the sufferer chewed on a squash, and the colonists of Jamestown used boiled squash mashed into paste as a poultice for sore eyes.

A hefty number of pumpkins and squashes were needed to supply all these dietary and medicinal needs, and the colonial cucurbit soon outgrew the kitchen garden and was elevated to the status of field crop. It usually sat in its field until October, bulging ripely over the remains of withered vines and stalks, and as such was fair game for the natural disasters recorded in colonial histories as "pumpkin floods."

Floods of any kind are rare in October, a notoriously dry month nationwide, but occasional torrential downpours do occur, with accompanying high water and river overflow. Such floods occurred at least twice in the 1780s, once overrunning the pumpkin fields of Maine and New Hampshire, the following year washing out the pumpkins of Pennsylvania and Maryland. Pumpkins, for all their apparent solidity, float, and the unexpected October overflows carried off enough of them that the floods were named for their buoyant orange cargo. In years without floods, pumpkins were harvested more conventionally, stored in straw in the root cellar, and served up in pies for Thanksgiving dinner, a holiday scornfully referred to by nonparticipating Episcopalians as St. Pumpkin's Day.

❀

Europeans were not initially taken with American cucurbits. Gardening manuals of the seventeenth and eighteenth centuries reiterate that the various "pompions" were principally a food of the poor, who planted them on dunghills. Summer squash reached England in the late seventeenth century, where it was ungratefully dubbed "harrow marrow." (The source of the English *marrow*, meaning squash, is obscure; one guess is that it was thought to have the taste or consistency of bone marrow,

Pumpkins float. October rain and river overflow can wash them out of their fields, creating "pumpkin floods."

a common ingredient in eighteenth-century recipes.) In France, squash seeds stuck in the gullets of the prized Strasbourg geese, destined for pâté de foie gras, and squash on the whole managed to offend the influential horticulturalist Olivier de Serries, who had obtained his garden specimens from Spain. He referred to the new vegetable as "Spain's revenge."

Squash and pumpkins, however, grew on people. Washington and Jefferson were both squash growers: the Monticello gardens featured pumpkins, "white pumpkins," and "cymlings," the last an early name for the bush scallop or pattypan. Cymlings or simnels, according to Virginian John Banister in his *Natural History* (1690), were so called for their resemblance to a traditional Lenten or simnel cake, a round cake decorated with balls of almond paste around the outer edge. John Gerard called them buckler squash, from their resemblance to bucklers, the small round shields favored by medieval swordsmen.

Many new squash varieties were picked up in the nineteenth century by sea captains in the West Indies or South America and brought back to enrich the gardens of their home ports. By such routes arrived the Valparaiso, Marblehead, pineapple, and Hubbard squashes. The Hubbard squash, cunningly described as "turned up like a Chinese shoe," and said when baked to taste like a sweet potato, had a long run as America's favorite winter squash.

It was formally introduced to American gardens by Marblehead, Massachusetts, seedsman James J. H. Gregory, who traced its homely history in *The Magazine of Horticulture*, December 23, 1857:

> "Of the origin of the Hubbard squash we have no certain knowledge. The facts relative to its cultivation in Marblehead are simply these. Upwards of twenty years ago, a single specimen was brought into town, the seed from which was planted in the garden of a lady, now deceased; a specimen from this yield was given to Captain Knott Martin, of this town, who raised it for family use for a few years, when it was brought to our notice in the year 1842 or '43. We were first informed of its good qualities by Mrs. Elizabeth Hubbard, a very worthy lady, through whom we obtained seed from Cpt. Martin. As the squash up to this time had no specific name to designate it from other varieties, my father termed it the 'Hubbard Squash.'"

Gregory's business fairly boomed after the acquisition of Hubbard squash seed, and Gregory went on to become something of an authority on squashes, publishing in 1893 an informative work titled *Squashes: How to Grow Them*.

❋

Most successful among squashes today is probably the zucchini, which became popular in American gardens in the 1950s, reintroduced to North America from Italy. The Italians had acquired the zucchini in mysteriously undocumented fashion more than three hundred years ago and formed an immediate affinity for it. The name is a derivative of an Italian word meaning sweetest. It's also legendarily productive: six zucchini plants, one expert figures, yield an average of fifty pounds of fruit per summer, and that's a conservative estimate. "The trouble is, you

"The first zucchini I ever saw," says one author,
"I killed it with a hoe."

cannot grow just one zucchini," humorist Dave Barry writes. "Minutes after you plant a single seed, hundreds of zucchini will barge out of the ground and sprawl around the garden menacing other vegetables. At night, you will be able to hear the ground quake as more and more zucchinis erupt."

Much of the squash-breeding effort in this country over the past twenty years has been devoted to zucchini, which is now available in a rainbow of colors other than the standard flecked green. It appears internationally on the tables of France, as the *courgette*; England, as the baby marrow; and Spain, as the *calabacin*. Still, it's not a squash for everybody. "The first zucchini I ever saw," says author John Gould, "I killed it with a hoe." Mr. Gould is also down on the pattypan ("a cross between a Scottish curling stone and the end cut from a roast of foam rubber") and insists that the best use for all squashes is to dry them and hang them from the trees as birdhouses.

A perhaps more acceptable, since less squashlike, alternative is the spaghetti squash or vegetable spaghetti, a variety of *C. pepo* whose insides, when baked or boiled, unravel into a mass of fine spaghetti-like strands touted as a low-calorie substitute for pasta. A hard-shelled winter squash shaped roughly like a football, the spaghetti squash was originally cultivated in Italy and Spain.

❁

Adventurous squash eaters do not necessarily confine themselves to the conventional fleshy fruits. Squash flowers, especially those of zucchini, pattypan, and summer crookneck squashes, are both edible and flavorful. Friar Bernardino de Sahagún reported squash blossom hors d'oeuvres at Montezuma's banquet table, though he was regrettably vague about their manner of preparation. These days the blossoms are sautéed, dipped in batter for fritters, or stuffed with rice and meat. The Zunis of the Southwest ate squash blossoms in soup, choosing the large male flowers, which were considered the most delectable.

Prospective soup cooks have a choice between male and female flowers because monoecious plants, such as squashes, pumpkins, cucumbers, and melons, bear both. Dioecious plants, in contrast, segregated like Victorian boarding schools, bear either male or female flowers, never both. This seeming botanical propriety is nature's way of preventing self-fertilization and promoting the beneficially varied genetic scrambling that is the point of sexual reproduction in the first place. Spinach, asparagus, and holly are all dioecious, which means that to get red berries for your Christmas wreaths, you need a breeding pair of trees.

In monoecious plants, often the male and female flowers mature at different times to encourage cross-fertilization. In squashes, for example, the male flowers, the pollinizers, open first. Male and female flowers are simple to tell apart: the males have straight skinny stems leading directly to the bud; the females have a prominent bulge at the top of the stem adjacent

The Zunis of the Southwest ate squash blossoms in soup, choosing the large male flowers, considered the most delectable.

to the petals, containing the ovary. Upon fertilization, this ovary develops into a mature squash or pumpkin.

❊

Squash and pumpkin blossoms are borne on indefatigable vines that given their head will happily overrun one hundred square feet or more of garden. This insidious habit, of particular concern to gardeners with limited growing space, has long been a target of breeders and plant scientists. The results of their professional manipulations are known as bush cultivars, plants in which the internodes — the lengths of stem between leaves — have been drastically shortened. The truncated cultivars take up a quarter, or less, of the space of the standard vines, but in many cases have been found to bear smaller and fewer fruits than their unconfined relatives.

A possible reason for this, researchers suggest, is the reduced photosynthetic area that follows reduction in vine length: shorter vines mean fewer leaves, which in turn means less sunlight-derived energy to fuel the development of fruit. To owners of pocket-handkerchief-sized vegetable plots, however, a small pumpkin is better than no pumpkin at all. Still, even a bush pumpkin can swallow sixty square feet of garden space, so genetics has yet to give us a jack-o'-lantern in a flowerpot.

Not everyone, of course, likes the pumpkin. In the 1890s, New York seedsman and squash activist Peter Henderson began to inveigh against it:

> "The pumpkin is yet offered in large quantities for sale in our markets, but it ought to be banished from them as it has been for some time from our garden. But the good lieges of our cities are suspicious in all innovations in what

is offered them to eat, and it will be many years yet before the masses will understand the modest and sometimes uncouth looking squash is immeasurably superior for all culinary purposes to the mammoth, rotund pumpkin."

❊

Over a century later, historian James McWilliams, author of *A Revolution in Eating: How the Quest for Food Shaped America* (2005), is saying the same. The edible pumpkin, warns McWilliams, may well be headed the way of the passenger pigeon — and the fault can be laid at the feet of grower Jack Howden. In the 1970s, he developed the Howden Field

Jack's Deal with the Devil

One indisputable advantage of the mammoth pumpkin over the modest squash is its suitability for the carving of jack-o'-lanterns. The jack-o'-lantern arrived in this country in the mid-nineteenth century along with the influx of potato-starved immigrants from Ireland. An old custom of Ireland and Great Britain, it is said to have originated with a blacksmith named Jack, who sold his soul, for a hefty sum, to the Devil. When the Devil came around to collect, Jack weaseled out of the bargain by sneakily trapping him in a pear tree.

This solved matters temporarily, but eventually Jack's irrevocable and final number came up. Barred from the Pearly Gates for all this truck with the Devil, Jack went straight to hell. The Devil, with the pear tree fresh in his mind, didn't want Jack around either. Just before the gates of Hell shut him out forever, Jack scooped up a burning coal with half of a turnip that he happened, providentially, to be eating. He has used it as a lantern ever since, while wandering around the earth waiting for Judgment Day. In America, the traditional turnip jack-o'-lantern rapidly gave way to the enormous and irresistible pumpkin.

pumpkin — a round, uniformly sized thick-skinned pumpkin — from the less prolific Connecticut Field, the traditional American baking pumpkin. Although they are perfect for jack-o'-lantern carving, porch décor, or flinging into a field via catapult, Howden's pumpkins, which now dominate the American market, don't taste all that good.

McWilliams suggests that it's time we replaced fake pumpkins with real ones. "Some traditions," he maintains, "like cultivating vegetables to eat, should never be destroyed."

RADISHES IDENTIFY WITCHES

plus

*The Awful Fruits of Adultery,
A Japanese Journey,
German Beer Gardens,
A Squint-Eyed Monk,
Dutch Breakfasts, and
A Heroine with Very Long Hair*

Our vegetable garden is coming along well, with radishes and beans up, and we are less worried about the revolution than we used to be.

E. B. WHITE

radish

Here in America, today's garden radish is barely considered a food. Instead, we know them as the peppery little red-skinned balls commonly relegated to the level of garnishes, or casually added, sliced, to salad. This is a comedown for the radish, which for much of its vegetable history has been admired, important, and huge.

The cultivated radish — *Raphanus sativus* — was formerly believed to have originated in China, where the bulk of wild radish relatives are found today. Recent genetic analyses, however, indicate multiple loci of domestication scattered across Europe, Eurasia, and Asia — in other words, lots of people in wildly widespread locations liked it enough to dig it up, take it home, and attempt to improve upon it.

No one is yet quite sure just *what* they first brought home. One candidate for the ancestral radish is *Raphanus raphanistrum*, wild radish or charlock, an invasive native of Asia, reportedly collected and used in early Europe as a potherb. Another guess is *Raphanus maritimus*, the so-called sea radish, native to the European seacoast — or possibly a hybrid of the two, or a hybrid of one or the other with another ancient radish, now extinct.

Like the multitudinous cabbages, the turnip, and the horseradish, the radish is a member of the Cabbage or Mustard family, Brassicaceae. Its relationship to other Brassicas is close enough for successful crossing, though such crosses (like those of zebras with Shetland ponies), while possible, are not the natural rule.

The genus name *Raphanus* comes from the Greek and means "rapidly appearing," which is no more than simple truth. Radishes, always a good pick for very young or inordinately impatient gardeners, germinate in as little as five days and turn out a crop in three to four weeks. Such rapidity is a prime reason that scientists consider the radish an ideal crop for future spacecraft gardens designed to feed traveling astronauts. The common name *radish* comes from the Latin *radix*, meaning root, which is somewhat less accurate. The edible portion of the radish, as in the turnip and rutabaga, is a mix of root and hypocotyl, the starch-stuffed base of the stem.

The peppery taste that we associate with radishes is the result of a defensive chemical reaction, initiated when the radish is bitten, which radishes don't like. Once radish cells are disrupted, a class of enzymes called glucosinolases comes in contact with sulfur- and nitrogen-containing precursors to form isothiocyanates. The effect, depending on the radish, is anything from a tang to a burn, though even the most vicious of radishes is mild compared to such radish relatives as horseradish and wasabi, whose volatile isothiocyanates can make the sinuses cringe.

Pliny condemns radishes as "a vulgar article of diet" since "all radishes breed wind wonderful much, and provoke a man that eateth of them to belch"— though he adds that this apparently persistent Roman problem could be minimized if a meal of vulgar radish is rapidly followed by a serving of half-ripe olives. The Greeks, he continues slightingly, were inordinately fond of radishes, as evidenced by the silly votive offerings in the temple of Apollo at Delphi, which included radishes made of solid gold, and a Greek author named Moschion apparently wrote an entire book devoted to the radish, which Pliny does not say but implies was a waste of time.

Pliny describes three kinds of radishes: a long and "semi-transparent" — which is possibly the long white radish that appears in a wall painting in Pompeii, heaped in a basket beside a bunch of grapes and a plate of figs; the turnip-shaped or Syrian radish, which keeps well over the winter; and a wild radish, "which grows more leaves than root." Pliny's turnip-shaped radish was most likely the black radish, *Raphanus sativus* var. *niger*, a winter radish, harvested late in the gardening season and known for its long-term staying power. Thought to be the oldest of cultivated radishes, the black radish was a popular crop in ancient Egypt. It appears in tomb paintings as early as 2800 BCE and Herodotus, in his *Histories*, written in the fifth century BCE, claims that radishes were a primary food of the pyramid builders.

The most common black radish grown today is the Round Black Spanish, which looks like a large licorice-colored beet. In its

In ancient Greece, the punishment for adultery was to have a radish thrust up one's behind.

original incarnation, however, the black radish was huge, weighing anywhere from 40 to 100 pounds. Pliny mentions radishes the size of human babies, and an ancient Jewish legend tells of a radish so immense that a fox hollowed it out and used it for a den. Rowdy Romans reputedly used radishes as projectiles during unpopular political debates, and among the Greeks, the punishment for adultery — which, given the size of the classical radish, was intimidating — was to have a radish thrust up one's behind. When not angrily airborne (or worse), radishes were eaten cooked like turnips, or raw in salad, seasoned with honey, vinegar, pepper, and salt.

Radishes today are generally differentiated by season: spring radishes, such as the fat little red globes of the French Breakfast or Cherry Belle radish and the carrot-shaped White Icicle, develop rapidly and don't store well; and winter radishes, such as the aforementioned Round Black Spanish and the awesome Asian daikon, which grow more slowly, are substantially bigger, and keep better.

❄

The radish is mentioned in the Chinese *Shih Ching* or *Book of Odes*, a collection of poems which dates to about 1000 BCE. By the time Western travelers arrived in Asia, radishes were a major food crop, available in many varieties, some of astounding size. Commodore Matthew C. Perry, arriving in Japan in 1853, observed radishes up to a yard long and a foot in circumference.

Perry's behemoth was almost certainly *R. sativus* var. *longipinnatus*, the daikon — known as the Japanese radish, though the

Japanese probably acquired it from China. The name translates as "long root," which makes perfect sense, since even an average daikon is an impressive foot and a half long. The Japanese have hundreds of ways of preparing their mega-radishes — and a daikon-heavy diet, according to Naomi Moriyama, author of *Japanese Women Don't Get Old or Fat* (2006), helps give Japanese women the lowest obesity rate (3 percent) and longest life expectancy (85 years) in the world.

Radishes may be annual or biennial. Table radishes — the small round red-skinned types — are annuals; the large late-season winter radishes, however, like daikons, are biennial, the seeds produced in their second year. In all radishes, the tiny seeds are borne in beanlike pods, formally known as siliques. In the seventeenth century, such radish pods, pickled, were a standard accompaniment to the dinner roast.

All radish pods are edible, though the rat-tailed radish, *R. sativus* var. *caudatus*, is grown specifically for its edible pods, which — pungent, pencil-thin, and curly — can be more than a foot long. Also known as the serpent, snake, or aerial radish, the rat-tail was originally Asian, introduced to England from Java in 1815. The pods are eaten raw in salads, where they taste much like radish roots, or are pickled or stir-fried. The München Bier Radish, a white winter variety, is also grown for its crispy green pods, which are popular as snacks in German beer gardens.

❊

In medieval Europe, the radish occupied both a substantial place on the dinner table and a sizeable niche in the medicine cabinet. Charlemagne demanded that radishes be planted in his estate gardens. In *Hortulus, or The Little Garden*, his instructional

Rapunzel, Rapunzel, Let Down Your Hair

In the traditional fairy tale "Rapunzel," included by the Brothers Grimm in their *Children's and Household Tales* (1812), the long-haired heroine, according to some versions, is named for a type of radish. Her mother craved radishes while pregnant, which led her father to steal some from a neighboring witch's garden. Caught in the act, radishes in hand, the father was forced to hand his infant daughter over to the witch.

poem about gardening, ninth-century Frankish monk Walafrid Strabo ("the Squint-Eyed") writes:

"Here in the last bed we find radishes, with their mighty roots and spread of leaves. When coughing shakes your insides, the sharp root of the radish suppresses it. If you eat some, or make a drink from crushed radish seeds, it will very often heal the suffering caused by this malicious illness."

According to various other authorities, radishes were also used to treat viper or adder bites and to alleviate the pains of childbirth, were administered as a general-purpose antidote for poison, and were applied to remove freckles. John Gerard in 1597 recommended radish roots for baldness, mashed with honey and mixed with a little powder of dried sheep's heart. In the seventeenth century William Salmon, a self-styled "Professor of Physick," prescribed "juyce of Radishes" for deafness, at the top of a list of less appealing remedies, including the "fat of a mole, eele, or serpent," essence of bullock's gall, and a boy's distilled urine. More excitingly, a medieval superstition claimed that wearing a wild radish allowed the bearer to see witches, at least on Walpurgis Night.

The radish reached North America with the European settlers. "8 oz. Radish seed" appears on John Winthrop, Jr.'s 1631 seed list. Naturalist Peter Kalm, tooling through New York in 1749, commented on the customary Dutch breakfast of tea with brown sugar, bread and butter, and radishes. (Dinner was meat with turnips or cabbages; supper, corn porridge and buttermilk.) At least ten varieties were grown in gardens by the late eighteenth century, of which Thomas Jefferson grew eight — the black, the common, the English scarlet, the salmon, the scarlet, the summer, the violet, and the white — and instructed that new plantings be started every two weeks beginning in March, to ensure a plentiful supply for salads.

According to Amelia Simmons, the "Salmon-coloured" was the best, next best the purple. "They grow thriftiest," she tells us, "sown among the onions." (Amelia gives much shorter shrift to the pungent radish relative, horseradish: "Horse Radish, once in the garden, can scarcely ever be totally eradicated; plowing or digging them up with that view, seems at times rather to increase and spread them.")

The colonists grew both the large mild winter radishes, suitable for months of storage in the family root cellar, and the smaller, zingier, and more quickly maturing summer radishes. The earliest of these summer varieties, white and carrot-shaped, was introduced in the late sixteenth century, white and red globular forms were developed by the eighteenth, and thereafter shapes, sizes, and colors proliferated.

By the nineteenth century, the catalog of Vilmorin-Andrieux listed twenty-five varieties of summer radishes, subdivided by shape into round or "turnip-rooted" radishes (ten kinds in scarlet, white, dark violet, or dull yellow), "olive-shaped" radishes (seven kinds, including the popular French Breakfast, which looks less like an olive than a cork); and "long" radishes (eight kinds, including the bizarre Mans Corkscrew, a pure white radish with a foot-long, sharply twisted, zigzag root, almost impossible to pull out of the ground without breaking in two).

In 1888, the Burpee seed catalog listed twenty-eight varieties of early or summer radishes, preceded by the reproachful sales pitch: "We wish that Americans appreciated good radishes and used them as largely as do the French. For breakfast, dinner, and supper, three times a day, they are a most appetizing and wholesome relish." Prominent among these was Burpee's yellow-skinned Golden Globe, first introduced in 1880, of which an ecstatic Missouri customer wrote that some of his were sixteen inches in circumference, or about the size of a grapefruit. Also offered were the rat-tailed radish and five varieties of winter radishes, including the famous Black Spanish (both round and sausage-shaped) and the rose-skinned China Rose.

Today there are hundreds of varieties of radishes in every color of the rainbow — the most gorgeous of which may be the watermelon radish, a green-skinned daikon variety with watermelon-pink flesh. Sliced, it looks like a very small watermelon. Bitten, it tastes like a radish.

One customer's Golden Globe radishes were sixteen inches in circumference, or about the size of a grapefruit.

SPINACH DECEIVES A GENERATION OF CHILDREN

plus

*Popeye's Power Snack, Persian Cats,
Florentine Dinners, A Contrary King,
Puritan Prayers, and Alice Roosevelt's Pet Snake*

I say it's spinach and I say the hell with it.
E. B. WHITE

Spinach

Popeye, according to the latest in sports-oriented nutrition, would have done better for himself with a plate of spaghetti. *Spinacia oleracea*, garden spinach, for all its vaunted muscle-building power, is far better known for vitamin A, of which it contains a lot: 14,500 units per cooked cupful. Vitamin A is great for night vision, which means that Popeye the Sailor Man would have had an edge as a night pilot, but it's not much as a pick-me-up prior to a dockside brawl. Still, the spinach-gulping sailor, who first appeared in the comic pages in 1929, convinced a generation of Depression-era kids to do likewise, boosting spinach consumption by a third over the next decade.

Legendarily, Popeye's spinach was famed for its iron content, the stuff that builds red blood and brawn. A persistent myth holds that the reputation of Popeye's spinach was the result of one of the worst typos in history: a misplaced German decimal point that led agricultural chemist Emil von Wolff in 1870 to inadvertently attribute to spinach ten times more iron that it deserved. Spinach, the beneficiary of this supposed egregious goof, was touted thereafter as a cheap equivalent for traditionally iron-rich T-bone steak.

Uses for Spinach Juice

Spinach juice — deeply and intensely green — was used as a food coloring up through the nineteenth century, and seasonally, at eighteenth- and nineteenth-century celebrations, to make touchpaper for fireworks. Soaked in spinach juice and dried, paper smoldered when lit, and was found just the thing for touching off Roman candles and Catherine wheels.

The truth is a bit more complex. Spinach *is* a rich source of iron, containing some 3.2 mg per serving (that is, per cooked half cup), actually slightly more than an equivalent serving of red meat. For the most part, however, we can't get at it. In heme iron, which constitutes up to 40 percent of the iron in meats, the essential iron is helpfully encased in an organic ring molecule, which we find easy to absorb. Non-heme iron — the iron of spinach — is largely out of our digestive reach. Ordinarily we absorb less than 5 percent of the total — though we can up the intake substantially by pairing non-heme iron with vitamin C. Popeye's swelling biceps, in other words, might have been a little more convincing if he'd paired his can of spinach with a glass of orange juice.

❀

Botanists believe that spinach probably originated in or near Iran. The modern name derives from the Persian *isfanakh*, which means green hand. The Persians, one story claims, initially cultivated spinach for the delectation of their exotically long-haired cats. (The cats around here, who like cantaloupe and popcorn, won't touch it.) They also ate it themselves and exported it to the Far East, where it caught on long before it established itself in western Europe. Chinese records, which refer to spinach as the "Persian herb," note its arrival in 647 CE as a gift (or possibly extorted tribute) from the intermediately located king of Nepal. The Chinese liked it and planted it around the edges of their vast rice paddies, where it flourished. They used it in soups.

It took another four hundred years for the Persian herb to reach Europe, where it arrived along with the conquering Moors in eleventh-century Spain. One report mentions a treatise on spinach by Ibn Hadjadj, a Spanish Moor, who addressed it enthusiastically as "the prince of vegetables." It's uncertain when the princely leaf reached northern Europe: *spinachium* appears on a 1351 list of the unexciting fare permitted monks on fast days, and "spynoches" can be found in the fourteenth-century *Forme of Cury*. In the late fourteenth-century *Tacuinum Sanitarium*, spinach appears as "Spinachie": the best, the text explains, are leaves still wet with rainwater.

❀

Europeans seem to have been of two minds about spinach. John Gerard in 1597, anticipating generations of American children,

Emily Spinach

Alice, the flamboyant oldest daughter of President Theodore Roosevelt, had a pet snake named Emily Spinach — Emily after a maiden aunt, and Spinach because the snake was spinach green.

Alice's behavior with and without snake often drove her father to distraction. "Do you know how much talk there has been recently in the newspapers about your betting and courting notoriety with that unfortunate snake?" he wrote the 20-year-old Alice in an exasperated letter in 1904.

"What! I am king of France and I cannot eat spinach?"

said it was watery and tasteless; but Catherine de Medici, originally from Florence, Italy, and sixteenth-century queen of France, was reportedly so mad for it that to this day the phrase "Florentine" attached to anything edible means "with spinach."

Perhaps it was all in the preparation. The ancient Medes recommended washing each spinach leaf twelve times before dropping it into the cooking pot: eleven times in clear water, for best results, with a final rinse in human tears. "The dayly eating of the hearbe Spinage doth marvelously profite such having a hoarse voice, and that hardly fetch breath," wrote an English spinach fan, "if the hearbe after proper seething and ordering be either fried with sweete butter or the oyle of Almonds, and that to it Pepper bruised be wittily added." Another claimed that spinach chopped in oatmeal made a "sublime Pottage," and the Dutch recommended it baked in tarts.

The French compared spinach poetically to *cire-vierge* — virgin beeswax — since it could adapt innocuously to any culinary situation. It was therefore said to require a great chef to do justice to its subtle and delicate flavor. Apparently such were around, as Louis XIV, denied spinach by a conscientious royal physician, bellowed in chagrin, "What! I am king of France and I cannot eat spinach?" (He could and, in the teeth of medical advice, he did.)

John Evelyn, usually enthusiastic about salad greens, was tepid about spinach, writing in *Acetaria* (1699), "of old not us'd in *Sallets*, and the oftner kept out the better." Boiled to a pulp and served with butter and vinegar or "Limon," he concedes, it may have a place in "a Sick Man's Diet." The notoriously non-mealymouthed farmer/politician William Cobbett, however, seems to have approved of it. "Every one knows the use of this excellent plant," he writes in *The English Gardener* (1833). "Pigs, who are excellent judges of the relative qualities of vegetables, will leave cabbages for lettuce, and lettuces for spinage."

Spinach arrived in North America at least by the early seventeenth century, as "1 oz. spynadg" appeared in John Winthrop, Jr.'s well-documented seed list. Chef and vegetable expert Bert Greene argues that an early Puritan children's prayer begging divine protection from fire, famine, flood, and "unclean foreign leaves" may just possibly refer to spinach, though tobacco seems a more likely guess. Spinach, though grown, seems not to have been high on the list for most colonial gardeners. Jefferson, of course, grew it, and Mary Randolph, after warning that "great care" must be taken in washing and picking it, says that it's good with poached eggs.

❀

Bernard M'Mahon, in his 1802 seed catalog, mentions only three existing cultivars, and David Landreth, in his 1824 list of "Esculent Vegetable Seeds," lists only two ("round" and "prickley"). Landreth, who established his seed company in

Chef and vegetable expert Bert Greene argues that an early Puritan children's prayer begging divine protection from fire, famine, flood, and "unclean foreign leaves" may refer to spinach, though tobacco seems a more likely guess.

Philadelphia in 1784, counted Washington, Adams, Jefferson, and Monroe among his early customers, and once patriotically granted a strapped Washington a thirty-day extension on his bill.

The D. Landreth Seed Company is still selling seeds today. Among its claims to fame are the introduction of the tomato and the zinnia to garden cultivation, the first American listing of cantaloupe seed (imported from a source in Tripoli), and the development of a superior and notably slow-bolting spinach. Named Bloomsdale after the company farm in Bristol, Pennsylvania, the new spinach, glossily dark green with thick crumpled leaves, was first made available to American gardeners in 1826.

Bloomsdale is a smooth- or round-seeded spinach, the smooth seeds a feature that appeared, presumably by spontaneous mutation, at some point in the sixteenth century. Older and more primitive spinaches produced prickly seeds. Neither, in a strict botanical sense, is a seed at all, but a utricle (fruit) encased in a smooth or spiny capsule. The prickly-seeded varieties, nicknamed "winter" spinaches in the mistaken belief that they were more resistant to cold, were once more common in the United States, though food critics deem them less flavorful than their smooth-seeded relations. Smooth-seeded "summer" spinach predominates today.

There are three basic types of spinach. Landreth's Bloomsdale is a Savoy spinach, characterized by large deeply crinkled leaves that are difficult to clean, since the crinkles tend to retain gritty particles of sand. Flat-leaf spinach has broad smooth leaves that are far easier to rinse; a small-leaved version of this is sold as "baby" spinach. Semi-Savoy, which teeters between Savoy and flat, is a slightly crinkled hybrid — not as flat as flat, not as wrinkled as Savoy. All are members of the Amaranthaceae family, along with beets, pigweed, and the signature amaranths — grown for grain and used by the Hopi Indians to make a deep red dye.

Sexually, spinach is dioecious, with most cultivars producing approximately equal numbers of male and female plants. Variations appear on either side of the sexual average: there are, for example, perfect-flowered hermaphroditic spinaches, which consolidate all the necessary sexual equipment in a single flower, and monoecious spinaches, which produce both male and female flowers on a single plant. All are annuals. Most American spinach — over 90 percent of the commercial crop — is grown in California and Arizona. "The Spinach Capital of the World," however, is in neither state: contenders for the title are Crystal City, Texas, and Alma, Arkansas, which boasts a town water tower painted to resemble an enormous can of spinach.

❀

Far from restricting itself chastely to *Spinacia oleracea*, the term spinach is frequently used in a generic sense to mean practically anything leafy and green. Captain Cook discovered New Zealand spinach, *Tetragonia expansa*, on his landmark voyage down under in 1771; though edible, it was grown back home in England initially as a houseplant. Good-King-Henry, *Chenopodium bonus-henricus*, is commonly known as wild spinach or poor man's asparagus; orach, *Atriplex hortensis*, whose elegant pearly gray leaves were popular in colonial salads, is nicknamed mountain spinach. *Amaranthus tricolor*, sometimes called Joseph's-coat for its gaudy multicolored leaves, is also called Chinese spinach.

"Spinach!" has meant "stuff and nonsense" since at least the 1920s, probably from the mid-nineteenth-century "gammon and spinach," as in Charles Dickens's rueful "What a world of gammon and spinage it is, though, ain't it!" Spinach thus fell in with such anti bombast expressions as humbug, twaddle, baloney, moonshine, balderdash, hogwash, horsefeathers, and "Go tell it to the Marines!" When Will Rogers, in 1924, told the nation, "I tell you, folks, all politics is applesauce," he could just as well have said spinach.

"Spinach!" has meant "stuff and nonsense" since at least the 1920s.

TOMATOES FAIL TO KILL COLONEL JOHNSON

plus

Wolf Bait, Mary Randolph's Marmalade,
Pills, Panaceas, and Suspect Syrup,
How Radiator Charlie Beat the Depression,
An Alternative Use for an Incense Burner,
and A Day in Court

A world without tomatoes is like a string quartet without violins.
LAURIE COLWIN

tomato

"It is difficult to think anything but pleasant thoughts while eating a homegrown tomato," wrote *Atlanta Journal-Constitution* columnist Lewis Grizzard. According to the U.S. Department of Agriculture, four out of five people prefer tomatoes to any other homegrown food. American tomato enthusiasm runs so high that gardenless fans have grown them in backyard barrels, patio pots, and window boxes, on apartment balconies, on houseboat decks, and even, in the case of a few intrepid souls, on the roofs of Volkswagens. Over 90 percent of home gardeners plant tomatoes, and the tomato is so popular among consumers that it's been voted the official state vegetable (or fruit) of Arkansas, Ohio, New Jersey, and Tennessee. It's quite a turnaround for a plant that most of our ancestors wouldn't have touched with a ten-foot pole.

The tomato came originally from the Andes of South America, where small-fruited wild forms, described by botanists as weedy and aggressive, still proliferate in a swath of territory across Peru, Chile, Bolivia, and Ecuador and north into Central America and Mexico. It seems to have been generally ignored on its home turf — the Incas didn't eat it — but instead was domesticated over a thousand miles to the north, by the Mayas of Central America and southern Mexico.

By the time the Europeans reached the New World, tomatoes in dozens of colors, shapes, and sizes were a staple of native cuisine, eaten in proto-enchiladas, stewed with peppers, beans, and corn, and chopped into a sauce with peppers and ground squash seeds that sounds a lot like an early form of salsa. Spanish priest Bernardino de Sahagún, in his sixteenth-century *General History of the Things of New Spain*, described the mind-boggling array of tomatoes routinely on sale in the Aztec market of Tenochtítlan:

"... large tomatoes, small tomatoes, leaf tomatoes, thin tomatoes, sweet tomatoes, large serpent tomatoes, nipple-shaped tomatoes, serpent tomatoes ... coyote tomatoes, sand tomatoes, those which are yellow, very yellow, quite yellow, red, very red, quite ruddy, ruddy, bright red, reddish, rosy dawn colored."

Hernando Cortés and company saw tomatoes growing in Montezuma's Mexican gardens in 1519 and later described them recognizably, though in less than glowing terms: they found the sprawling vines scraggy and ugly. Nonetheless, Cortés may have brought the first tomatoes to Spain, from whence they spread to continental Europe and the Middle East.

The earliest mention of tomatoes in Europe comes from Italian botanist Pietro Andrea Mattioli in 1544 — apparently a yellow variety, since he later dubbed it *pomo d'oro*, "golden apple." (*Pomodoro* to this day is Italian for a tomato of any color, though most modern European languages call tomatoes by some version of the Aztec *tomatl*.) Based on morphology, Mattioli perceptively linked the tomato to the eggplant, as well as to a number of more disreputable relatives, among them mandrake, henbane, and the aptly named deadly nightshade — *Atropa belladonna*, popular among upper-class Romans for permanently eliminating rivals.

✿

The tomato's association with known poisonous plants was distinctly off-putting and most likely the reason for the three-hundred-year hiatus before it was accepted as an everyday article of European diet. In fact, by mid-sixteenth century, the tomato was ominously nicknamed the wolf peach — "peach" from its luscious appearance, "wolf" from its presumptive poisonous qualities — in analogy to pieces of aconite-sprinkled meat thrown out as bait to destroy wolves. This nickname, Latinized, has persisted as *lycopersicon*, which figures in *Solanum lycopersicon*, the modern scientific moniker for the tomato.

Early names for the tomato indicated vast confusion about where the tomato came from and what it was or wasn't good for. Italians called it the Moor's apple or the apple of Peru; German herbalist Joachim Camerarius (the Younger) — who rewrote and helpfully beefed up Mattioli — called it the apple of India; and the Iranians called it the Armenian eggplant.

Love Apple

The tomato's nickname "love apple" may stem from its association with the sinister mandrake, which also bears red or yellow fruits. The hallucinogenic mandrake is traditionally associated with magic and witchcraft — it did Joan of Arc no good at her trial when it was revealed that she carried one around for good luck — and it has a history as an aphrodisiac, possibly because a low dose of it made people woozy and lowered their inhibitions.

The tomato's poisonous aura was not without its element of truth. Tomatoes belong to the Nightshade family, Solanaceae, known for their manufacture of potentially toxic alkaloids, examples of which include morphine, quinine, nicotine, and strychnine. Compared to such alkaloid superstars, however, tomatine, the major alkaloid in tomatoes, is wimpy. It's found primarily in tomato leaves and stems, and in the green fruit, from which it disappears as the tomato ripens.

Green tomatoes, however, fried and pickled, have been enjoyed without lethal incident for generations: Mary Randolph's *Virginia Housewife* (1824) includes a recipe for a spicy green tomato marmalade. Researcher Mendel Friedman of the U.S. Department of Agriculture points out that tomatine may actually have substantial health benefits. Studies in animals indicate that tomatine lowers the blood levels of low-density lipoprotein (LDL) — a.k.a. "bad cholesterol" — and it inhibits the growth of cancer cells in culture. It also kills bugs. Pre-pesticide nineteenth-century gardeners used broth from cooked tomato foliage to destroy aphids and bedbugs; and tomatine *in situ* fends off *Fusarium* wilt, a destructive fungal disease and common bane of tomatoes.

❁

In Europe, the Spaniards and the Italians ate tomatoes first. They were certainly eating them by the late sixteenth century, when John Gerard noted of the "Apples of Love" in his *Great Herball:* "In Spaine and those hot Regions they use to eat the Apples prepared and boiled with pepper, salt, and oile" — but, he adds disapprovingly, "they yeeld very little nourishment to the bodie, and the same nought and corrupt." He admitted that tomatoes were attractive to look at ("of a bright red colour and the bigness of a goose egg or a large pippin"), but smelled awful ("of ranke and stinking savour") and were probably dangerous to eat.

In similarly reluctant France, agronomist Olivier de Serres wrote in 1600 that "love apples are marvelous and golden" but were primarily grown as ornamentals, noting that "they serve commonly to cover outhouses and arbors." Richard Bradley, professor of botany at Cambridge University, wrote in 1728 that the tomato "makes an agreeable Plant to look at, but the Fruit of most of them is dangerous" and the leaves and stalks "yield a very strong and very offensive smell."

❀

Early American colonists followed the lead of their mother country: tomatoes, fetid and potentially death-dealing, are conspicuously absent from early seed lists. The fruits were condemned by ministers and physicians, and the Puritans — perhaps influenced by the designation "love apple" — considered them an abomination, on par with dancing, card-playing, and theatergoing. At least one liberal pastor in early Massachusetts Bay was fired by his congregation for thoughtlessly growing some in his kitchen garden.

Southerners were more amenable to the tomato. According to tomato authority Andrew Smith, the first reference to colonial tomatoes appears in William Salmon's *Botanologia* (1710),

The Puritans — perhaps influenced by the designation "love apple" — considered tomatoes an abomination, on par with dancing, card-playing, and theatergoing.

in which he mentions viewing some while traveling through the Carolinas in the late 1680s. The first evidence that anyone was actually eating them comes from Harriott Pinckney Horry's *Receipt Book* of 1770, whose instructions "To Keep Tomatoos for Winter use" involve stewing chopped tomatoes with salt and pepper, then storing them in "pint Potts" topped with melted butter for later use in soups. The fact that there were enough tomatoes around to keep implies that they were prolific inhabitants of at least some Southern gardens.

The first formal American reference to tomatoes as food plants appears in Thomas Jefferson's *Notes on the State of Virginia* in 1781, in which he writes that "The gardens yield muskmelons, watermelons, tomatas, okra, pomegranates, figs, and the esculent plants of Europe." He himself purchased "tomatas" for presidential dinners and planted them annually at Monticello, beginning in June, 1809. Mary Randolph's *Virginia Housewife* lists seventeen recipes for tomatoes, among them gumbo, gazpacho, scalloped tomatoes, stewed tomatoes, eggs and tomatoes, and "Ochra and tomatos."

The North — possibly in part because the climate was less congenial to tomatoes — remained reluctant to adopt them. Amelia Simmons's *American Cookery* (1796) doesn't so much as mention a tomato. Tales of tomato failures include that of a vegetable-promoting refugee from Santo Domingo who brought some to Philadelphia in 1798, only to find that nobody liked them much, and an account of an Italian painter who brought some to Salem, Massachusetts, in 1802, but couldn't persuade anyone even to taste them.

Two thousand people assembled to watch Colonel Johnson suffer these awful fates, to the accompaniment of a local firemen's band playing dirges.

The turning point for the tomato, according to time-honored legend, occurred on September 26, 1820, on the steps of the courthouse in Salem, New Jersey, when Colonel Robert Gibbon Johnson ate, in public and without ill effect, an entire basketful of tomatoes. The colonel, a notorious eccentric, was not a man to be trifled with. During the Revolutionary War, at the tender age of seven, he had patriotically slapped a British officer in the face, and as an adult he habitually dressed in imitation of General Washington in a black suit with impeccable white ruffles, a tricorn hat, black gloves, and a gold-topped walking stick.

Tomatoes, claimed the colonel, had been eaten by the ancient Egyptians and Greeks, but the original accounts of this beneficial diet had been lost in the mists of history. The colonel's personal physician, a Dr. James Van Meeter, took a dim view of the proposed tomato eating and was quoted as saying, "The foolish colonel will foam and froth at the mouth and double over with appendicitis." Also threatened were aggravated high blood pressure and brain fever. Two thousand people assembled to watch Colonel Johnson suffer these awful fates, to the accompaniment of a local firemen's band playing dirges. Undaunted, the colonel ate and stalked away, to live in undisputed health to the ripe old age of seventy-nine.

It's a great story, but the truth seems to be that none of this ever happened. Andrew Smith cites it as "fakelore," one of our cultural collection of exaggerations, hoaxes, tall tales, and flat-out lies that frankly are just so appealing that we can't bear to let them go. The tomato-eating colonel, in other words, is in the same boat as George Washington's cherry tree, Newton's apple, Nero's fiddle, and the landing of the Pilgrims on Plymouth Rock.

❄

What does seem to be true is that by the 1820s, even without the help of the probably apocryphal colonel, the tomato had effected a turnaround. Even New Englanders had begun to plant and eat it. Bernard M'Mahon of Philadelphia was selling tomato seeds by 1805, William Booth of Baltimore by 1810, and Philadelphia's D. Landreth Seed Company by 1825. From New York, Grant Thorburn's 1832 *Catalogue of Kitchen Garden, Herb, Flower, Tree and Grass Seeds* not only offered tomato seeds, but — just in case customers didn't know what to do with the resultant tomatoes — listed two recipes for tomato relish.

Boston's Hovey & Co., by the 1830s, was touting two kinds of tomatoes ("small and large"), soon thereafter upping the tally to four. By 1835, tomatoes were being grown in the gardens of Maine, and the editor of the *Maine Farmer* had pronounced them "a useful article of diet" — probably, for Down East conservatives, gushing praise.

Seedsman Robert Buist — a specialist in rare plants and the first to sell poinsettias in America — wrote of the tomato in his *Family Kitchen Gardener* (1847):

"In taking a retrospect of the past eighteen years, there is no vegetable on the catalogue that has obtained such popularity in so short a period as the one now under consideration. In 1828-9 it was almost detested; in ten years more every variety of pill and panacea was 'extract of Tomato.' It now occupies as great a surface of ground as Cabbage, and is cultivated the length and breadth of the country . . . It is brought to the table in an infinite variety of forms, being stewed and seasoned, stuffed and fried, roasted and raw . . . It is also made into pickles, catsup, and salted in barrels for Winter use, so that with a few years more experience, we may expect to see it as an every-day dish from January to January."

Buist cites four common varieties: the large smooth Red, the Large Red (an enormous ribbed tomato, measuring up to 18 inches in circumference), the pear-shaped, and the cherry-shaped (recommended for pickling). He also mentions offhand-edly "several other fancy sorts, generally of a yellow color."

The upsurge in tomato popularity was due in no small part to the above-mentioned pills and panaceas. Beginning in the 1830s, physicians, both amateur and professional, touted the tomato as a remedy for practically anything, including indigestion, diarrhea, liver and lung diseases, and cholera. Popular nostrums included "Dr. Miles's Compound Extract of Tomato" and "Dr. Phelps' Compound Tomato Pills," neither of which actually contained any form of tomato. Catharine Beecher — sister of Harriet Beecher Stowe and an active proponent of education for women — recommended Tomato Syrup for the sick in her *Domestic Receipt-Book* (1858). It contained tomato juice and sugar, to be bottled for several weeks before use, and, despite Catharine's staunch advocacy of Temperance Drinks, sounds suspiciously like tomato wine.

Fruit? Or Veggie?

The tomato, botanically, is a fruit — that is, an organ that develops from the ovary of the flower and encloses the developing seeds. More specifically, like the avocado and papaya, the tomato is a berry, composed of seeds surrounded by parenchymatous cells. Legally, however, it's a vegetable.

In 1886, importer John Nix landed a load of West Indian tomatoes in New York, for which the presiding customs agent demanded the payment of a 10 percent tax in accordance with the Tariff Act of 1883, which levied a duty on foreign vegetables. Nix, who knew his botany, protested that the tariff applied only to vegetables; tomatoes, as fruits, should be exempt. The controversy eventually reached the Supreme Court, where, in 1893, Justice Horace Gray decreed the tomato a vegetable:

"Botanically speaking, tomatoes are the fruit of the vine, just as are cucumbers, squashes, beans and peas. But in the common language of the people . . . all these vegetables . . . are usually served at dinner, in, with, or after the soup, fish, or meat, which constitute the principal part of the repast, and not, like fruits, generally as dessert."

Nix paid up.

The state of Arkansas, which continues to sit on the fence, has declared the tomato both its official state fruit and its official state vegetable.

The garden tomato, once it became a beneficiary of positive medical press, flourished. It was so ubiquitous by the 1850s that an English tourist, stuffed with tomatoes at every turn, commented acidly, "Its very name I now perfectly dread — so constantly, so regularly, does it come up every day, prepared in every imaginable way." Even tomato-resistant England — where in 1826 John James Audubon had flabbergasted his hosts by eating a whole tomato, raw — had given way by midcentury.

Mrs. Isabella Beeton's famous *Book of Household Management* (1859–1861), an immense and invaluable tome that covered everything for the beginning housewife, from the appropriate amount of a butler's salary to a diagram of the vascular system of plants, recommended tomatoes stewed, baked, and turned into ketchups and sauces. She noted of tomatoes, "In this country it is much more cultivated than it formerly was; and the more the community becomes acquainted with the many agreeable forms in which the fruit can be prepared, the more widely will its cultivation be extended." Stewed tomatoes, she adds, should be served on a silver vegetable dish.

The common garden tomato of the early nineteenth century was lobed, lumpy, and flattish, and looked something like the tuffet that Miss Muffet perched on in old-fashioned nursery-rhyme books. Its ungainly appearance was one cause of slow tomato acceptance, and as tomatoes became more popular in the kitchen, gardeners began to select for bigger, rounder, more symmetrical, and generally better-looking fruits.

The first major breeding success story was the Trophy tomato, developed in the 1850s by a Dr. Hand of Baltimore County, Maryland, who painstaking crossed a small, smooth-skinned ornamental tomato with a larger, lobed garden variety. The product — smooth-skinned, solid, glossy, and attractively shaped like an apple — was passed on to a Colonel George E. Waring of Rhode Island by Dr. Hand's son, who had met the colonel at a meeting of the American Jersey Cattle Club.

Waring, the future sponsor of Hand's tomato, was a scientific farmer and sanitation engineer, the author of *Book of the Farm*, *A Farmer's Vacation*, and *Draining for Profit and Draining for*

Health, and a master marketer. He offered seeds of the Trophy for sale at an outrageous price of 25 cents apiece, while simultaneously offering a prize of $100 "for the heaviest tomato grown from seed purchased directly from me." The response was overwhelming and soon Waring was announcing that "it is evident that henceforth the Trophy will be the only tomato grown in America." It wasn't, but it did dominate tomato patches for decades and figures in the parentage of hundreds of tomato varieties grown today.

By the 1880s seed catalogs routinely offered upwards of a dozen tomato varieties, with numbers increasing annually. In 1885, Vilmorin-Andrieux, in *The Vegetable Garden,* listed five varieties of ribbed tomatoes; four of round tomatoes, including the Apple-Shaped Red, Apple-Shaped Rose, and Apple-Shaped Purple; two pear-shaped or fig tomatoes; one plum tomato; one cherry tomato (yellow); the curiously shaped King Humbert tomato, flat on four sides and in cross-section nearly square; and the Turk's-Cap tomato, which bore a topknotlike protuberance in the middle much like that of the turban gourds.

In 1888, W. Atlee Burpee's *Farm Annual* offered fifteen large-fruited and seven small-fruited tomato cultivars, among them the pulchritudinous Trophy, as well as the Perfection, Cardinal, Mayflower, and Golden Queen. Also available was the Faultless Early, which, Burpee stated with admirable objectivity, was far from faultless, the fruits being disappointingly rough. By 1901, Burpee felt comfortable declaring that "The tomato now rivals all other vegetables and fruits in popularity, having reached a use beyond that of the potato and apple combined."

Despite its past and present popularity, the average tomato, nutritionally, is no great shakes. Though plugged as the "oranges of the vegetable garden" for their reputedly high vitamin C content, tomatoes are actually unimpressive. A tomato provides only about one-third as much vitamin C as a green pepper or a cantaloupe half, one-fourth as much vitamin C as a cup of orange juice, and one-fifth as much as a stalk of broccoli. In a comparative study, tomatoes were found to rank sixteenth in overall concentration of ten selected vitamins and minerals, considerably behind such traditional good-for-yous as spinach (#2) and lima beans (#4). (Top of the list was broccoli.) As specific sources of vitamins C and A, tomatoes ranked thirteenth and sixteenth, respectively.

The tomato makes up for its deficiencies in nutritional quality, however, by the quantities in which we consume it. Tomatoes rank high in contribution of nutrients to the American diet simply because we eat a lot of them. Tomatoes, to their credit, are among the foods that weight-watchers can eat of lot of with a clear conscience: they contain 93.5 percent water (only cucumbers and a few leafy vegetables contain more) and log in at a piddling 4 calories per ounce. That means that for the caloric price of a chocolate ice cream cone you can wolf down about three hundred cherry tomatoes.

Nutritionally, it's also possible to stack the deck by using some care in selecting your tomatoes. Homegrown types, for example, ripened all the way on the vine, have about one-third more

For the caloric price of a chocolate ice cream cone, you can wolf down three hundred cherry tomatoes.

vitamin C than the artificially ripened supermarket varieties; and organic tomatoes — those that get their nitrogen from manure and compost — are higher in antioxidants than conventionally grown tomatoes, fed on commercial fertilizers. A study conducted at the University of California at Davis found that organic tomatoes contained nearly twice as much quercetin and kaempferol — flavonoids with potent antioxidant activity — as their conventionally grown cousins.

Some tomato cultivars have also been specifically bred for high nutrient content. The P20 Blue tomato, for example, a cross between a garden red and a wild tomato from Peru, has exceptionally high levels of antioxidant flavonoids — in the form of anthocyanin, which turns the fruit a deep purple-blue. The Doublerich, an early red medium-sized tomato, contains twice the vitamin C of ordinary tomatoes — most of it, as in all tomatoes, concentrated in the jellylike material in the middle, surrounding the seeds. The USDA-developed 97L97 tomato contains forty times more vitamin A than other varieties; and the high-yielding plum-shaped Health Kick tomato is essentially a juicy vegetable vitamin pill, with enhanced levels of vitamins A, B, and C, potassium, iron, and lycopene.

Lycopene, a carotenoid and an antioxidant, is the chemical that makes tomatoes tomato red, as well as putting the color in pink watermelon, pink grapefruit, and red bell peppers. Some recent evidence indicates that lycopene may be a cancer preventive, reducing the risks of prostate and breast cancer. It has also been shown to lower the risks of heart disease and age-related macular degeneration, a retinal condition that can lead to visual impairment or blindness.

Eating Paste

To get the most lycopene out of a tomato, you have to cook it. In fact, it's best if you process your tomatoes at high heat, with a bit of oil thrown in. The reason has to do with the chemical structure of lycopene. In the luscious raw tomato, fresh off the vine, lycopene is in its *trans* configuration — that is, in the form of long straight skinny molecules that are poorly absorbed by the human digestive tract. In the boiled and oiled tomato, however, lycopene curls up into an alternative *cis* configuration, in which state it can be far more easily absorbed. Those who eat their tomatoes as paste or sauce absorb over 50 percent more lycopene than those who eat their tomatoes as nature made them.

It may even function as a low-grade internal sunscreen. Some studies have shown that tomato eating staves off UV-induced skin damage, boosting the levels of essential skin structural proteins — the compounds that keep us supple and smooth — and countering the wrinkly effects of aging.

❈

Today there are literally thousands of tomato varieties. In seed catalogs, these are usually roughly categorized according to size and shape. Beefsteak tomatoes are the biggest of the bunch: garden whoppers, dense, meaty, and favored for tomato sandwiches. The current world record for largest tomato is held by a beefsteak variety: grown by Gordon Graham of Edmond, Oklahoma, in 1986, the winner was the size of a goldfish bowl and weighed seven pounds, twelve ounces.

Oxheart tomatoes are large, but not as gargantuan as beefsteaks, and are shaped like ox hearts, although most catalogs understandably prefer to compare them to strawberries. Salad or slicing tomatoes, a large and miscellaneous group, are generally medium-sized juicy types, too slurpy to cook down properly and so best eaten raw. Cherry tomatoes are the round, more or less cherry-sized varieties, also popular for salads, and plum or paste tomatoes are solid, thick-walled oblongs, good for strewing into sauce and soup.

Generally ignored in seed catalogs is the most spectacular success among paste-style hybrids: the so-called "square" tomato, a tough and vaguely blocky fruit, permutations of which are the standard tomatoes of the commercial processing industry. These are the tomatoes you find today in cans on supermarket shelves. Originally developed in the 1950s, the square tomato, officially known by the Star Trekkish designation "Cultivar VF-145," was designed solely with machines in mind. Mechanical harvesters squished most ordinary tomato cultivars, which tend to be fragile, which led UC Davis crop specialist Gordie "Jack" Hanna to develop the thick-skinned and solid VF-145.

The thugs of the tomato world, these are the fruits you want to grab if you need a projectile in a food fight. California grows about 95 percent of America's processing tomatoes, and each of us eats — in pizza, salsa, spaghetti sauce, and ketchup — about 71 pounds of them a year.

❋

The world's largest tomato was grown by Gordon Graham of Edmond, Oklahoma, in 1986. It was the size of a goldfish bowl and weighed seven pounds, twelve ounces.

Far more popular among gardeners are heirloom tomatoes, old-fashioned open-pollinated varieties, each at least 50 years in cultivation. Among these are such time-honored favorites as the Green Zebra, Brandywine, Cherokee Purple, Crimson Cushion, Ponderosa, Black Prince, Arkansas Traveler, and Ivory Egg. We can enjoy these today, just as they were picked off the vine back in the days of FDR's fireside chats, because of a sexual glitch. Tomatoes, when it comes to reproduction, are suspiciously self-indulgent.

The making of a tomato begins, conventionally enough, with the fertilization of a female ovule by male pollen. Pollen grains land on the sticky surface of the stigma — the smokestack-like tip of the pistil, the female organ containing the ovary — and germinate, extending long tubes that terminate at the ovary. Down these tubes travel a pair of fertilization-bent male nuclei,

Radiator Charlie's Mortgage Lifter

Perhaps the catchiest name among heirloom tomatoes is Radiator Charlie's Mortgage Lifter, an enormous pinkish tomato developed by M. C. Byles of West Virginia in the financially dismal days of the Great Depression.

Byles, a mechanic whose knack with blown-out radiators gave him the nickname "Radiator Charlie" (his given name was Marshall Cletis), bred the tomato in his backyard garden. The new tomato was so delicious and so huge, averaging an awesome two and a half pounds a fruit, that Byles was soon selling his seedlings for a dollar apiece to clamoring customers from as much as 200 miles away. The tomatoes — presumably with a little help from radiators — allowed Byle to pay off his mortgage and gave the tomato its name.

one of which fuses with the female "egg" to form the seed embryo, the other with an adjacent cell to form the endosperm, future food for the developing infant plant.

Tomato forebears, both wild South American tomatoes and the early Central American cultivated varieties, were cross-pollinated by insects. To facilitate this, the ancestral tomato blossom possessed an extended (exserted) stigma that stuck up well beyond the anther cone, where the (male) pollen is produced. In that elevated position, it was much more likely to contact pollen grains from tomato neighbors. Pollen grains from the home blossom, to hit the receptive target, would have had to defy gravity and fall up.

When translocated to Europe, the abrupt dearth of pollinating insects left the tomato stranded — no bugs means no mates, means no seeds — and its eventual solution was incest. The stigma gradually retracted, to sit well down within the anther cone, which shift in position allowed for self-fertilization; in fact, made it a virtual necessity. It allowed the bugless tomato to survive, but also made it genetically boring. The self-fertilized tomato, having no new genetic material to work with, simply repeats itself. For all their seeming diversity, cultivated tomatoes are pretty much endless iterations of more of the same.

Scientists estimate that garden tomatoes have less than 5 percent of the genetic variation of their wild relatives. At a

When translocated to Europe, the abrupt dearth of pollinating insects left the tomato stranded — no bugs means no mates, means no seeds — and its eventual solution was incest.

guess, a mere ten genes control all tomato characteristics available to gardeners today: small to stupendous; round, ribbed, pear, or plum; pink, purple, red, yellow, orange, black, white, or green. In the world of plants, the cultivated tomato is the inbred equivalent of the pharaohs of Egypt, who married their sisters, and an exemplar of all those jokes about redneck family trees. If tomatoes were dogs, they'd have hip dysplasia; and if they were nineteenth-century European royalty, they'd have mental disorders, hemophilia, and funny-looking ears.

✤

Hybrid tomatoes nowadays owe their admirable germplasm in large part to plant geneticist Charles Rick of UC Davis, who spent the bulk of his multi-decade career trekking through the Andes in search of their wild relatives. Rick, who died in 2002 at the age of 87, was famously known on campus for his beard, bicycle, and crumpled army fatigue hat. In the world of tomatoes, he was a legend, singlehandedly preserving seventeen different wild tomato species — among them a tomato of the Galapagos Islands, off the coast of Ecuador, whose seeds frustratingly refused to germinate until Rick discovered that they first had to be partially digested in the gut of the Galapagos tortoise. The result of Rick's dedication and effort is UC Davis's Tomato Genetics Resource Center, now a repository of thousands of wild and mutant tomato samples.

Genomics, for all that it makes many on-the-ground jeans-and-trowel gardeners nervous, has done a lot for the tomato. Genes that confer resistance to nearly fifty different tomato maladies — among them nematodes, *fusarium* wilt, and tobacco mosaic virus — have been found in Rick's wild tomatoes, and

Its seeds refused to germinate until they were partially digested in the gut of the Galapagos tortoise.

bred into their previously frail and susceptible domestic relatives. Researchers have also identified a potentially valuable salt-tolerant tomato species on the Galapagos Islands — it grows on the coast, five yards above the high-tide line, and can survive in seawater — and a drought-resistant variety in western Peru, which essentially survives on what little water it gets from fog. A continuing worry among plant geneticists is that such species and traits, many of them already endangered, will vanish before their best features can be incorporated into the domestic gene pool.

⁂

The tomato is an unusual plant in that cell division in the future fruit is over almost at the moment of fertilization. A tiny, but fully formed, infant tomato can be seen at the base of the flower as soon as it opens. Further development is largely a matter of cell growth — existing tomato cells, rather than multiplying, simply get bigger.

Usually the tomato reaches full size in twenty to thirty days, about half the length of the total ripening period. During this time, the growing fruit accumulates quantities of water, minerals, and starch. New cell-wall material is also laid down, in the form of cellulose — the primary stiffening component in plant cells, digestible only with difficulty by cows and termites, and not at all by people — embedded in an equally indigestible layer of insoluble cement-like pectin. Cellulose and pectin are the main contributors to the green tomato's crunchy texture.

Once the tomato reaches mature peak size, it passes through a one- to two-week maturation period, during which starch storage continues and a number of developmental changes pave the way for the nitty-gritty of ripening. Mature peak size varies considerably from cultivar to cultivar. These range from huge — among them the Big Boy, the Mammoth Wonder, and the Watermelon Beefsteak, which puts out pink two-pounders — to tiny, with their names reminiscent of miniature poodles, such as Toy Boy, Tiny Tim, Sweetie, and Small Fry.

�֍

At whatever size, however, once growth and maturation are complete, ethylene production goes up, along with an abrupt rise in respiration, which, scientists tell us, signals the beginning of the end in the life of a tomato. This respiratory upsurge, termed a climacteric rise, is displayed by a number of fruits — the cantaloupe, honeydew melon, watermelon, peach, pear, plum, and apple, as well as the tomato. (Nonclimacteric fruits, among them oranges and lemons, ripen without an initial respiratory skyrocket.)

About two days after the tomato reaches the mature green stage, the color change, the most obvious of the ripening processes, commences. Initially the fruit lightens in a star-shaped pattern at the blossom end — the "starbreaker" stage, to those in the tomato trade. It then proceeds gradually through yellowish pink to orange to the deep rich red ordinarily associated with the mouthwatering ripe garden tomato.

Chemically, this color change is due to the breakdown of chlorophyll (green) and the synthesis of carotenoids (yellow and red), including the tomato-red lycopene. Yellow tomatoes produce yellow carotenoids, but no red lycopene; orange tomatoes are similarly lycopene-less, but high in the carotenoid beta-carotene, which also puts the orange in carrots and sweet potatoes. White tomatoes degrade chlorophyll normally but synthesize no carotenoids — a behavior governed by an eerie genetic locus termed *gh* for ghost. There is even a variety of tomato that ripens, but does not degrade chlorophyll and so remains confusingly green. It is called, appropriately, Evergreen.

Along with the color change, ripening involves marked changes in texture and taste. The fruit softens due to the activity of the enzymes pectinesterase and polygalacturonase, which convert the insoluble cell-wall pectins to soluble form. In the unripe fruit, the insoluble pectins act to strengthen cell walls and to bind adjacent cells together; soluble pectins, on the other hand, weaken the whole structure and allow the cells to separate easily when bitten. In the absence of pectinesterase and polygalacturonase, tomatoes would have to be gnawed. There are some tomato mutants that suffer from just that: one of these, designated Neverripe, produces only miniscule amounts of the required enzymes and softens extremely slowly. Understandably, scientists are more interested in it than gardeners are.

Finally, ripening involves the development of true tomato taste, the quality we all fantasize about, but don't get, from the winterbound Safeway, Shop 'n Save, or Piggly-Wiggly. Flavor in any fruit is a complicated mix of sugars, organic acids, and many miscellaneous volatile compounds — as many as a hundred in the ripe tomato and more than two hundred in the equally ripe banana.

In the green tomato, most of the sugar is stashed in the storage form of (unsweet) starch. As ripening progresses, the enzyme alpha-amylase — found fulfilling the same function in human saliva — rapidly hydrolyzes this starch, converting it to (sweet) glucose and fructose. Simultaneously, the concentration of (sour) organic acid drops off, and the result, a nice balance of sugar, acid, and volatiles, is what makes up the perfect tomato. Optimal tomato acidity generally ranges around pH 4.0 to 4.5 (pH 7.0 = neutrality), in the same ballpark as red cabbages, onions, and pears. (Lemon juice, in contrast, logs in at a puckering pH of 2.3, and vinegar at 2.5.)

The genetic key to tomato yumminess, according to recent research by Zach Lippman of New York's Cold Spring Harbor Laboratory and colleagues at Hebrew University in Israel, is a single gene for a chemical called florigen, whose purpose is to tell the growing plant when to stop making leaves and start making flowers. A mutation in one copy of the florigen gene (each tomato plant has two) results in astonishingly higher yields of fruits that are notably sweeter and more scrumptious than those of their nonmutant peers.

❀

Few foods are as delicious as a ripe, fresh-picked garden tomato. Conversely, few are as dreadful as the anemic substitutes found on supermarket shelves in February. Winter tomatoes, which have to be stored and shipped long distances, are picked in the green stage, then exposed to ethylene gas, a process delicately known in the tomato industry as "de-greening."

Ethylene, primarily a breakdown product of the amino acid methionine, is present normally in fruits and acts much like a hormone, triggering the many activities that lead to natural ripening. It can also lead to unnatural ripening. The ancient Chinese were aware that fruit would ripen more rapidly if placed in a closed chamber with burning incense. In this country, considerably later, orange growers noticed that green oranges placed in rooms with oil heaters rapidly turned into orange oranges. The reason for this color change, at first assumed to be simply heat, was soon discovered to be the presence of ethylene gas, an incomplete oil-combustion product.

Tomatoes are much more resistant to ethylene than are oranges, but will, if determinedly treated, eventually turn reddish. The infamous Walter tomato, developed in Florida where the bulk of U.S. winter tomatoes are grown, was selected for its cooperative uniform response to gassing and its resilience to travel. (It's a tough tomato; you can play catch with it.) In the chilly off-season, it's better than nothing — but it's also proof that, just like trees, only God can make a tomato.

To Sprawl or Not to Sprawl

In the absence of genetic manipulation, growers agree that the best-tasting tomatoes ripen on the vine — preferably on indeterminate vines. Indeterminate plants are lanky sprawlers that grow steadily throughout the gardening season, grinding to a halt only with the advent of unseasonably cold weather. The larger size and higher leaf count of indeterminate plants mean more sugar production and sweeter fruit. Many heirloom tomato varieties are indeterminate, which may explain their reputation for tastiness.

Determinate tomatoes, in contrast, are bushy, compact, and tidy, usually growing no more than three feet tall. This habit is governed by a specific gene designated *sp* (self-pruning) which appeared out of the blue as a spontaneous mutation in Florida in 1914.

Transgenic Tomatoes

The first genetically engineered crop ever sold in American markets was a tomato. Called the Flavr Savr, the tomato was created by the California company Calgene and introduced in 1994 as an improved alternative to the standard cardboardlike, picked-green-and-gassed product ordinarily available to consumers in winter.

The new tomato had a gene, inserted via bacterial carrier, that blocked the production of polygalacturonase, an enzyme essential for softening of the fruit during ripening. In the absence of this enzyme, the Flavr Savr could be allowed to ripen naturally on the vine — thus developing a normal tomato's battery of flavor molecules — but would still be tough enough for shipping. Though deemed both safe and nutritious by the FDA, the Flavr Savr didn't make the cut with consumers, and transgenic tomatoes — in a flood of hype about mutants, monsters, and Frankenstein — vanished.

Today, rather than genetic engineering, tomato experts favor "smart breeding," a technique that combines genetic analyses of plants for desirable traits with traditional crossbreeding.

Fruit is not an end in itself, but a tomato plant's clever way of making more tomato plants — a fancy mechanism for seed dispersal. Within each tomato are 250 to 300 tiny seeds, which weigh in at about 5,000 to the ounce. These seeds develop most rapidly during the second half of the tomato maturation period, the one- to two-week pause between the attainment of full growth and the onset of ripening. During this time, the seed embryo reaches full size and the seed coat develops and hardens.

Animal-assisted seed dispersal, of the sort aspired to by the tomato, is known as endozoochory, "seeds inside animals," or what one researcher terms the "Jonah syndrome." Here, the seeds are covered by an appealing coat of fleshy food and, at some point during the eating process, are spat out, spilled, or voided (a.k.a. dispersed) by a hungry and helpful animal. For this dispersal to be effective the seeds must escape wholesale digestion or destruction by overenthusiastic eaters, a problem the tomato gets around by producing immense numbers of small seeds. Some inevitably spill during feeding and go on to reproduce the species, and those that are actually swallowed possess coats tough enough to resist the fatal activity of the digestive tract enzymes. By the seed dispersal stage, that's it for the tomato — until, of course, gardening time next year.

✵

The correct tomato pronunciation, linguists believe, is to-*mah*-to, from the sixteenth-century Spanish *tomate*. The word picked up its *o* in eighteenth-century England, where the insular English believed that all Spanish words ended that way, but retained its short *a*.

Around here, though, we eat to-*may*-toes. After all these years of phonetic error, it's just too blasted late to call the whole thing off.

TURNIPS MAKE A VISCOUNT FAMOUS

plus

Castles, Lighthouses, and Locomotives,
A Roman Wrinkle Cure,
A Curmudgeonly Cryptographer,
A Diet for Diamond Hunters, and
A Weekly Dish of Woolton Pie

Tulip or turnip,
Rosebud or rhubarb,
Filet or plain beef stew,
Tell me, tell me, tell me, Dream Face,
What am I to you?
DUKE ELLINGTON

turnip

T he turnip's finest hour occurred at dinnertime in the sixteenth century when, carved in the shape of a castle ("gilded with egg yolk"), cathedral, or sailing ship, it served as a fantastic centerpiece on the grandest of aristocratic tables. Since then it's been a steady slide from glory. The turnip, historically, is the favored food of cows, pigs, and desperate peasants. Fewer and fewer gardeners these days bother to grow them, and younger diners, presented with them, have a tendency to push them fretfully about on their plates and hide them under the mashed potatoes.

Still, people have been growing turnips since the Neolithic era, and turnip seeds, saved in pots, have been found in Swiss lake dwellings. Plant scientists hypothesize dual centers of origin for the now-neglected turnip, one in the eastern Mediterranean, the other in Afghanistan and Pakistan. Oldest of the cultivated turnips is thought to be the Asian *Brassica rapa* ssp. *oleifera*, commonly known as rape, grown for its oil-bearing seeds. Rapeseed oil, used in lamps since ancient times, was the oil of choice in the nineteenth century for illuminating lighthouses and lubricating steam locomotives. It's still around today: tastefully renamed canola oil, it's commonly used in cooking.

�֎

The first turnip cultivated in Europe, however, was *Brassica rapa* ssp. *rapa* — the garden turnip — grown for its edible roots. The Romans ate them, but — even though the first-century cookbook *Apicius* includes upper-class recipes for duck with turnips, turnip pickle with myrtle berries, and boiled turnips seasoned with cumin, honey, and vinegar — the Roman turnip was ordinarily considered poverty food. It was similarly a cottage, rather than a castle, vegetable during the Middle Ages; in England, turnips appeared on the occasional family coat-of-arms to indicate a benefactor of the poor.

Medicinally, the turnip, mashed and mixed with suet, was recommended for winter maladies: frozen feet, chilblains, and aching joints. It was also used to treat "goute," smallpox, and measles, and to make a nice "sope" for "beautifying the face," a custom that may have been handed down from Roman times, when Apicius urged the wrinkle-conscious to use facial masks of cooked turnip, cream, and mashed rosebuds. Two applications, he claimed, would leave the aging face as smooth as a baby's thigh. Less frivolously, professional sixteenth-century cutlers used turnip juice to temper steel, and individuals with nothing better to drink fermented turnips and turned them into alcohol.

John Gerard (1597) describes "Turneps" of several types — large and small, round, "peare-fashion," and "longish;" as does John Parkinson (1629), who mentions white, yellow, and red turnips, and the "Navew gentle," which is shaped like a carrot. The white kind, a globular turnip with a "pigges tale-like roote" underneath it, is the most common, Parkinson tells us; and both he and Gerard agree that turnips are primarily eaten by the "poore." In Wales, according to Gerard, the utterly broke didn't even bother to boil their turnips, but simply gnawed upon them, raw.

Because of the turnip's generally lousy press, "turnip eater" traditionally meant lower-class dullard. "Let the lowborn dig turnips!" was a German catchphrase dating to the fourteenth century; and in Old French, anything conspicuously worthless was deemed "not worth a turnip." François Rabelais, in his bawdy sixteenth-century satire *Gargantua and Pantagruel*, referred to country bumpkins as turnip-chewers, and German scholar Johannes Trithemius, who wrote the world's first printed book on ciphers and cryptology, began with an introductory poke at the dim-witted common man:

> "This I did that to men of learning and men deeply engaged in the study of magic, it might, by the Grace of God, be in some degree intelligible, while on the other hand, to the thick-skinned turnip-eaters it might for all time remain a hidden secret, and be to their dull intellects a sealed book forever."

In the popular BBC series *Blackadder*, which traces the fortunes of the hapless Blackadder family dynasty from 1485 to World War I, doofy dogsbody Baldrick (Tony Robinson), servant to Edmund Blackadder (Rowan Atkinson), is noted for his multigenerational lowbrow love of turnips. The Elizabethan Baldrick was famed for his recipe for Turnip Surprise, which — the surprise — contains absolutely nothing but a turnip.

❀

With its vulgar associations and silly appearance — bulbous below, shaggy above — the turnip is an unlikely literary hero, but apparently it has been one since at least the fourteenth century. The Grimm Brothers' tale "The Turnip," for example, harks back to a trio of medieval Latin poems, the gist of which is deserved comeuppance. A poor but honest farmer brings an enormous turnip as a gift to the king, and receives a purse of gold as a reward. The farmer's wealthy neighbor (or, occasionally, half-brother) then decides to give the king a horse, hoping for an even bigger and better reward. Instead, he gets the turnip.

Turnip tall tales date to sixteenth-century Germany, where folk stories variously feature a turnip so big that it filled an entire cart, a turnip that took three days to ride around on horseback, and a turnip so huge that a cow could eat its way into the middle of it and vanish, with nothing left showing but the tip of a tail. Still around today are picture-book versions of the Russian story of the gigantic turnip, a cumulative tale in which an old man and woman plant a turnip and then find that it's so huge that they can't pull it up. The result is a tug-of-war with every person and animal on the farm hauling on the turnip, until finally a vegetable the size of a small house explodes out of the ground.

The turnip tales, argues Harvard classics professor Jan Ziolkowski in *Fairy Tales Before Fairy Tales* (2009), may reflect the human fascination with novelty — we like oddly enormous vegetables — or they may simply give the prolific turnip its due. The turnip is famous for bulk, and for what it has historically provided best: lots and lots of good cheap food.

Introduced to England by the invading Romans along with apples, lavender, and peas, the turnip led a career of relative obscurity until it came to the attention of Charles, second Viscount Townshend. Townshend — later nicknamed "Turnip"

Townshend — was a passionate agriculturist who, in the early 1700s, promoted the turnip both as livestock feed and as part of a four-crop cycle of crop rotation with sequential plantings of wheat, barley, turnips, and clover. Daniel Defoe, tramping through Townshend's home county of Norfolk in 1724, wrote: "this part of England is remarkable for being the first where the feeding and fattening of sheep and other cattle with turnips was first practiced . . . a very great part of the improvement of their lands to this day."

King George II was so impressed with the Norfolk turnips that he had an instructional report written about them for the edification of his subjects across the Channel in Hanover. Even the irascible William Cobbett admired the Norfolk turnip fields. Jane Austen's Mr. Knightley, the love interest in *Emma* (1815), grew turnips.

Turnips were first planted in America by Jacques Cartier, who tended a kitchen garden in Quebec in 1541 while fielding expeditions to collect what he fondly believed to be gold and diamonds. (They turned out to be iron pyrites and quartz crystals, which inspired the contemporaneous French expression "fake as Canadian diamonds.") The Jamestown colonists planted turnips in Virginia. "Our English seeds thrive very well heere," wrote Alexander Whitacker in *Good Newes of Virginia* (1612), a bolstering report to the colonists' backers in London, citing the pleasant climate, the abundant wildlife, and the success of "Pease, Onions, Turnips, Cabbages."

Turnips also grew in the gardens of Massachusetts Bay: a letter from Governor John Winthrop to his wife in Boston sends kisses, inquires after the children, and reminds her to get in the turnips. John Randolph, in his *Treatise on Gardening* (1793), lists "the white and purple rooted Turnep" as best for the table.

At Monticello, Thomas Jefferson, who ate turnips with sugar in ragouts, grew ten kinds.

By the nineteenth century, seed catalogs offered dozens of different turnip varieties. D. M. Ferry, in 1881, listed twenty-one turnips, and Burpee, in 1888, carried sixteen, including the White Egg; the Cowhorn, a white carrot-shaped variety; and the Golden Ball or Orange Jelly, noted for "rich, sweet, pulpy flesh." Vilmorin-Andrieux's *The Vegetable Garden* (1885) describes forty-five, among them carrot-shaped, round, and flat turnips, which last in illustrations look somewhat like hockey pucks.

The notable success of the turnip paved the way for the rutabaga, which is neither turnip nor cabbage but somewhere in between. While the cabbage has eighteen chromosomes and the turnip twenty, the rutabaga — which cheerfully incorporates both — has thirty-eight. Scientists guess that the crucial combinatorial mating took place at some point in the Middle Ages, possibly in Scandinavia, where the cool climate particularly suits them.

The first written mention of the rutabaga occurs in 1620, usually attributed to Swiss botanist Gaspard (or Caspar) Bauhin, who saw some growing in Sweden. This makes sense, since the common name comes from the Swedish *rotabagge*, "root bag." It's also variously known as the swede, the yellow turnip, or the

Rootabaga Country

Carl Sandburg's *Rootabaga Stories* (1922) is collection of American fairy tales, first told to Sandburg's three daughters and set in the fabulous Rootabaga Country, which is named after a turnip.

turnip-rooted cabbage, though officially it has a species name all its own: *Brassica napobrassica*.

The swollen edible bottoms of both turnip and rutabaga are part stem, part taproot. The lower two-thirds, all root, lurks underground, while the upper third, derived from the stem base, remains above. The aboveground portion, exposed to sunlight, accumulates an assortment of purple and red anthocyanin compounds and becomes pigmented, while the shielded root remains pale: hence the familiar turnip's purple top. The term *turnip-pate*, common in the seventeenth century, took into account only the snowy nether region, and was applied to individuals with very fair hair, those today called towheads or platinum blondes.

Both turnip and rutabaga are biennials, the starch-laden lower stem (hypocotyl) and root botanically intended for the nourishment of subsequent flowers and seeds. Turnip flowers, like those of the related cabbage, kohlrabi, kale, Brussels sprouts, cauliflower, and broccoli, are perfect flowers, which means that each blossom contains both male and female reproductive organs. These are usually cross-pollinated by proverbially busy bees. Turnips are occasionally known to jump the gun and flower the first year, a circumstance once viewed with alarm. John Gerard, commenting ominously upon it in 1633, said "the Turneps that floure the same year that they are sowen, are a degenerate kind, called Madneps, of their evill qualitie in causing frensie and giddinesse of the brayne for a season."

In many western European languages, the turnip, like many other ostensibly sexless objects, possesses gender — masculine in French (*navet*), masculine in Spanish (*nabo*), feminine in German (*Ruhe*). This linguistic curiosity once led the touring

Mark Twain to remark: "In German, a young lady has no sex, while a turnip has. Think what overwrought reverence that shows for the turnip, and what callous disrespect for the girl."

❀

There's less overwrought reverence for the turnip nowadays. It comes in dead last on the National Gardening Association's list of most popular American garden vegetables, and a lot of seed catalogs leap insouciantly from tomatoes to watermelons without a turnipward glance.

Some historians hypothesize that public repudiation of turnips is a holdover from World Wars I and II, when people periodically were condemned to live on nothing but. In the "Turnip Winter" of 1916–17, for example, due to Allied blockade and potato failure, starving Germans turned to turnips, transmogrifying them, with varying degrees of success, into everything from coffee to marmalade and bread. Food shortages in World War II Britain led to a resurgence of turnips, often baked into Woolton Pie, named after Frederick Marquis, Baron Woolton, the wartime Minister of Food.

"A horrible dish has appeared on the dining room table," wrote an unhappy consumer, "and it is to be repeated once a week. It is called Woolton Pie. It is composed entirely of root vegetables in which one feels turnip has far too honoured a place." One mother claimed that at the very mention of Woolton Pie, her six-year-old son would burst into uncontrollable sobs. Understandably, postwar everybody hated turnips, along with Spam, blackout curtains, and sirens.

But given what turnips have done for us, they deserve a whole lot better.

GENERAL SOURCES

Albala, Ken. *Beans: A History.* Berg, 2007

Allen, Stewart Lee. *In the Devil's Garden: A Sinful History of Forbidden Food.* Ballantine Books, 2002.

Andrews, Jean. *Peppers: The Domesticated Capsicums.* University of Texas Press, 1984.

Barkas, Janet. *The Vegetable Passion.* Charles Scribner, 1975.

Behr, Edward. *The Artful Eater.* Art of Eating, 2004.

Block, Eric. *Garlic and Other Alliums: The Lore and the Science.* Royal Society of Chemistry, 2009.

Brillat-Savarin, Jean Anthelme. *The Physiology of Taste: Or Meditations on Transcendental Gastronomy.* Translated by M. F. K. Fisher. Everyman's Library, 2009.

Brothwell, Don and Patricia Brothwell. *Food in Antiquity,* rev. ed. John Hopkins University, 1998.

Brown, John Hull. *Early American Beverages.* Bonanza Books, 1966.

Civitello, Linda. *Cuisine and Culture: A History of Food and People,* 3rd ed. John Wiley, 2011.

Coe, Sophie D. *America's First Cuisines.* University of Texas Press, 1994.

Collingham, Lizzie. *Curry: A Tale of Cooks and Conquerors.* Oxford University Press, 2006.

Conniff, Richard. "Mammoths and Mastodons: All American Monsters." *Smithsonian,* April 2010.

Cutler, Karan Davis. *Tantalizing Tomatoes.* Brooklyn Botanic Garden, 1997.

Damerow, Gail. *The Perfect Pumpkin.* Storey Publishing, 1997.

de Forest, Elizabeth Kellam. *The Gardens and Grounds at Mount Vernon.* Mount Vernon Ladies' Association of the Union, 1982.

Dewitt, Dave and Nancy Gerlach. *The Whole Chile Pepper Book.* Little, Brown, 1990.

Drummond, J. C., and Anne Wilbraham. *The Englishman's Food: Five Centuries of English Diet,* rev. ed. Pimlico, 1994.

DuBose, Fred. *The Total Tomato.* Harper & Row, 1985.

Dyer, T. F. Thiselton. *The Folk-lore of Plants.* Echo Library, 2007.

Donovan, Mary, Amy Hatrack, Frances Mills, and Elizabeth Shull. *The Thirteen Colonies Cookbook.* Praeger, 1975.

Editors of American Heritage. *The American Heritage Cookbook and Illustrated History of American Eating and Drinking.* American Heritage Publishing, 1964.

Favretti, Rudy J. and Gordon P. DeWolf. *Colonial Gardens.* Barre Publishers, 1972.

Federoff, Nina and Nancy Marie Brown. *Mendel in the Kitchen: A Scientist's View of Genetically Engineered Foods.* Joseph Henry Press, 2004.

Fowler, Damon Lee, ed. *Dining at Monticello.* Thomas Jefferson Foundation, 2005.

Fussell, Betty. *The Story of Corn.* Knopf, 1992.

Garnsey, Peter. *Food and Society in Classical Antiquity.* Cambridge University Press, 1999.

Goldman, Amy. *The Heirloom Tomato: From Garden to Table.* Bloomsbury, 2008.

———. *The Compleat Squash: A Passionate Grower's Guide to Pumpkins, Squash, and Gourds.* Artisan, 2004.

Green, Harvey. *Fit for America: Health, Fitness, Sport, and American Society.* Pantheon Books, 1986.

Greene, Bert. *Greene on Greens.* Workman, 1984.

Hanson, James Ralph. *Chemistry in the Garden.* Royal Society of Chemistry, 2007.

Harbury, Katherine E. *Colonial Virginia's Cooking Dynasty.* University of South Carolina Press, 2004.

Haughton, Claire Shaver. *Green Immigrants: The Plants That Transformed America.* Harcourt, Brace, Jovanovich, 1978.

Hedrick, U. P. *A History of Horticulture in America to 1860.* Oxford University Press, 1950.

Heiser, Charles B. *The Fascinating World of the Nightshades: Tobacco, Mandrake, Potato, Tomato, Pepper, Eggplant, Etc.* Dover, 1987.

———. *Of Plants and People.* University of Oklahoma Press, 1985.

———. *Seed to Civilization,* 2nd ed. W.H. Freeman, 1981.

Henderson, John. *The Roman Book of Gardening.* Routledge, 2004.

Hendrickson, Robert. *The Great American Tomato Book.* Doubleday, 1977.

Henig, Robin Marantz. *The Monk in the Garden*. Mariner Books, 2001.

Hess, Karen, ed. *Martha Washington's Booke of Cookery*. Columbia University Press, 1981.

Hiatt, Judith. *Cabbage: Cures to Cuisine*. Naturegraph Publishers, 1989.

Hickman, Peggy. *A Jane Austen Household Book*. David and Charles, 1977.

Hooker, Richard J. *Food and Drink in America*. Bobbs-Merrill, 1981.

———, ed. *A Colonial Plantation Cookbook: The Recipe Book of Harriott Pinckney Horry, 1770*. University of South Carolina Press, 1984.

Jabs, Caroline. *The Heirloom Gardener*. Sierra Club Books, 1984.

Jashemski, Wilhelmina Feemster and Frederick G. Meyer, eds. *The Natural History of Pompeii*. Cambridge University Press, 2002.

Jefferson, Thomas. *The Garden and Farm Books*. Edited by Robert C. Baron. Fulcrum, 1987.

Jones, Benton J. *Tomato Plant Culture*, 2nd ed. CRC Press, 2008.

Josselyn, John. *New-Englands Rarities Discovered*. Massachusetts Historical Society, 1972. First published 1672.

Kalm, Peter. *Peter Kalm's Travels in North America*. Dover, 1987. First published in 1770.

Kaufman, Cathy K. *Cooking in Ancient Civilizations*. Greenwood, 2006.

Kingsbury, Noel. *Hybrid: The History and Science of Plant Breeding*. University of Chicago Press, 2009.

Ladizinsky, Gideon. *Plant Evolution under Domestication*. Kluwer Academic Publishers, 1998.

Lane, Maggie. *Jane Austen and Food*. Hambledon Pres, 1995.

Laws, Bill. *Spade, Skirret, and Parsnip: The Curious History of Vegetables*. Sutton Publishing, 2004.

Lang, James. *Notes on a Potato Watcher*. Texas A&M University Press, 2001.

Lee, David. *Nature's Palette: The Science of Plant Color*. University of Chicago Press, 2007.

Leighton, Ann. *Early American Gardens: "For Meate or Medicine"*. Houghton Mifflin, 1970.

Leslie, Eliza. *Miss Leslie's Complete Cookery*, 49th ed. Applewood Books, 2008. First published 1853.

Lovelock, Yann. *The Vegetable Book: An Unnatural History*. St. Martin's Press, 1973.

Lyte, Charles. *The Kitchen Garden*. Oxford Illustrated Press, 1984.

Manning, Richard. "Super Organics." Wired Magazine, 12.05, May 2004.

Martineau, Belinda. *First Fruit: The Creation of the Flavr Savr Tomato and the Birth of Biotech Foods*. McGraw-Hill, 2001.

McGee, Harold. *On Food and Cooking: The Science and Lore of the Kitchen*, rev. ed. Scribner, 2004.

McKendry, Maxime. *Seven Hundred Years of English Cooking*. Exeter Books, 1973.

McWilliams, James E. *A Revolution of Eating: How the Quest for Food Shaped America*. Columbia University Press, 2005.

Mennell, Stephen. *All Manners of Food: Eating and Taste in England and France from the Middle Ages to the Present*. Basil Blackwell, 1985.

Phipps, Frances. *Colonial Kitchens: Their Furnishings and Their Gardens*. Hawthorn Books, 1972.

Pizer, Vernon. *Eat the Grapes Downward: An Uninhibited Romp Through the Surprising World of Food*. Dodd, Mead, and Co., 1983.

Pliny the Elder. *Natural History, With an English Translation in Ten Volumes*. Translated by H. Rackham, W. H. S. Jones, and D. E. Eichholz. Harvard University Press, 1938–1963.

Pollan, Michael. *In Defense of Food*. Penguin Press, 2008.

Proulx, Annie. *The Fine Art of Salad Gardening*. Rodale Press, 1985.

Quinn, Vernon. *Leaves: Their Place in Life and Legend*. Frederick A. Stokes Co., 1937.

Randolph, Mary. *The Virginia Housewife, Or, Methodical Cook*. Dover, 1993. First published 1824.

Reader, John. *Potato: A History of the Propitious Esculent*. Yale University Press, 2009.

Revel, Jean-François. *Culture and Cuisine*. Doubleday, 1982.

Root, Waverley. *Food*. Simon & Schuster, 1980.

Root, Waverley and Richard de Rochemont. *Eating in America*. Morrow, 1976.

Roueché, Berton. *The Orange Man and Other Narratives of Medical Detection*. Little, Brown and Co., 1971.

Sass, Lorna J. *To the King's Taste: Richard II's Book of Feasts and Recipes Adapted for Modern Cooking*. Metropolitan Museum of Art, 1975.

Russell, Howard S. *A Long, Deep Furrow: Three Centuries of Farming in New England*. University Press of New England, 1976.

Sauer, Jonathan D. *Historical Geography of Crop Plants*. CRC Press, 1993.

Simmons, Amelia. *The First American Cookbook: A Facsimile of "American Cookery," 1796*. Dover, 1984. First published 1796.

imoons, Frederick J. *Plants of Life, Plants of Death*. University of Wisconsin Press, 1998.

inger, Marilyn. *The Fanatic's Ecstatic Aromatic Guide to Onions, Garlic, Shallots, and Leeks*. Prentice-Hall, 1981.

Smith, Andrew F. *Souper Tomatoes: The Story of America's Favorite Food*. Rutgers University Press, 2000.

———. *The Tomato in America*. University of South Carolina Press, 1994.

———. *The Oxford Companion to American Food and Drink*. Oxford University Press, 2007.

Smith, C. Wayne, Javier Betrán, and E. C. A. Runge. *Corn: Origin, History, Technology, and Production*. John Wiley, 2004.

Sokolov, Raymond. *Why We Eat What We Eat: How Columbus Changed How the World Eats*. Simon & Schuster, 1991.

Spencer, Colin. *British Food: An Extraordinary Thousand Years of History*. Columbia University Press, 2002.

Spurling, Hilary, ed. *Elinor Fettiplace's Receipt Book: Elizabethan Country House Cooking*. Viking, 1986.

Standage, Tom. *An Edible History of Humanity*. Walker & Co., 2009.

Staveley, Keith and Kathleen Fitzgerald. *America's Founding Food: The Story of New England Cooking*. University of North Carolina Press, 2004.

Staub, Jack. *Alluring Lettuces: And Other Seductive Vegetables for Your Garden*, rev. ed. Gibbs Smith, 2010.

Sturtevant, E. Lewis. *Sturtevant's Notes on Edible Plants*. Edited by U. P. Hedrick. Dover, 1972. First published 1919.

Tannahill, Reay. *Food in History*. Three Rivers Press, 1988.

Toussaint-Samat, Maguelonne. *A History of Food*, rev. ed. Wiley-Blackwell, 2009.

Trager, James. *The Food Book*. Grossman Publishers, 1970.

Trollope, Fanny. *Domestic Manners of the Americans*. Penguin, 1997. First published 1832.

Vilmorin-Andrieux, M. M. *The Vegetable Garden*. Ten Speed Press, 1981. First published 1885.

Warren, Susan. *Backyard Giants: The Passionate, Heartbreaking, and Glorious Quest to Grow the Biggest Pumpkin Ever*. Bloomsbury, 2007.

Wheaton, Barbara Ketcham. *Savoring the Past: The French Kitchen and Table from 1300 to 1789*. University of Pennsylvania Press, 1983.

Weiner, Michael A. *Earth Medicine, Earth Food*, rev. ed. Ballatine, 1991.

Woodham-Smith, Cecil. *The Great Hunger: Ireland 1845–1849*. Penguin, 1991.

Woodward, Penny. *Garlic and Friends: The History, Growth, and Use of Edible Alliums*. Hyland House, 1996.

Zohary, Daniel and Maria Hopf. *Domestication of Plants in the Old World*, 3rd ed. Oxford University Press, 2000.

Zuckerman, Larry. *The Potato: How the Humble Spud Rescued the Western World*. North Point Press, 1998.

NOTES

Vegetables In and Out of the Garden

Samuel Reynolds Hole's thoughts on gardening can be found in his book *Our Gardens* (J. M. Dent & Co., 1899), available as a free e-book at www.onread.com/book/Our-Gardens-1068952.

Detailed statistics on American gardening can be found in the National Gardening Association's "The Impact of Home and Community Gardening in America" (NGA, 2009), available in pdf format online at www.gardenresearch.com/files/2009-Impact-of-Gardening-in-America-White-Paper.pdf.

For information on vegetables and nutrition, see the USDA's Food and Nutrition Information Center at http://fnic.nal.usda.gov. Other sources include:

Duyff, Roberta Larson. *American Dietetic Association Complete Food and Nutrition Guide*, 3rd ed. John Wiley, 2006.

Guthrie, Joanne F., Claire Zizza, and Nancy Raper. "Fruit and Vegetables: Their Importance in the American Diet." *Food Review*, Jan–June 1992.

The pejorative "rude herbs and roots" was originally mentioned in the *Gesta Stephani* (Deeds of Stephen), a mid-twelfth-century English history.

Robert Campbell's strictures against the French appeared in *The London Tradesman* (1747), quoted in *Seven Centuries of English Cooking* by Maxime de la Falaise (Grove Press, 1992. First published 1973).

Food psychologist Paul Rozin points out the benefits of taking hot dogs (and milk chocolate) to a desert island in Michael Pollan's *In Defense of Food* (Penguin, 2008).

Benjamin Franklin's abortive experience with vegetarianism is described in *The Autobiography of Benjamin Franklin* (Yale University Press, 1964), and the history of Sylvester Graham and his food reforms can be found in Harvey Green's *Fit for America: Health, Fitness, Sport and American Society* (Pantheon Books, 1986).

Joni Mitchell's plea for getting back to the garden is in the song "Woodstock," first issued in 1970 on the album "Ladies of the Canyon."

Elizabeth, Countess von Arnim, is the author of *Elizabeth and Her German Garden*, originally published in 1898, still available in several reprint editions.

A biography of Eliza Leslie and information about her cookbooks can be found at the Feeding America: The Historical American Cookbook Project website at http://digital.lib.msu.edu/projects/cookbooks.

Asparagus

Reports on the asparagus-worthiness of Martian soil come from the Phoenix Wet Chemistry Lab (WCL) at Tufts University. The WCL website is located at http://planetary.chem.tufts.edu/Phoenix/WetChemLab.html.

Apicius or *De Re Coquinaria* is the oldest known Roman cookbook, a collection of recipes dating to the first century CE, but first compiled in the late fourth century. The author – though there is some debate over this – was purportedly Marcus Gavius Apicius, a flamboyant epicure who lived, ate, and threw lush parties during the reign of Tiberius. A translation of the surviving text can be found at http://penelope.uchicago.edu/Thayer/E/Roman/Texts/Apicius.

For all about hangovers, see Joan Acocella's "A Few Too Many" (*The New Yorker*, May 26, 2008: 32–37).

For the anti-hangover efficacy of asparagus, see: Kim, B. Y., Z. G. Cui, S. R. Lee, S. J. Kim, et al. "Effects of *Asparagus officinalis* Extracts on Liver Cell Toxicity and Ethanol Metabolism." *Journal of Food Science*, 74, no. 7 (September 2009): H204–H208.

For an account of the life of Ziryab the Blackbird, see Robert W. Lebling, Jr.'s "Flight of the
Blackbird" in *Saudi Aramco World*, 54, no. 4 (July/August 2003): 24–33. The article can be
found online at www.scribd.com/doc/22570702 Flight-of-the-Blackbird-Saudi-Aramco-
World-Jul-Aug-2003.

The complete text of Samuel Pepys's diary is online at www.pepysdiary.com.

Euell Gibbons's *Stalking the Wild Asparagus* (25th anniversary ed., Alan C. Hood & Co.,
1987), a paean to returning to nature and eating from the wild, was popular among
environmentalists in the 1960s and remains so today.

For the complete text of Marriott Edgar's poem "Asparagus," see www.poemhunter.com/
poem/asparagus.

The text of Mary Randolph's *The Virginia Housewife, Or, Methodical Cook* (Dover, 1993. First
published 1824) is available online at www.fullbooks.com/The-Virginia-Housewife.html.

The story of Bernard le Bovier de Fontanelle and his apoplectic guest is found in Waverley
Root's *Food* (Simon & Schuster, 1980).

Benjamin Franklin's underpublicized "Fart Proudly" appears in: *Fart Proudly: Writings of
Benjamin Franklin You Never Read in School.* (Carl Japikse, ed. Frog Ltd., 2003.)

For the science of asparagus and urine, see Harold McGee's *The Science and Lore of the
Kitchen* (rev. ed., Scribner, 2004): 314–315. Also see: Mitchell, S.C. "Food Idiosyncrasies:
Beetroot and Asparagus." *Drug Metabolism & Disposition* 29, no. 4 (2001): 539–543. The
article is available online at http://dmd.aspetjournals.org/content/29/4/539.full.

Waring, R. H., S. C. Mitchell, and G. R. Fenwick. "The Chemical Nature of the Urinary
Odour Produced by Man After Asparagus Ingestion." *Xenobiotica* 17, no. 11 (November
1987): 1363–1371.

An account of the discovery of asparagine can be found in: Street, H. E. and G. E. Trease.
"The discovery of asparagine." *Annals of Science* 7, 1951: 70–76.

For the woes of the American asparagus farmers in the wake of the War on Drugs, see
Timothy Egan's "War on Peruvian Drugs Takes a Victim: U.S. Asparagus," reported in
The New York Times, 25 April 2004.

Information about Anne de Mare and Kirsten Kelly's film *Asparagus!* can be found online
at www.ironweedfilms.com/films/asparagus or www.asparagusthemovie.com.

The Locavore website is found at www.locavores.com.

For more accounts of local eating, see Alisa Smith and J. B. MacKinnon's *Plenty: Eating
Locally on the 100-Mile Diet* (Three Rivers Press, 2007), Barbara Kingsolver's *Animal,
Vegetable, Miracle: A Year of Food Life* (HarperCollins, 2007), and Ben Hewitt's *The Town
That Food Saved: How One Community Found Vitality in Local Food* (Rodale Books, 2009).

Beans

An excellent all-purpose source of information on the history of beans is Ken Albala's
Beans: A History (Berg, 2007).

For information on the domestication of food plants in eastern North America, see: Smith,
Bruce D. "Eastern North America as an Independent Center of Plant Domestication."
Proc. Natl. Acad. Sci. 103, no. 33 (15 August 2006): 12223–12228. Also by Bruce D.
Smith, see *Rivers of Change* (Smithsonian Institution Press, 1992).

For general information on fava beans, see Raymond Sokolov's "Broad Bean Universe."
Natural History, December 1984: 84–86.

Umberto Eco's "How the Bean Saved Civilization" appeared in *The New York Times
Magazine*, 18 April 1999: 36–42.

Information on nitrogen and nitrogen fixation can be found in John Emsley's *Nature's
Building Blocks: An A-Z Guide to the Elements* (Oxford University Press, 2001), 287–293;
and in Lubert Stryer's *Biochemistry* (W. H. Freeman, 1995), 713–716.

Christine Goldberg discusses the history of "Jack and the Beanstalk" in "The Composition
of 'Jack and the Beanstalk'" in *Marvels & Tales*, 15, no. 1 (2001): 11–26. For the online
text, see http://muse.jhu.edu/journals/mat/summary/v015/15.1goldberg.html. A history

of "Jack and the Beanstalk" and alternative versions of the tale can also be found at the SurLaLune Fairy Tales website at www.surlalunefairytales.com/jackbeanstalk/history. html.

For images and information on the Babylonian culinary tablets, see the Yale Babylonian Collection, established in 1909 with a gift from J. P. Morgan. The website is found at www.yale.edu/nelc/babylonian.html.

For an account of humanity's uneasy relationship with fava beans, see: Katz, Solomon H. "Fava Bean Consumption: A Case for the Co-Evolution of Genes and Culture." In *Food and Evolution: Toward a Theory of Human Food Habits*, edited by Marvin Harris and Eric B. Ross, 133–162. Temple University Press, 1989.

Melody Voith discussed the biochemistry of L-dopa in "L-Dopa" in the special "Top Pharmaceuticals That Changed The World" issue of *Chemical & Engineering News*, 83, no. 25 (June 2005).

An English version of *Le Menagier de Paris* (1393), translated by Janet Hinson, can be found online at www.daviddfriedman.com/Medieval/Cookbooks/Menagier/Menagier. html. Also see *The Good Wife's Guide (Le Menagier de Paris): A Medieval Household Book*, translated by Gina L. Greco and Christine M. Rosa (Cornell University Press, 2009).

Alexander Lobrano's history of cassoulet, "Spilling the Beans," appeared in *Forbes* magazine, 8 December 2008. The article can be found online at www.forbes.com/forbes-life-magazine/2008/1208/071.html.

The text of Amelia Simmons's *American Cookery* (1796) can be found at www.fullbooks. com/American-Cookery.html.

Statistics on national and international bean production can be found at the United Nations Food and Agriculture Organization's website at http://faostat.fao.org.

Jay D. Mann's *How to Poison Your Spouse the Natural Way: A Guide to Safer Food* (JDM & Associates, 2004) discusses poisons in everyday foods, including the cyanide-prone bean.

On de-gassing the bean, see David Cohen's "Irradiation Produces Low-Gas Beans" in the *New Scientist*, 27 March 2002.

The science, history, and pros and cons of oxygen are the subject of Nick Lane's *Oxygen: The Molecule That Made the World* (Oxford University Press, 2002). Also see "Oxygen" in John Emsley's *Nature's Building Blocks: An A–Z Guide to the Elements* (Oxford University Press, 2001): 297–304.

From the U.S. Department of Agriculture's Nutrient Data Laboratory, "Oxygen Radical Absorbance Capacity (ORAC) of Selected Foods — 2007" (2007) is a comprehensive overview with tabulated test results. It is available online in pdf format at www.ars.usda. gov/sp2userfiles/place/12354500/data/orac/orac07.pdf. Also see:

Decker, Eric A., Kathleen Warner, Mark P. Richards, and Fereidoon Shahidi. "Measuring Antioxidant Effectiveness in Food." *J. Agric. Food Chem.* 53, no. 10 (2005): 4303–4310.

Halvorsen, B. L., K. Holte, M. C. Myhrstad, I. Barikmo, et al. "A Systematic Screening of Total Antioxidants in Dietary Plants." *Journal of Nutrition* 132, no. 3 (2002): 461–471

Marandino, Cristin. "Eleven Healing Foods." *Vegetarian Times*, June 2002:56–61.

Wu X., G. R. Beecher, J. M. Holden, D. B. Haytowitz, S. E. Gebhardt, and R. L. Prior. "Lipophilic and Hydrophilic Antioxidant Capacities of Common Foods in the United States." *J. Agric. Food Chem.* 52 (2004): 4026–4037.

Beets

For disliked beets, see the original AOL "America's Most Hated Foods" poll at http://community.livejournal.com/about_food/76665.html.

For more food dislikes, see "America's Least Favorite Foods" at www.slashfood. com/2009/02/02/americas-least-favorite-foods.

Sullivan, Amy. "Food Phobias: How to Make Peace with Beets." *The Atlantic*, 6 July 2010.

For information on geosmin and beets, see: Lu, G., C. G. Edwards, J. K. Fellman, D. S. Mattinson, and J. Navazio. "Biosynthetic Origin of Geosmin in Red Beets (*Beta vulgaris* L.)" *J. Agric. Food Chem.* 51, no. 4 (2003): 1026–1029.

R. R. M. Paterson, A. Venâncio, and N. Lima. "Why Do Food and Drink Smell Like Earth?" in *Communicating Current Research and Educational Topics and Trends in Applied Microbiology*, ed. A. Mendez-Vilas (Formatex, 2007): 120–128. Available online at www. formatex.org/microbio/pdf/Pages120-128.pdf.

Ritter, Stephen K. "How Nature Makes Earth Aroma." *Chemical & Engineering News*, 19 September 2007. The article is online at http://pubs.acs.org/cen/news/85/i39/8539notw8.html.

Stephen Nottingham's online book, *Beetroot* (2004), is available at http://stephennottingham.co.uk/beetroot.htm.

Excerpts from Charlemagne's Capitularies can be found online at Professor Paul Halsall's Internet Medieval Sourcebook at www.fordham.edu/halsall/sbook.html.

Also see Pierre Riché's *Daily Life in the World of Charlemagne* (University of Pennsylvania Press, 1988).

On beet-derived pink urine, see: Mitchell, S. C. "Food Idiosyncrasies: Beetroot and Asparagus." *Drug Metabolism & Disposition* 29, no. 4 (April 2001): 539–543. The article is available online at http://dmd.aspetjournals.org/content/29/4/539.full.

For statistics on the world's major crops, see the United Nations Food and Agriculture Organization website at http://faostat.fao.org.

For more information on the sugar beet, see Henry Hobhouse's *Seeds of Change: Six Plants That Transformed Mankind* (reprint, Shoemaker & Hoard, 2005).

Cabbages

The text of Robert Burton's *The Anatomy of Melancholy* (1621) is available online at Project Gutenberg at www.gutenberg.org/ebooks/10800.

For the complete text of Samuel Pepys's diary, including the account of his unhappy cabbage dinner, see www.pepysdiary.com.

John Winthrop, Jr.'s complete 1651 seed list can be found in Ann Leighton's *Early American Gardens*, (Houghton Mifflin, 1970): 190.

For more detail on W. Atlee Burpee and his seed company, see Ken Kraft's *Garden to Order: The Story of Mr. Burpee's Seeds and How They Grow* (Doubleday, 1963).

For the account of Mrs. Davidson and her difficult encounter with cabbage, see "The Social Status of a Vegetable" in M. F. K. Fisher's *Serve It Forth* (Reprint, North Point Press, 2002. First published 1937.).

For more detail on Captain Cook and scurvy, see Francis E. Cuppage's *Captain Cook and the Conquest of Scurvy* (Greenwood Press, 1994). Also see Jonathan Lamb's "Captain Cook and the Scourge of Scurvy" on the BBC's website: www.bbc.co.uk/history/british/empire_seapower/captaincook_scurvy_01.shtml.

For lightning that resembles broccoli, see Ivan Amato's "Sprites Trigger Sky-High Chemistry." *Chemical & Engineering News* 84, no. 12 (2006): 40–41.

For cabbages in space, see: Wheeler, R. M., C. L. Mackowiak, J.C. Sager, W. M. Knott, and W. L. Berry. "Proximate Composition of CELSS Crops Grown in NASA's Biomass Production Chamber." *Advances in Space Research* 18 (1996): 43–47.

For more information on biomimetics, see Tom Mueller's "Biomimetics: Design by Nature" in *National Geographic* magazine (April 2008); Rowan Hooper's "Ideas Stolen Right from Nature." *Wired* (November 2004); and "Technology that Imitates Nature." *The Economist* (9 June 2005).

Carrots

For more on the non-carrot-eating Peter, see Leslie Linder's *The History of the Tale of Peter Rabbit* (Warne, 1976).

An account of Henry Ford's carrot obsession can be found in William C. Richards's *The Last Billionaire* (Grizzell, 2007. First published 1948). Also see David L. Lewis's *The Public Image of Henry Ford: An American Folk Hero and His Company* (Wayne State University Press, 1976).

The Vegetable Orchestra, www.vegetableorchestra.org

For information on using paintings in the study of the history of vegetables, see: Zeven, A. C. and W. A. Brandenburg. "Use of Paintings from the 16th to 19th Centuries to Study the History of Domesticated Plants." *Economic Botany* 40, no. 4 (1986): 397–408.

For more detail on carotenoids in carrots, see entries in Harold McGee's *On Food and Cooking: The Science and Lore of the Kitchen* (rev. ed., Scribner, 2004) and David Lee's *Nature's Palette: The Science of Plant Color* (University of Chicago Press, 2007). Also see: Simon, Philipp W. and Xenia Y. Wolff. "Carotenes in Typical and Dark Orange Carrots." *J. Agric. and Food Chem.* 35, no. 6 (1987): 1017–1022.

For the nutritional differences between raw and cooked vegetables, see Sushma Subramanian's "Fact or Fiction: Raw Veggies Are Healthier than Cooked Ones" in *Scientific American* (March 2009). See the text online: http://www.scientificamerican.com/article.cfm?id=raw-veggies-are-healthier.

For the story of "Cat's Eyes" Cunningham, see Gavin Mortimer's "Cat's Eyes" in the November 2010 issue of the Smithsonian's *Air & Space* magazine, available online at www.airspacemag.com/history-of-flight/Cats-Eyes.html.

For an account of carotenemia, see Berton Roueché's *The Orange Man and Other Narratives of Medical Detection* (Little, Brown and Co., 1971).

For more on enhanced supervegetables, see Richard Manning's "Super Organics" in *Wired* (12.05, May 2004), available online at http://online.sfsu.edu/~rone/GEessays/SuperOrganics.htm. Also see Don Baker's "Beet Generation" in *Vegetarian Times* (November 2004), online at www.vegetariantimes.com/features/editors_picks/377.

See Natural News Network online for "Scientists Genetically Engineer 'Super Carrot' Rich in Calcium" by David Gutierrez (1 August 2008) at www.naturalnews.com/023750_calcium_scientists_carrots.html.

Also see: Morris, J., K. M. Hawthorne, T. Hotze, S. A. Abrams, and K. D. Hirschi. "Nutritional Impact of Elevated Calcium Transport Activity in Carrots." *Proc. Natl. Acad. Sci.* 105, no. 5 (2008): 1431–1435.

For World War II's Dr. Carrot and company, see the BBC's "Dig for Victory!" at www.bbc.co.uk/dna/h2g2/A2263529.

Fearnley-Whittingstall, Jane. *The Ministry of Food: Thrifty Wartime Ways to Feed Your Family.* (Hodder & Stoughton, 2010).

For more on parsnips, see Roger B. Swain's "A Taste for Parsnips" in his book *Earthly Pleasures: Tales from a Biologist's Garden* (Scribner, 1981).

More details on Queen Anne's lace can be found in Jack Sanders's *Hedgemaids and Fairy Candles: The Lives and Lore of North American Wildflowers* (Ragged Mountain Press, 1993) and in Claire Shaver Houghton's *Green Immigrants: The Plants That Transformed America* (Harcourt, Brace, Jovanovich, 1978).

Visit the World Carrot Museum (www.carrotmuseum.co.uk) for the Trojan horse story and other carrot tidbits.

Celery

For an account of Dr. Brown's Celery Tonic and general information on celery, see Eugene Garfield's "From Tonic to Psoriasis: Stalking Celery's Secrets" in *Current Contents* 8, no. 18 (6 May 1985): 3–12.

For images and information on celery vases, see "The Celery Vase: A Prominent Way to Serve an Exotic Vegetable" at the WorthPoint Corporation's website: www.worthpoint.com/blog-entry/the-celery-vase-a-prominent-way-to-serve-an-exotic-vegetable. Also see Dorothy Dougherty's *Celery Vases: Art Glass, Pattern Glass, and Cut Glass* (Schiffer Publishing, 2007).

On psoralens in celery, see: E. Finkelsein, U. Afek, E. Gross, N. Aharoni, L. Rosenberg, and S. Halevy. "An Outbreak of Phytophotodermatitis Due to Celery." *Int. J. Dermatol.* 33, no. 2 (1994): 116–118.

Scheel, Lester D., Vernon B. Perone, Robert L. Larkin, and Richard E. Kupel. "The Isolation and Characterization of Two Phototoxic Furanocoumarins (Psoralens) from Diseased Celery." *Biochemistry* 2, no. 5 (1963): 1127–1131.

Jay D. Mann's *How to Poison Your Spouse the Natural Way: A Guide to Safer Food* (JDM Associates, 2004) discusses poisons in everyday foods, including celery psoralens.

For information on John Evelyn, *Acetaria*, and his unfinished masterpiece, *Elysium Britannicum or the Royal Gardens*, see: O'Malley, Therese and Joachim Wolschke-Bulmahn, eds. "John Evelyn's 'Elysium Britannicum' and European Gardening". Volume 17 of the *Dumbarton Oaks Colloquium on the History of Landscape Architecture* series, Dumbarton Oaks Research Library and Collection, 1998. The text is available online at www.doaks.org/publications/doaks_online_publications/Evelyn/evel013.pdf.

William R. Snyder discusses celeriac in "Celery's Taking Root" in the *The Wall Street Journal*, 29 April 2010.

The sad truth about celery's negative calories is explained in Anahad O'Connor's *Never Shower in a Thunderstorm: Surprising Facts and Misleading Myths About Our Health and the World We Live In* (Times Books, 2007).

Corn

An excellent general reference on corn is Betty Fussell's wide-ranging *The Story of Corn* (Knopf, 1992).

For state-by-state crop statistics, see the National Agricultural Statistics Service website at www.nass.usda.gov. The U.S. Grains Council, at www.grains.org, has production statistics on corn and other grains. The Environmental Protection Agency at www.epa.gov/agriculture/ag101/cropmajor.html also lists statistics on major crops grown in the United States.

For the history of popcorn, see Andrew F. Smith's *Popped Culture: A Social History of Popcorn in America* (Smithsonian Institution, 2001).

For popcorn production statistics, see the Agricultural Marketing Resource Center's Popcorn Profile at www.agmrc.org/commodities__products/grains__oilseeds/corn_grain/popcorn_profile.cfm.

For the history of whiskey, see Sarah Hand Meacham's *Every Home a Distillery* (Johns Hopkins University Press, 2009), Tom Standage's *A History of the World in 6 Glasses* (Walker & Co., 2005), and Mary Miley Theobald's "When Whiskey Was King of Drink" in the *Colonial Williamsburg Journal* (Summer 2008).

All three cantos of Joel Barlow's poem "The Hasty Pudding" (1793) can be found online at www.poemhunter.com/poem/the-hasty-pudding.

For more information on corn and vampires, see: Hampl, J. S. and W. S. Hampl, 3rd. "Pellagra and the Origin of a Myth: Evidence from European Literature and Folklore." *J. of the Royal Soc. of Medicine* 90, no. 11 (November 1997): 636–639.

For general information on pellagra, see Daphne A. Roe's *A Plague of Corn: The Social History of Pellagra* (Cornell University Press, 1973) and Walter Gratzer's *Terrors of the Table: The Curious History of Nutrition* (Oxford University Press, 2005).

On hybrid corn, see: Crow, James F. "90 Years Ago: The Beginning of Hybrid Maize." *Genetics* 148, March 1998: 923–928.

On diversity and transgenic corn, see Peter Canby's excellent article "Retreat to Subsistence" in *The Nation*, 5 July 2010: 30–36.

For more on corn palaces, see Henry Wiencek's "House of Corn" in *Americana*, September/October 1992: 110–112. Also see the home page of Mitchell, South Dakota's Corn Palace, at www.cornpalace.org.

For an account of the Kellogg Brothers and cornflakes, see Harvey Green's *Fit for America: Health, Fitness, Sport and American Society* (Pantheon Books, 1986). Also see Gerald Carson's "Cornflake Crusade" in *American Heritage* 8, no. 4 (June 1957): 66–85.

Cucumbers

For more information on Landon Carter, see *Landon Carter's Uneasy Kingdom: Revolution and Rebellion on a Virginia Plantation* by Rhys Isaac (Oxford University Press, 2004).

Excerpts from Landon Carter's diary can be found on the National Humanities Center website at http://nationalhumanitiescenter.org/pds/becomingamer/economies/text5/landoncarterdiary.pdf.

The account of the deadly cucumbers is found in Samuel Pepys's diary, online at www.pepysdiary.com.

For additional information on Bernard M'Mahon or McMahon, see Peter J. Hatch's "Bernard McMahon, Pioneer American Gardener" in the *Twinleaf Journal* (January 1993) from Monticello. The text can be found online at www.monticello.org/site/house-and-gardens/bernard-mcmahon-pioneer-american-gardener.

For more on pickles, see David Mabey and David Collison's *The Perfect Pickle Book* (Grub Street, 2007), a celebration of all things pickled.

For more detailed information on Henry Heinz, see Robert C. Alberts's *The Good Provider: H. J. Heinz and His 57 Varieties* (Houghton Mifflin, 1973).

The story of Burma's Cucumber King is found in G. E. Harvey's *History of Burma* (Asian Educational Services, 2000. First published 1925): 18–19.

Eggplants

For additional general information about eggplants, see: Daunay, Marie-Christine and Jules Janick. "History and Iconography of Eggplant." *Chronica Horticulturae* 47, 2007: 16–22.

For an account of the Chinese eggplant domestication hypothesis, see: Wang, Jin-Xiu, Tian-Gang Gao, and Sandra Knapp. "Ancient Chinese Literature Reveals Pathways of Eggplant Domestication." *Annals of Botany* 102, no. 6 (2008): 891–897.

Illuminations and text from the medieval *Tacuinum Sanitatis* can be found online at www.godecookery.com/tacuin/tacuin.htm.

The history of Delmonico's is described in the *American Heritage Cookbook and Illustrated History of American Eating and Drinking* (American Heritage Publishing, 1964).

An account of the Middle Eastern fat-tailed sheep appears in Reay Tannahill's *Food in History* (Three Rivers Press, 1988).

For more on phenolic compounds in eggplants, see: Stommel, J. R. and B. D. Whitaker. "Phenolic Acid Content and Composition of Eggplant Fruit in a Germplasm Core Subset." *J. of Amer. Soc. for Horticultural Science* 128, 2003: 704–710.

For information on the Colorado potato/eggplant beetle, see Andrei Alyokhin's "Colorado Potato Beetle Management on Potatoes: Current Challenges and Future Prospects." *Fruit, Vegetable and Cereal Science Biotechnology* 3: 10–19. See an online version at www.potatobeetle.org/Alyokhin_CPB_Review_reprint.pdf.

The description of the "cannibal tomato" is found in Berthold Seemann's "Fiji and Its Inhabitants," included in *Vacation Tourists and Notes of Travel in 1861* (Francis Galton, ed., Macmillan and Co., 1862): 249–292.

For more on Carl Sandburg's wonderful *Rootabaga Stories*, see Ross Simonini's "Carl Sandburg Stops Making Sense" at www.poetryfoundation.org/journal/article.html?id=238530. The 1922 edition of *Rootabaga Stories*, complete with illustrations, is available online at www.gutenberg.org/files/27085/27085-h/27085-h.htm.

Lettuce

A translation of the *Historia Augusta* can be found online at http://penelope.uchicago.edu/Thayer/E/Roman/Texts/Historia_Augusta.

For information on lettuce latex, see: Hagel, J. M., E. C. Yeung, and P. J. Facchini. "Got Milk? The Secret Life of Lactifers." *Trends in Plant Science* 13, no. 12 (December 2008): 631–639.

An article on the mysterious aphrodisiacal Egyptian lettuce is Rosella Lorenzi's "Egyptians Ate Lettuce to Boost Sex Drive" *ABC Science*, 29 June 2005. Find it here: www.abc.net.au/science/articles/archive/.

de Vries, I. M. "Origin and Domestication of *Lactuca sativa L.*" *Genetic Resources and Crop Evolution* 44, no. 2 (1997): 165–174.

Illuminations and text from the medieval *Tacuinum Sanitatis* can be found online at www.godecookery.com/tacuin/tacuin.htm.

For more on Thomas Jefferson's lettuce, see "Lettuce: Monday Morning Madness" by Peter J. Hatch, *Twinleaf Journal*, 2008. The text can be found online at www.monticello.org/site/house-and-gardens/twinleaf-journal-online.

For information on chlorophyll f, see Ferris Jabr's "A New Form of Chlorophyll?" in *Scientific American* (19 August 2010). The article is online at www.scientificamerican.com/article.cfm?id=new-form-chlorophyll. Also see Rachel Ehrenberg's "Chlorophyll gets an 'F'" in *ScienceNews* 178, no. 6 (September 2010): 13. The article is online at www.sciencenews.org/view/generic/id/62400/title/Chlorophyll_gets_an_'f'.

For the chlorophyll craze of the 1950s, see Paul Sann's "The Time of the Green" in *Fads, Follies, and Delusions of the American People* (Bonanza Books, 1967: 131–135) and Dick Dempewolff's "The Bright Green Chlorophyll World" in *Popular Mechanics Magazine* (January 1953: 8–10, 30).

Also see: Galston, Arthur W. "An Uncolored View of Chlorophyll." *Engineering & Science*16, no. 4 (1953): 17–19. Available online at http://calteches.library.caltech.edu/144/01/Galston.pdf.

Melons

For the tangled interrelationships of cucumbers and melons, see: Ghebretinsae, Amanuel G., Mats Thulin, and Janet C Barber. "Relationships of Cucumbers and Melons Unraveled: Molecular Phylogenetics of *Cucumis* and Related Genera (Benincasea, Cucurbitaceae)." *Amer. J. of Botany* 94, 2007: 1256–1266.

Sebastian, P., H. Schaefer, I. R. H. Telford, and S. S. Renner. "Cucumber (*Cucumis sativus*) and Melon (*C. melo*) Have Numerous Wild Relatives in Asia and Australia, and the Sister Species of the Melon Is from Australia." *Proc. Natl. Acad. Sci.* 107, no. 32 (August 2010): 14269–14273.

For general information on watermelon, see: Maynard, Donald N., Xingping Zhang, and Jules Janick. "Watermelons: New Choices, New Trends." *Chronica Horticulturae* 47, no. 4 (December 2007): 26–29.

For information on lycopene in watermelons, see "Watermelon Packs a Powerful Lycopene Punch" in the June 2002 issue of the USDA's *Agricultural Research* magazine. The article is online at www.ars.usda.gov/is/ar/archive/jun02/lyco0602.htm.

For information on citrulline, see "Watermelon May Have Viagra-Effect" in *ScienceDaily* (1 July 2008), online at www.sciencedaily.com/releases/2008/06/080630165707.htm.

The National Watermelon Promotion Board website is at www.watermelon.org.

Mark Twain's disgraceful watermelon performance is shamelessly described in "The Watermelon" in his book *Plymouth Rock & the Pilgrims and Other Salutary Platform Opinions* (Charles Neider, ed. Harper & Row, 1984): 278–282.

Queen Anne's Pocket Melon is described in Jack Staub's *Alluring Lettuces: And Other Seductive Vegetables for Your Garden* (rev. ed., Gibbs Smith, 2010).

Onions

For general information on onions and kin, sources include Eric Block's *Garlics and Other Alliums: The Lore and Science* (Royal Society of Chemistry, 2009), Penny Woodward's *Garlic and Friends: The History, Growth, and Use of Edible Alliums* (Hyland House, 1996), and Marilyn Singer's *The Fanatic's Ecstatic Aromatic Guide to Onions, Garlic, Shallots, and Leeks* (Prentice-Hall, 1981).

For images and information on the Babylonian culinary tablets, see the Yale Babylonian Collection, established in 1909 with a gift from J. P. Morgan. The website is found at www.yale.edu/nelc/babylonian.html.

The Forme of Cury (1390) is online at Project Gutenberg at www.gutenberg.org/ebooks/8102. Also see Lorna J. Sass's *To the King's Taste: Richard II's Book of Feasts and Recipes Adapted for Modern Cooking* (Metropolitan Museum of Art, 1975).

For onion superstitions, see Frederick J. Simoons's *Plants of Life, Plants of Death* (University of Wisconsin Press, 1998).

O. Henry's short story "The Third Ingredient," originally published in 1920, can be read online at www.classicreader.com/book/978/1.

On the medicinal (nutraceutical) onion, see:

Desjardins, Yves. "Onion as a Nutraceutical and Functional Food." *Chronica Horticulturae* 48, no. 2 (2008): 8–14.

Galeone, C., C. Pelucchi, F. Levi, E. Negri, S. Franceschi, R. Talamini, A. Giacosa, and C. La Vecchia. "Onion and Garlic Use and Human Cancer." *American Journal of Clinical Nutrition* 84, no. 5 (November 2006): 1027–1032.

The story of the *Semper-Augustus*-chewing sailor is repeated in Mike Dash's *Tulipomania* (Three Rivers Press, 1999): 109.

Peas

For the vast diversity of legumes, see: Doyle, Jeff J., and Melissa A. Luckow. "The Rest of the Iceberg: Legume Diversity and Evolution in a Phylogenetic Context." *Plant Physiology* 131, no. 3 (March 2003): 900–910.

A translation of the *Historia Augusta* can be found online at http://penelope.uchicago.edu/Thayer/E/Roman/Texts/Historia_Augusta.

For more on Jefferson's annual pea contest, see "Jefferson's Horticultural Neighborhood: A Rational Society of Gardeners" by Peter J. Hatch in *Twinleaf Journal* (2007), online at www.monticello.org/site/house-and-gardens/twinleaf-journal-online.

Philip Miller's *The Gardener's Dictionary* (1754) "printed for the author and sold by John and James Rivington" is available online through the Internet Archive at www.archive.org/details/gardenersdictio03millgoog.

An account of Thomas Knight's work can be found in Noel Kingsbury's *Hybrid: The History and Science of Plant Breeding* (University of Chicago Press, 2009).

Mendel's famous pea experiments are described in Robin Marantz Henig's *The Monk in the Garden* (Mariner Books, 2001).

For the genetic secret behind Mendel's wrinkle-seeded pea, see: Bhattacharyya, M. K., A. M. Smith, T. H. Ellis, C. Hedley, and C. Martin. "The Wrinkled-Seed Character of Pea Described by Mendel is Caused by a Transposon-Like Insertion in a Gene-Encoding Starch-Branching Enzyme." *Cell* 60, no. 1 (January 1990): 115–122.

Peppers

Good general references on peppers include Jean Andrews's classic *Peppers: The Domesticated Capsicums* (University of Texas Press, 1984), and almost anything by Dave DeWitt, such as DeWitt and Nancy Gerlach's informative *The Whole Chile Pepper Book* (Little, Brown, and Co., 1990).

Jack Turner's *Spice: The History of a Temptation* (Vintage Books, 2004) is a fascinating story of the profitable spice trade from ancient times through the Renaissance, with considerable information about black pepper.

A list of English words derived from the indigenous languages of the Americas (including Aztec or Nahuatl) can be found at http://en.wikipedia.org/wiki/ List_of_English_words_from_indigenous_languages_of_the_Americas.

For information on using starch grain samples to track plant domestication, see Donald Smith's "Chili pepper starch grains linked to ancient settlement sites across the Americas" in *Inside Smithsonian Research* 16, Spring 2007. Also see: Perry, Linda, Ruth Dickau, Sonia Zarrillo, Irene Holst, et al. "Starch Fossils and the Domestication and Dispersal of Chili Peppers (*Capsicum* spp. *L.*) in the Americas." *Science* 315, no. 5814 (February 2007): 986–988.

Bernardino de Sahagún's *Florentine Codex (General History of the Things of New Spain)* is available as a 12-volume set (Arthur J. O. Anderson, ed., University of Utah Press, 1950–1982). Also see: Reeves, H. M. "Sahagún's 'Florentine Codex,' a Little Known Aztecan Natural History of the Valley of Mexico." *Arch Nat Hist.* 33, no. 2 (2006): 302–321.

On pepper hotness, see: Mullin, Rick. "Red-Hot Chili Peppers." *Chemical & Engineering News* 81, 44 (3 November 2003): 41.

On discouraging bears, see: Smith, Tom S., Stephanie Herrero, Terry D. DeBruyn, and James M. Wilder. "Efficacy of Bear Deterrent Spray in Alaska." *The Journal of Wildlife Management* 72, no. 3 (2008): 640–645.

For more information on Joshua Tewksbury and directed deterrence, see: Borrell, Brendan. "What's So Hot About Chili Peppers?" *Smithsonian* magazine, April 2009.

Tewksbury, J. J., and G. P. Nabhan. "Seed Dispersal: Directed Deterrence by Capsaicin in Chilies." *Nature* 412, no. 6845 (July 2001): 403–404.

Tewksbury, J. J., K. M. Reagan, N. J. Machnicki, T. A. Carlo, D. C. Haak, A. L. Calderon-Penaloza, and D. J. Levey. "The Evolutionary Ecology of Pungency in Wild Chilies." *Proc. Natl. Acad. Sci.* 105, no. 33 (2008): 11808–11811.

Paul Rozin's "constrained risk" theory is described in Harold McGee's *On Food and Cooking: The Science and Lore of the Kitchen* (rev. ed., Scribner, 2004).

On the pepper-induced heat sensation, see: Caterina, Michael J., Mark A. Schumacher, Makoto Tominaga, Tobias A. Rosen, Jon D. Levine, and David Julius. "The Capsaicin Receptor: A Heat-Activated Ion Channel in the Pain Pathway." *Nature* 389, October 1997: 816–824.

On peppers and tarantula bites, see: Siemens, Jan, Sharleen Zhou, Rebecca Piskorowski, Tetsuro Nikai, Ellen A. Lumpkin, Allan I. Basbaum, David King, and David Julius. "Spider Toxins Activate the Capsaicin Receptor to Produce Inflammatory Pain." *Nature* 444, November 2006: 208–212.

Albert-Szent Györgyi's Nobel Prize-winning discovery of vitamin C in peppers is described on the Nobel Prize's official website: http://nobelprize.org/nobel_prizes/medicine/laureates/1937/szent-györgyi-bio.html.

On capsaicin and prostrate cancer, see: A. Mori, S. Lehmann, J. O'Kelly, T. Kumagai, J. C. Desmond, M. Pervan, W. H. McBride, M. Kizaki, and H. P. Koeffler. "Capsaicin, a Component of Red Peppers, Inhibits the Growth of Androgen-Independent, p53 Mutant Prostate Cancer Cells." *Cancer Research* 66, no. 6 (March 2006): 3222–3229.

The story of pirate Lionel Wafer and the bell pepper is recounted in Diana and Michael Preston's biography of William Dampier, *A Pirate of Exquisite Mind* (Walker & Co., 2004).

For more on son-of-a-bitch stew, see Jane and Michael Stern's *Chili Nation* (Clarkson Potter, 1999), which covers the history of chili and includes a chili recipe for every state in the United States.

Potatoes

Helpful potato books include James Lang's *Notes of a Potato Watcher* (Texas A&M University Press, 2001), John Reader's *Potato: A History of the Propitious Esculent* (Yale University Press, 2009), and Larry Zuckerman's *The Potato: How the Humble Spud Rescued the Western World* (North Point Press, 1998).

The theories of Pye Henry Chavasse are described in Judith Flanders's *Inside the Victorian Home* (W. W. Norton, 2004).

Thor Heyerdahl describes his sweet-potato-chasing journey to Polynesia in *Kon-Tiki: Across the Pacific by Raft* (reprint ed. Skyhorse Publishing, 2010). Also see: Montenegro, Alvaro, Chris Avis, and Andrew J. Weaver. "Modeling the Prehistoric Arrival of the Sweet Potato in Polynesia." *Journal of Archaeological Science* 35, no. 2 (2008): 355–367.

For the history of scurvy, see Stephen R. Bown's *Scurvy: How a Surgeon, a Mariner, and a Gentleman Solved the Greatest Medical Mystery of the Age of Sail* (Thomas Dunne Books, 2003) and David I. Harvie's *Limeys: The Conquest of Scurvy* (Sutton Publishing, 2005).

For a history of Mr. Potato Head, see *Funny Face! An Amusing History of Potato Heads, Block Heads, and Magic Whiskers* by Mark Rich and Jeff Potocsnak (Krause Publications, 2002).

For the story of the Irish potato famine, see Cecil Woodham-Smith's *The Great Hunger* (Penguin, 1991) and James S. Donnelly, Jr.'s *The Great Irish Potato Famine* (History Press, 2008).

For information on *Phytophthera infestans* as a potential biological weapon, see the Monterey Institute of International Studies (Middlebury College) Chemical & Biological Weapons Resource Page at http://cns.miis.edu/cbw/possess.htm.

For more on Luther Burbank, see Jane S. Smith's *The Garden of Invention: Luther Burbank and the Business of Breeding Plants* (Penguin Press, 2009).

On the Defender potato, see: Novy, R. G., S. L. Love, D. L. Corsini, J. J. Pavek, et al. "Defender: A High-Yielding, Processing Potato Cultivar with Foliar and Tuber Resistance to Late Blight." *American Journal of Potato Research* 83, 2006: 9–19.

For information on the genetics of *P. infestans*, see: Haas, Brian J., Sophien Kamoun, Michael C. Zody, Rays H. Y. Jiang, et al. "Genome Sequence and Analyis of the Irish Potato Famine Pathogen *Phytophthora infestans*." *Nature* 461, September 2009: 393–398.

For a history of French fries, see Maryann Tebben's " 'French' Fries: France's Culinary Identity from Brillat-Savarin to Barthes" in *Convivium Artium* (Spring 2006). The article is online at http://flan.utsa.edu/conviviumartium/Tebben.html.

For more information on Civil War army rations, see "Army Rations" in John D. Billings's *Hard Tack and Coffee: Or, the Unwritten Story of Army Life* (1887) (Corner House Publishers, 1980).

Pumpkins and Squashes

Paul Dudley's prolific pumpkin is mentioned in *Jonathan Edwards: A Life* by George M. Marsden (Yale University Press, 2003), 66, and in L. H. Bailey's *The Standard Cyclopedia of Horticulture* (Macmillan Company, 1914), 1505.

For Thomas Jefferson, the Comte de Buffon, and the degeneracy debate, see Richard Conniff's "Mammoths and Mastodons: All American Monsters" in *Smithsonian* magazine (April 2010), Keith Thomson's "Jefferson, Buffon and the Moose" in the *American Scientist* 96, no. 3 (2008), and Lee Alan Dugatkin's *Mr. Jefferson and the Giant Moose* (University of Chicago Press, 2009).

For the story of enormous pumpkins, see Susan Warren's *Backyard Giants: The Passionate, Heartbreaking, and Glorious Quest to Grow the Biggest Pumpkin Ever* (Bloomsbury, 2007); also see Jules Janick's "Giant Pumpkins: Genetic and Cultural Breakthroughs." *Chronica Horticulturae* 48, no. 3 (2008): 16–17.

On early American cucurbits, see: Smith, Bruce D. "The Initial Domestication of *Cucurbita pepo* in the Americas 10,000 Years Ago." *Science* 9 (May 1997): 932–934.

Radishes

On radishes and witches, see T. F. Thiselton Dyer's *The Folk-Lore of Plants* (Echo Library, 2008. First published 1889) and Ruth Edna Kelley's *The Book of Hallowe'en* (Lothrop, Lee & Shepard Co. First published 1919).

The adulterers' radish is described in Danielle S. Allen's *The World of Prometheus: The Politics of Punishing in Democratic Athens* (Princeton University Press, 2000).

For the history of the fairy tale "Rapunzel," see: www.surlalunefairytales.com/rapunzel.

Spinach

For a summary of the Popeye controversy, see "Spinach, Iron, and Popeye" by law professor Mike Sutton at www.internetjournalofcriminology.com/Sutton_Spinach_Iron_and_Popeye_March_2010.pdf.

The Forme of Cury (1390) is online at Project Gutenberg at www.gutenberg.org/ebooks/8102. Also see Lorna J. Sass's *To the King's Taste: Richard II's book of feasts and recipes adapted for modern cooking* (The Metropolitan Museum of Art, 1975).

Illuminations and text from the medieval *Tacuinum Sanitatis* can be found online at www.godecookery.com/tacuin/tacuin.htm.

Tomatoes

For the detailed scoop on tomatoes, you can't do better than Andrew F. Smith. See *The Tomato in America* (University of South Carolina Press, 1994) and *Souper Tomatoes: The Story of America's Favorite Food* (Rutgers University Press, 2000). Also see Karan Davis Cutler's *Tantalizing Tomatoes* (Brooklyn Botanic Garden, 1997) and David Gentilcore's *Pomodoro! A History of the Tomato in Italy* (Columbia University Press, 2010).

On the positive aspects of tomatine, see: M. Friedman, C. E. Levin, S. U. Lee, H. J. Kim, et al. "Tomatine-Containing Green Tomato Extracts Inhibit Growth of Human Breast, Colon, Liver, and Stomach Cancer Cells." *J. Agric. Food Chem.* 57, no. 13 (2009): 5727–5733.

Friedman, Mendel, T. E. Fitch, and W. E. Yokoyama. "Lowering of Plasma LDL Cholesterol in Hamsters by the Tomato Glycoalkaloid Tomatine." *Food and Chemical Toxicology* 38, no. 7 (2000): 549–553.

Jefferson's *Notes on the State of Virginia* (1781) is available online at http://etext.virginia.edu/toc/modeng/public/JefVirg.html.

For Andrew F. Smith's exposé of the apocryphal Colonel Johnson, see "The Invention of Culinary Fakelore and Food Fallacies" at www.foodhistorynews.com/debunk.html#typology.

For more on the influential Mrs. Beeton, see Kathryn Hughes's *The Short Life and Long Times of Mrs. Beeton* (Alfred A. Knopf, 2006).

The story of the Trophy tomato appears in L. H. Bailey's *The Survival of the Unlike: A Collection of Evolution Essays Suggested by the Study of Domestic Plants* (Macmillan, 1896), 485–60.

On lycopene and cooking: Dewanto, Veronica, Xianzhong Wu, Kafui K. Adom, and Rui Hai Liu. "Thermal Processing Enhances the Nutritional Value of Tomatoes by Increasing Total Antioxidant Activity." *J. Agric. Food Chem.* 50, no. 10 (2002): 3010–3014.

Unlu, N. Z., T. Bohn, D. M. Francis, H. N. Nagaraja, S. K. Clinton, and S. J. Schwartz. "Lycopene from Heat-Induced Cis-Isomer Rich Tomato Pasta Sauce Is More Bioavailable than from All-Trans Rich Pasta Sauce in Humans." *Br. J. Nutr.* 98, 2007: 140–146.

For the nutritional differences between raw and cooked vegetables, see Sushma Subramanian's "Fact or Fiction: Raw Veggies Are Healthier than Cooked Ones" in *Scientific American* (March 2009). See the text online in *Scientific American*'s report "Science of Our Food" at www.scientificamerican.com/report.cfm?id=food-science.

For a discussion of the square tomato (VF-145), see Raymond Sokolov's *Why We Eat What We Eat: How Columbus Changed How the World Eats* (Simon & Schuster, 1991).

For more on Radiator Charlie's Mortgage Lifter tomato, see NPR's "Living on Earth. Mortgage Lifter Tomatoes" at www.loe.org/shows/segments.htm?programID=05-P13-00038&segmentID=8.

On the inestimable Charles M. Rick, founder of the Tomato Genetics Resource Center, see http://tgrc.ucdavis.edu/charlie.html and www.universityofcalifornia.edu/senate/inmemoriam/CharlesM.Rick.htm. Also see: Estabrook, Barry. "On the Tomato Trail: In Search of Ancestral Roots." *Gastronomica: The Journal of Food and Culture* 10, no. 2 (Spring 2010): 40–44. For the C. M. Rick Tomato Genetics Resource Center, see http://tgrc.ucdavis.edu.

The tomato ripening process is described by A. Karim Khudairi in "The Ripening of Tomatoes" in the *American Scientist* 60, no. 6 (1972): 696–707.

On flavor in tomatoes, see Craig Canine's "A Matter of Taste . . . Who Killed the Flavor in America's Supermarket Tomatoes?" in *Eating Well*, January/ February 1991: 41–55.

On the flavorful gene for florigen, see: Krieger, Uri, Zachary B. Lippman, and Dani Zamir. "The Flowering Gene SINGLE FLOWER TRUSS Drives Heterosis for Yield in Tomato." *Nature Genetics* 42, 2010: 459–463.

For more information on transgenic tomatoes, see Belinda Martineau's *First Fruit: The Creation of the Flavr Savr Tomato and the Birth of Biotech Foods* (McGraw-Hill, 2001), Alan McHughen's *Pandora's Picnic Basket: The Potential and Hazards of Genetically Modified Foods* (Oxford University Press, 2000), and Nina Federoff and Nancy Marie Brown's *Mendel in the Kitchen: A Scientist's View of Genetically Engineered Foods* (Joseph Henry Press, 2004).

Turnips

For the turnip as castle, see an example in *Elinor Fettiplace's Receipt Book: Elizabethan Country House Cooking* (Viking, 1986), 97.

Johannes Trithemius's sneer at turnip eaters in his seminal cryptography book appears in Ivars Peterson's Math Trek column "Cracking a Medieval Code" (4 May 1998). See the article online on the Mathematical Association of America's website: www.maa.org/mathland/mathtrek_5_4_98.html.

On marvelous and enormous turnips, see Jan M. Ziolkowski's "The Wonder of the Turnip Tale" in her book *Fairy Tales Before Fairy Tales: The Medieval Latin Past of Wonderful Lies* (University of Michigan Press, 2009).

On Woolton Pie, see Charles Lyte's *The Kitchen Garden*. Oxford Illustrated Press, 1984.

ACKNOWLEDGMENTS

I am deeply grateful to all of the many people who provided the help, advice, encouragement, inspiration, and information without whom this book would not have been possible.

Special thanks go to Deb Burns, my kind and patient editor, and the wonderful staff at Storey Publishing; to Pat Stone and colleagues at *GreenPrints* magazine, who so beautifully combine digging and literature; to Ethan Rupp, who so generously, competently, and continually fixed my computer; and to the helpful and sympathetic librarians at the Bennington Free Library in Bennington, Vermont, the Fletcher Free Library in Burlington, Vermont, and the Bailey/Howe Library at the University of Vermont.

INDEX

Page numbers in *italics* indicate illustrations and photographs.

beans *(continued)*
    scarlet runner, 47–48
    string, shell, and dried, 44–45
    superstitions about, 36–38
    taxonomy of, 32
Beaver, Hugh, 274
Beecher, Catharine, 322
beets
    benefits of, 59–60
    Charlemagne and, 57–58
    coloration of, 59, 60
    hatred of, 54–55
    mangel-wurzel, 62–63
    medicinal uses of, 57
    sugar, 61–62
    taxonomy of, 55–56
bell peppers, 228
Benton, Isabella, 324
bergapten, 104
Berkeley, Miles Joseph, 261–262
beta-carotene, 88–89, 90–91, 176, 238,
        335
betacyanins, 59, 60
betalains, 59
Beverley, Robert, 249
Bhaba Atomic Research Centre
        (BARC), 49
biodiversity, 131, 262, 331–332
Birdseye, Clarence, 222
blanching, 101, 105
Block, Eric, 203
blush, 59, 60
Bockenheim, Johannes, 40
Booth, William, 321
Borgel (Pinkwater), 150
Bradley, Richard, 280, 318
Brillat-Savarin, Jean Anthelme, 21–22,
        169–170
broccoli, 76–78
Brown, Samuel, 230
Brussels sprouts, 79–80
Buchanan, James, 76
Buist, Robert, 321–322
Burbank, Luther, 263
Burpee, W. Atlee, 62–63, 72–73, 79,
        96, 101, 108–109, 145, 171, 186,
        301, 325

Burton, Robert, 48, 70
Bush, George W., 77
butterfly people, 127

C

cabbages
    Arabidopsis thaliana and, 80
    broccoli and, 76–78
    Brussels sprouts and, 79–80
    cauliflower and, 78–79
    chromosomes of, 347
    cleanliness of leaves, 73
    fruit of, 80
    heading, 70
    kale, 68
    kohlrabi, 68–69
    medicinal uses of, 67–68
    odor of, 74
    sauerkraut and, 75–76
    sugar content of, 93
    taxonomy of, 69
Caesar, Julius, 14, 70
Calgene, 338
Campbell, Robert, 3
cannibal tomato, 157
cantaloupe, 182–183
Canterbury Tales (Chaucer), 200
capsaicin, 232–236, 239–240
capsanthin, 237–238, 239
Carlsson, Arvid, 38
carotenemia (carotenosis), 90
carotenoids, 88–89, 237–239, 335
carrots
    alcohol and, 93
    butter and, 90–91
    in colonial America, 95–96
    coloration of, 87–89, 90–91
    cooked vs. raw, 89
    love of, 84–85
    modern varieties of, 97
    parsnips and, 92–93
    sweetness of, 91–94
    taproots of, 94–95
    taxonomy of, 85–86
    vision and, 89–90
Carson, Kit, 238
Carter, Landon, 20–21, 136, 282